RENEWALS 691-4574

DATE DUE

OCT 12		
DEC 11		
DEC 2		
OCT 21		
AUG 14		
JUL 28 2008		

Demco, Inc. 38-293

D0712247

The Brazilian Economy:
Its Growth and Development

THE BRAZILIAN ECONOMY:
ITS GROWTH
AND DEVELOPMENT

Werner Baer
Department of Economics
University of Illinois

Grid Publishing, Inc., Columbus, Ohio

1 2 3 4 5 6   3 2 1 0 9

Library of Congress Cataloging in Publication Data

Baer, Werner, 1931-
    Economic growth and development in Brazil.

    (Grid series in economics)
    Bibliography: p.
    Includes index.
    1. Brazil—Economic conditions. I. Title
HC187.B147   330.9'81'06   78-6857
ISBN 0-88244-173-6

DEDICATION

to

Marianne and Peter Kilby

Pia and David Maybury-Lewis

Heloisa and Annibal Villela

Contents

Part I: HISTORICAL PERSPECTIVE

PART II: CONTEMPORARY ISSUES

List of Tables

LIST OF TABLES (Cont'd)

Preface

The purpose of this book, *The Brazilian Economy: Its Growth and Development*, is to provide a survey of the Brazilian economy, with an emphasis on its historical evolution and its present-day institutional setting. Part I consists of five chapters recounting the growth process from colonial times to the 1970s. Part II's five chapters delve into some of the principal problems faced by the Brazilian economy in the 1960s and 1970s.

No volume can claim to adequately cover every aspect of an economy as complex as that of Brazil. I hope this book can at least provide a useful introduction to the study of the economy of Brazil.

My previous study of the Brazilian economy, *Industrialization and Economic Development in Brazil*, published in 1965, concentrated more specifically on the industrialization process of the 1950s. Except for chapter 4 and parts of chapter 9, which appeared in that volume and which are reproduced here with the permission of Richard D. Irwin, Inc., most of this book is based on the work of many scholars since that time and on articles which I have written in the 1970s.

Special thanks go to David Denslow who carefully went over the manuscript and enabled me to substantially improve the initial product. I would also like to thank Joseph Sweigart for many useful suggestions. Any failings in the final product are, of course, entirely attributable to me.

BRAZIL

States, Territories and
Regional Divisions

miles
0   200   400   600

0   200   400   600   800 1000
kilometers

PART I
HISTORICAL
PERSPECTIVE

INTRODUCTION AND OVERVIEW

Brazil has undergone profound socio-economic changes since the Great Depression of the thirties and especially since World War II. Its economy, which for centuries had been geared to the exportation of a small number of primary products, has in a relatively short period of time become dominated by a large and diversified industrial sector. At the same time its society, which had been predominantly rural, has become increasingly urbanized.

This rapid socio-economic transformation can be illustrated with a few numbers. In 1940 only 30 percent of the country's population was urban; by 1970 this proportion had increased to 56 percent.[1] The contribution of agriculture to the gross national product declined from 28 percent in 1947 to about 11 percent in the mid-seventies (measured in current prices), while that of industry rose from not quite 20 percent in 1947 to about 38 percent in the mid-seventies. After three decades of intense industrialization Brazil in 1976 was producing 985,000 motor vehicles, over 71,000 tractors, 9.1 million tons of steel, 17.5 million tons of cement, 1.8 million TV sets, and over 1.1 million refrigerators. It had close to 19,000 mW of installed electric power capacity, and over one-third of its exports consisted of manufactured products. Its road network increased from 36,000 kms in the early sixties to about 70,000 kms in the mid-seventies.[2]

Though agriculture was not the leading sector in these years, its growth was substantial. The country's land area in crops expanded from 16 million acres in 1920 to over 90 million acres in the seventies. The country became the world's largest sugar producer and the second largest exporter of soybeans, after the United States.

These achievements, however, did not transform Brazil

into an advanced industrial society. In terms of the welfare level of its average citizens, Brazil remained a less
developed country. Although per capita GNP in 1976 was
about US$1,200, this number is not a good indicator of gen-
eral well-being since the distribution of income was highly
concentrated both among income groups and among regions of
the country. In 1970, 20 percent of the population received
62 percent of the national income. Per capita income varied
regionally to such an extent that in many states of northeast Brazil it was less than half the national average,
while in the more advanced regions it was more than three
times the national average.[3] In 1972 fewer than 40 percent
of Brazil's urban households had access to a general water
supply system, fewer than 43 percent were connected with a
general sewage system or had septic tanks, only 53 percent
had electricity and only 5 percent had telephones.[4] In 1970
the population-physician ration was 1,962 as compated to 650
in the United States and 620 in Argentina; the population-
nurse ratio was 13,697, as compared to 122 in Sweden and
294 in the United States. There were 253 people per hos-
pital bed, compared to 80 in Switzerland and 110 in the
United States. The infant mortality rate per 1,000 was
around 90, compared to 60 in Argentina and 52 in the United
States. These social indicators only describe national
averages. In large areas of the country the population was
living in conditions much worse than these averages indicate.

Policy-makers had hoped that besides contributing to
the general growth and development of Brazil, industrialization would also substantially lessen the economic dependence of the country on the traditional industrial centers
of the world. The international division of labor originating in the nineteenth century had given to Brazil, and
most Third World countries, the role of supplier of primary
products. Thus its rate of economic activity was largely
dependent on the performance of the industrialized centers
of the world. It had been hoped that import substitutive
industrialization would result in a greater economic independence for the country. In fact, industrialization only
changed the nature of the dependency relationship. The import coefficient (import/GNP ratio) did not decline very
much, while the commodity composition of imports changed
and resulted in the country's being at least as dependent
on foreign trade as before for its rate of economic activity.
In addition, since industrialization was achieved by massive
foreign investment in the most dynamic sectors of industry,
foreign influence on the development and use of the means of
production increased substantially.

The Brazilian industrialization model was based on the ideology of market economies; that is, under most of its governments in the period when industrialization was being promoted, respect for private property and reliance on private domestic and foreign enterprises were stressed. The state, however, has become directly involved in economic activities to a far greater extent than was originally planned by the country's policy makers. This was due to the financial limitations and technical backwardness of the private domestic sector, the unwillingness of foreign capital to enter certain fields of activity, and the unwillingness of governments to allow foreign capital into some sectors.

This book will examine the historical evolution of the Brazilian economy, focusing especially on the process of its industrialization in the twentieth century, the methods used to achieve it, its impact on the socioeconomic environment, and the adjustments of the socioeconomic institutions to the structural changes in the economy. This will lead us to study the type of economic system which emerged in the process, i.e., the mixture of private and state capitalism, some of whose features are distinct from those of mixed economies of Western Europe. Finally, we plan to examine some aspects of Brazil's economic policies and economic system which account for the persistence of underdevelopment in the midst of economic growth.

PHYSICAL AND DEMOGRAPHIC SETTING

Brazil's territorial extension of 3.27 million square miles makes it the fifth largest country of the world, surpassed only by the Soviet Union, Canada, China, and the United States. It covers 47 percent of South America.[5] The largest proportion of the territory is made up of geologically ancient highlands. About 57 percent of the land is on a plateau varying between 650 and 3,000 feet; 40 percent consists of lowlands with an elevation of less than 650 feet; and 3 percent exceeds 3,000 feet. North of the city of Salvador there is a gradual rise from the coast to the interior. However, when approaching Brazil from the Atlantic along the central and southern coasts, one has the impression of a mountainous country since the highland plateau of central and southern Brazil drops off sharply into the Atlantic. The wall-like slope is called the Great Escarpment. It has made access to the interior difficult and has often been cited as a major reason for the slow development of the interior south-central plateau prior to the twentieth century.

With the exception of the Amazon, most of the principal river systems have their sources in central and southeastern Brazil, many fairly close to the ocean. Since, however, the rivers drain inward, there is no natural focus of routes in the most dynamic area of the country; therefore river transportation has not played an important role in the development of Brazil. The Parana system is fed by tributaries which flow westward into the interior until they reach the main river, which flows southward toward Argentina. The source of the São Francisco river is also located in the south. It flows northward, paralleling the cost for more than one thousand miles before turning eastward. Most of the river systems descend rapidly as they go through the Great Escarpment, making interior navigation for ocean vessels impossible. For instance, the São Francisco river is navigable for about 190 miles into the interior, until shortly before the Paulo Afonso falls. Only the Amazon river is navigable far into the interior, and it unites a sparsely populated, underdeveloped, and unexploited region of Brazil.

Brazil is mainly a tropical country and its climates contain few extremes, but "...they are by no means so monotonously uniform, or so umbearably hot and damp, that the human spirit is deadened. If the Brazilian people in certain regions appear to be lacking energy, this cannot be interpreted as the inevitable result of the climate until such other elements as diet and disease have been evaluated."[6]

The average temperature on the Amazon at Santarem, a few degrees from the equator, is 78.1 degrees; in the dry northeast, the highest temperature recorded is 106.7 degrees, but further southward along the coast the maximum temperatures are much lower. The average in Rio de Janeiro in the warmest month is 79 degrees. In the highlands of the interior the temperatures are lower than at the same latitudes on the coast. Only the states south of São Paulo ever experience frost.

Rainfall is adequate in most of Brazil. Deficiency is limited to part of the northeast, where there are areas receiving less than 10 inches a year. Most of the northeast receives between 20 and 25 inches. The principal problem of that region is rainfall irregularity, variations between excessive rains and droughts.[7] Very moist areas, with more than 80 inches of rainfall a year, exist in four regions: the upper Amazon lowlands, the coast from Belem northward, scattered parts of the Great Escarpment, and a small section in the western part of the state of Parana.

NATURAL RESOURCES

Brazil has an abundance of many different types of mineral resources. It has an immense reserve of iron ore (the potential reserves in the 1960s were thought to be about 28 billion tons, out of about 100 billion tons of world reserves), manganese (in 1975 estimated reserves were about 68 million tons) and other industrial metals. The country also possesses substantial quantities of bauxite, copper, lead, zinc, nickel, tungsten, tin, uranium, quartz crystals, industrial diamonds and gem stones.

Until the late sixties knowledge of Brazil's total mineral reserves was still limited. The use of modern techniques of surveying and prospecting (e.g., the use of satellites) has recently resulted in substantial new discoveries.[8] For example, most of the known deposits of minerals until recently were thought to be located in the mountain range running through central Brazil (especially in the state of Minas Gerais). In 1967, however, huge deposits of iron ore (estimated at 18 billion tons) were discovered in the Serra dos Carajas, located in the Amazon region. Also in the late sixties the Amazon was found to contain large deposits of bauxite. Tin reserves near the Bolivian border have been estimated to be larger than those of Bolivia and in the seventies substantial copper deposits were found in the state of Bahia.

In the three decades since World War II there has been a dramatic reshaping of Brazil's sources of energy consumption. In 1946, 70 percent of the country's energy supply was drawn from firewood and charcoal. By the seventies, however, 70 percent was being drawn from oil and hydroelectric power. Unfortunately, the fuel resources of the country have not matched its mineral resources. Until recently the only known coal deposits were located in the southern state of Santa Catarina. This coal is of poor quality, containing a high proportion of ash and sulfur and, therefore, cannot be fully used for the production of coking coal by the steel industry. About 65 percent of metallurgical coal requirements are met by imports. In the seventies some new coal deposits were discovered deep in the Amazon region but have yet to be exploited fully.

Brazil's known oil reserves are inadequate for its needs. Until the early seventies most of the known reserves were located in the states of Bahia and Sergipe, but domestic production from these sources furnished only 20 percent of the country's needs in the midseventies. Off-shore exploration by PETROBRAS, the government-owned company, has resulted in new discoveries near the town of Campos in the state of Rio de Janeiro, in the state of Sergipe, and near the mouth of the Amazon. The sizes of these discoveries were still in doubt at this writing. Also unknown are the potential findings by foreign companies which since 1975 were allowed to explore in Brazil under special risk contracts with PETROBRAS.

The hydroelectric potential of Brazil is one of the largest in the world. It is estimated at 150,000 megawatts. Until the post-World War II period the best sites were considered to be too remote from the major population centers for development, but since the fifties the development of such sites has proceeded rapidly with the construction of the hydroelectric works at Paulo Alfonso Falls and Boa Esperanca in the northeast, Furnas and Ilha Solteira in the southeast, and Tres Marias in the state of Minas Gerais. In the mid-seventies work began on the world's largest hydroelectric projects at Itaipu, on the Paraguayan border. By the mid-seventies, only 7 percent of the country's hydroelectric potential was being used.

THE POPULATION

The 1970 demographic census of Brazil revealed a population of 93 million and population projections of the Brazilian census bureau (FIBGE) estimated the total inhabitants in 1976 was 110 million. This makes Brazil the sixth largest nation in terms of population size. Given the country's enormous territory, its population density is relatively low. It stood at 11 persons per square kilometer in 1970 and was estimated at 12.8 in 1975 (as compared to 9.1 in Argentina, 30 in Mexico, 22.8 in Colombia). Considerable variation can be found in population density, ranging from 1 per square kilometer in the Amazon region to 18.2 in the northeast and to 71.9 in São Paulo state. In the 1970 census year 3.9 percent of the population lived in the Amazon region, 30.3 percent in the northeast, 42.7 in the southeast, 17.7 percent in the south and 5.5 percent in the center-west.

A distinctive feature about the regional distribution of Brazil's population is the degree of concentration within a few hundred miles of the seacoast. Population penetration into the interior has been notable only in the twentieth century, especially in the south. The building of the interior city of Brasilia (which became the federal capital

in 1960), the connecting roads to that city, and the high
rate of road construction activity in the 1960s and 1970s
has substantially increased the migration of the population
to the interior.[9]

The high growth rate of the population (3.1 percent
per year in the fifties and 2.8 percent per year in the
sixties and early seventies) is due to the continuing high
birth rate, coupled with a declining mortality rate. This
has resulted in a high proportion of the population in the
dependent age group of 14 years and below, 42 percent in
1975 (compared to 25 percent in the United States and 28.5
percent in Argentina). The rate of literacy of the population 15 years and above increased from 49 percent in 1950
to 66 percent in 1970. This is closely connected with recent high growth rates of educational enrollment. In the
1960-70 period primary school enrollment increased by 7.13
percent, secondary school enrollment by 247 percent, and
higher education by 487 percent. Thus, by 1971 primary
school enrollment as a percent of the 7-13 year age group
stood at 76 percent; secondary school enrollment as a proportion of the 14-19 year age group was 36 percent; and
higher education enrollment as a proportion of the 20-24
year age group was almost 7 percent.

The high proportion of the population in the younger
age groups and the increasing school enrollment account in
part for the low and even declining labor force participation rate (measured as percent of population of 10 years
and above). This rate shrank from 32.9 percent in 1950 to
31.8 percent in 1970 (the U. S. labor force participation
rate in the 16 year and older ages was about 43 percent in
1974).

The racial composition of Brazil is quite varied. One
expert on Brazil's population has stated that "...There are
few places in the world in which the racial makeup of the
population is more involved and complex than it is in Brazil.
All the principal varieties of mankind, all the basic stocks
into which the human race may be divided--red, white, black,
and yellow--have entered into the composition of the population of this great half-continent."[10] Until the latter
part of the nineteenth century the population was mainly
made up of descendents of Portuguese, Africans and Amer-
indians. During colonial times and into the nineteenth century a considerable amount of miscegenation took place, resulting in a large proportion of today's population being of
mixed ancestry. In the latter part of the nineteenth century
and first decade of the twentieth century large immigration

from Italy, Portugal, Spain, Germany, Poland and the Middle East occurred. These immigrants settled mainly in south-eastern and southern Brazil. In the second decade of the twentieth century large numbers of Japanese immigrated, settling mainly in the states of São Paulo and Parana. It is estimated that there are today over 800,000 Brazilians of Japanese descent.

The diversity in the background of the population has not prevented Brazil from achieving a high degree of cultural unity. With the exception of a small number of Indians deep in the Amazon region, all Brazilians speak Portuguese, with small regional variations of accents (possibly less than in the United States). According to one of the leading interpreters of Brazilian society "...There is a strong and deep feeling among Brazilians of all racial backgrounds and national origins that they form a 'people' and a nation. They share common ideals, common tastes, common problems, common heroes, a common past, and a common sense of humor."11

ENDNOTES

1. The source of population data is: FIBGE, Rio de Janeiro, *Demographic Census*, 1940, 1950, 1960, 1970. These data exaggerate the degree of urbanization, since the Brazilian census definition of urban extends to all populations living in administrative centers. These might consist of small towns with populations of 500 to 1,000 or large cities. Since the economic activities of the former are often much more rural than urban in character, Brazil's degree of urbanization in 1970 is probably less than the official data indicate. For example, if one were to define urban population as that part which lives in cities of 10,000 and more, the proportion of the population which is urban would fall to 41 percent.

2. FIBGE, *Anuario Estatistico do Brasil*, 1975.

3. Carlos Geraldo Langoni, *Distribuição da Renda e Desenvolvimento do Brasil*, Rio de Janeiro: Editôra Expressâo e Cultura, 1973.

4. FIBGE, *Pesquisa Nacional Por Amostra de Domicilios*, Rio de Janeiro, 1972.

5. More detailed information on Brazil's geography can be obtained from: FIBGE, *Sinopse Estatistica do Brasil, 1975;* Preston E. James, *Latin America*, New York: The Odyssey Press, 1969; Donald R. Dyer, "Brazil's Half-Continent," in *Modern Brazil: New Patterns and Development*, edited by John Saunders, Gainesville, Florida: University of Florida Press, 1971, pp. 29–50.

6. James, op. cit., p. 389; see also Dyer op. cit., p. 33.

7. In commenting on northeastern droughts, the geographer Dyer states that "...the dry season is regular but drought is not. However, droughts are too frequent to be unexpected, with periods ranging from a one- to four-year duration..." in Dyer, op. cit., pp. 41–2.

8. "Pesquisas de Recursos Minerais no Brasil," *Conjuntura Economica*, Janeiro de 1974, pp. 66–70.

9. T. Lynn Smith, "The People of Brazil and Their Characteristics," in John Saunders (ed.), *Modern Brazil*, op. cit., pp. 52–3.

10. Ibid., pp. 53–4.

11. Charles Wagley, *An Introduction to Brazil*, New York: Columbia University Press, 1971, Revised Edition, p. 5.

2

HISTORICAL PERSPECTIVE

THE COLONIAL ECONOMY

In early colonial times, during the sixteenth century, Brazil was not considered a rich prize by Portugal. Although the territory acquired by the Portuguese crown was immense, it did not bring it the economic windfall which the Spaniards obtained through their conquest of Peru and Mexico, i.e., precious metals and a large, settled, and well-organized population which could be used in the mining and the supportive agricultural sectors.[1] The Brazilian territory was sparsely inhabited by nomadic indians, whose number declined due to diseases contracted from early Portuguese colonists, and who could not easily be disciplined and trained for plantation work.[2]

Brazil derives its name from its first export product – brazil-wood (*pau-brasil*). The bark of this tree was used as a dye-stuff in Europe. The collection of brazil-wood was a rudimentary activity which did not create many permanent settlements and complementary sectors.[3]

The first major export product of Brazil was sugar. Its cultivation was introduced around 1520, brought to the Brazilian continent by immigrant cane-milling artisans and sugar traders from the Portuguese-held islands in the Atlantic. The rapid spread of sugar cultivation and exports soon developed into the first of a series of great primary export cycles which were to dominate Brazil's economic growth until the twentieth century.[4]

EARLY SOCIO-ECONOMIC ORGANIZATION

The dearth of manpower and the low economic benefits which early Brazil seemed to offer Portugal led to a decentralized political-economic organization of this colony. Trade was mainly in private hands and the establishment of early settlements was left to *donatarios*. The latter were individuals who received concessions to settle and develop specific areas *(capitanias)* at their own expense. They sold land to colonists and engaged in the promotion of various types of commercial undertakings. Thus, early colonization in Brazil "...was essentially a business venture, combined with aspects of private subgovernment."[5] Although in the middle of the sixteenth century a governor-general was appointed to preside over the colony from the city of Salvador, local government was stronger until the latter half of the eighteenth century. Thus, "...only the main outlines of policy were set forth in Europe, and the actual implementation and interpretation were left to the governors and municipal councils."[6]

The latter, in turn, were dominated by the owners of large rural estates *(fazendeiros)* and of sugar mills *(senhores de engenhos)*, and the center of economic and social life was in the large coastal sugar plantations.[7]

THE SUGAR CYCLE

The first great export product of Brazil - sugar - was produced mainly in the humid coastal zone of northeast Brazil, known as the "*zona da mata*". Besides the excellent growing conditions, the region was also favorably located for shipping the product to Europe and for receiving African slave labor. With the scarcity of local Indian laborers, the Portuguese had resorted to importing slaves from Africa (mainly from Angola) to work on the sugar estates.

The rapid spread of sugar growing turned the "*zona da mata*" into a monocultural area. The volume of sugar exports expanded steadily for a century. The increased production was based on the extension of land under cultivation (since there was a large available supply) and the growth of the slave population rather than on changes in the production process and increased productivity. Most of the sugar was grown on large estates (the number of slaves working on an average-sized estate at the time amounted to about 80 to 100).[8]

The only domestic economic linkage at the time was with the northeastern interior (the *agreste* and *sertão* areas) whose surplus agricultural output fed the population of the sugar zones. The population of the interior consisted of Portuguese immigrants and their slaves, fugitive slaves and *caboclos* of mixed blood. They practiced both cultivation and ranching on a fairly primitive basis, but were able to produce enough of a surplus to support the growth of the export sector.

The sugar export sector was profitable for a variety of economic actors: the estate owners, those engaged in marketing, financing, shipping and slave trading. Traders also made substantial profits from importing, since the colony was almost totally dependent on foreign manufactured products and even on some imported foodstuffs.

In his analysis of Brazil's colonial past Celso Furtado calls attention to a fundamental difference between the productive structure of Brazil and the English colonies in North America. A large part of the latter consisted of small agricultural properties, whereas Brazil's export agriculture consisted of large monocultural estates. As a consequence, income in North America was much more evenly distributed than in Brazil. This explains the early appearance of a large internal market in the former which set the basis for an early development of an independent commercial and industrial sector. The smallness of the Brazilian market due to the concentration of property and income served to maintain the stagnant colonial economic structure in Brazil.[9]

While appealing, this argument may not be totally relevant for the colonial period. Economies of scale were less important in industry and commerce at that time as they were to be in the nineteenth and twentieth centuries. One could also argue that since the economy had a natural comparative advantage in sugar and cotton, the development of industries would not have been an efficient way to allocate resources.

Furtado also provides a most convincing analysis of the failure of the early sugar export economy to have significant repercussions on the economy. He suggests that most of the surplus went either to the commercial classes, who invested their gains abroad, or to estate owners, who spent large sums on imports, both consumption and investment goods (which included slaves).[10] He points out how in an export-oriented slave economy the relation between investment and income is very weak since most of the expendi-

ture is made on the importation of manpower and capital,
while the maintenance of slaves was paid for mostly in kind.
The investment represented by the use of slaves to work on
local infrastructure had also no counterpart in money flows.

Since the monetary economy was thus very circumscribed,
export stagnation had little effect on the economy at large,
and was felt only through a decline in the import of goods
and slaves, and a general decline in the relative importance
of the money economy.[11] The only internal repercussions
which the sugar economy had were on the cattle economy of
the interior. Export declines would cause an atrophying of
this sector as it would shift increasingly towards a subsistence type of economy (i.e., a self-sufficient sector
outside the money economy). Migration from the depressed
sugar economy to the interior and the switching of economic
activity from export cattle raising to subsistence would
result in a process of what Furtado calls "economic invol-
ution"--the exact opposite of growth and development.[12]
This process would often occur in the country's economic
history. It shows, in effect, how Brazil's particular
socio-economic organization did not permit export booms to
have lasting secondary effects on the society. For export-
led development to occur many prerequisites were necessary
which were not present in Brazil.

By the early part of the seventeenth century Brazil
had become the world's leading sugar supplier and, according
to Glade "...had supplanted Asiatic spices as the staples
of Anglo-Portuguese trade and Brazilian exports were equally
well-known on the European continent."[13]

As the seventeenth century wore on the export boom
began to fade. The decline of sugar exports was not due to
the failure of technological improvements to occur in Brazil.
The cost of Brazilian sugar was still 30 percent lower than
from British-owned plantations in the Caribbean. The cause
of the decline was the development of an increasing quantity
of sugar supplies in the British, Dutch and French colonies,
which had preferential access to the respective "mother
country" markets.

The sugar plantations did not disappear. Their declining cash income was offset in part by declining money
costs "...as slave breeding within the firm offered at least
a partial substitute for purchased slave imports..."[14] As
described above, some lands were redirected towards subsistence agriculture or to the growing of foodstuffs for
the expanding coastal population. Around Salvador some

lands were switched to the production of tobacco and, later
on in the middle of the eighteenth century, to the growing
of cacao. Some cotton had always been grown in northeast
Brazil and would, on occasion, produce brief export booms
in the late eighteenth century (at the time of the American
revolution) and in the nineteenth century (e.g., during the
American Civil War).[15]

The legacy of the sugar export cycle was negative. The
organization of agriculture on the northeast's interior remained primitive and in the coastal plantations agriculture
techniques continued to be archaic. The slave system had
maintained human resources underveloped[16] and the distribution of assets and money income were extremely concentrated. Much of the windfall profits of the sugar cycle had
been appropriated by Portuguese and foreign intermediaries,
while a large part of the profits accruing to the *fazendeiro*
and *engenho* owners were spent on imported consumer goods
rather than for technical and infrastructural improvements.

THE GOLD CYCLE AND THE RISE OF MERCANTILISTIC CONTROL

A new burst of growth was launched in the 1690s with
the discovery of gold in what is now the state of Minas
Gerais. Despite the precariousness of the communication
system of the day, the news of the discovery spread rapidly
and soon the previously empty region was full of migrants
searching for the precious metals. Gold metal production
increased steadily between 1690 and 1760 (there was also
some diamond output, though on a minor scale). It has been
claimed that Brazil was responsible for half of the world's
gold output in the eighteenth century.[17]

The gold export cycle shifted the center of economic
activity to Brazil's center-south. Migrants came from all
over Brazil. Many northeasterners left their declining
area for the gold regions. These included even planters,
who brought along their slaves. Also streaming in were
farmers and ranchers from the rustic south and new immigrants
from Portugal. Many new towns emerged in the mining districts. Acting as service centers for the extraction
activities, they contained more complex occupational
structures than had existed in previous Brazilian towns.
An artisan sector emerged for the first time and private
banking groups appeared, catering to the needs of the mining
and commercial sectors.

A large proportion of mining was of the placer variety,

which could be operated on a small scale. Since the capital and labor requirements per production unit were therefore small, an increased participation in mining enterprises was possible and as a consequence the concentration of income was smaller than in the northeast.[18]

The mining sector of Minas Gerais had considerable linkage effects. The demand for food in the towns and mining centers was a stimulus to agricultural production not only in Minas Gerais, but also in what is now the state of São Paulo, areas further to the south and even in the northeast. As the shipment of gold to the ports was done by pack animals, the demand for such animals as mules had an impact on many supplying regions in the south. The export of gold and diamonds also financed a growing volume of imports of consumer goods and mining supplies.

The mining boom resulted in the emergence of Rio de Janeiro as a major port. It became the principal center through which the minerals were exported and through which manufactured imports came. It was not long before Brazil's major mercantile houses, financial institutions and various other service activities were located there. In 1763 the administrative center of this Portuguese colony was shifted from Salvador to Rio de Janeiro.

With the substantial increase in the value of its Brazilian colony, the Portuguese government drastically tightened its administrative controls. The mining districts were carefully supervised in order to minimize evasion from payment of one-fifth of the gold mined to the crown. Individual sailings were forbidden; all ships had to be part of officially supervised convoys. Special trading monopolies were established. Local manufacturing was tightly controlled and goods which could be supplied by the metropolis were not allowed to be produced in Brazil.[19]

The minimization of internal linkages with a new manufacturing sector kept the factors of production of the colony in a very primitive state. The latter was also the result, in part, of the neglect of education, which had been practically non-existent before 1776 (except for the scattered efforts of the Jesuits prior to their expulsion in 1759). Even after 1776 the few schools which functioned had little impact on the cultural level of the population.[20] The transportation infrastructure was purposely kept primitive in order to better control smuggling. This kept the dimensions of the internal market very limited for a long time.[21]

The gold cycle came to an end in the latter part of the eighteenth century, when most of the economically viable mines had become exhausted. Some of the mining population then drifted towards the central plateau of Brazil where they carried on ranching; others went to southern Brazil where they engaged in agricultural pursuits. Many remained in Minas Gerais, also turning towards agricultural activities, much of it of subsistence nature.

In the second half of the eighteenth century there also occurred a revival of export agriculture in northeast Brazil. This was especially the case with cotton exports. Most notable was the rise of cotton growing and exporting from Maranhão, Pernambuco and Bahia.[22] Sugar exports, which had never disappeared completely, revived in the late eighteenth century, originating not only from the northeastern areas, but also from São Paulo.

Glade well summarizes the situation of Brazil at the end of the eighteenth century. He states that "...the curtain...fell upon two distinctly separate Brazilian stages. In the north, the coastal-*agreste-sertão* complex lay prostrate, a society nearly immobilized by its internal institutional structure once the old-time dynamism had gone from the external trade links...southward, the first act, based on gold and diamonds, had also come to a close. But there, a rather more versatile and open society remained, poised, as it were, in a sort of developmental entr'acte. Already the stage was being readied for the second presentation - a longer work with coffee as its theme...."[23]

THE COLONY'S LAST YEARS

When Napoleon occupied Portugal in 1807, the royal family, under British protection, set sail for Brazil. In 1808 it established the capital of the Portuguese empire in Rio de Janeiro. The creation of government jobs and the effects of the government payroll on the service and manufacturing sectors stimulated the growth of this city. The crown also undertook construction designed to improve the infrastructure serving the new seat of government.

The abolition of mercantilistic controls helped to increase trade. Both Portuguese and foreign merchants and finance houses increased their activities, aided by the founding of the first Banco do Brasil in 1808. This bank functioned both as a bank of issue and as a commercial bank until 1829.

During this period a printing press was brought to Brazil for the first time. The crown also founded a number of higher educational institutions, and brought numerous European scientists and technicians to Brazil as consultants. It also tried to stimulate various types of industrial establishments. These did not take root, however, due to the flood of imported goods, mainly from Britain. The British had been granted special access to the Brazilian market in return for guaranteeing the naval defense of Brazil.

The king returned to Portugal in 1821, leaving his son behind as regent. As, after a while, it became obvious that Portugal would restore Brazil to a subordinate colonial status again, the increasing discontent throughout Brazil drove the regent to declare independence in 1822. From that date until 1889 Brazil was an independent country governed by a monarchical system, whose head was an emperor, at first Dom Pedro I who, after a regency period of nine years from 1831 to 1840, was followed by his son Dom Pedro II.

THE CENTURY AFTER INDEPENDENCE

At the time of independence, in fact the year after its declaration in 1822, the population of Brazil was estimated at 3.9 million, of which 1.2 million were slaves.[24] Considering the immensity of the country's territorial extension in relation to the number of inhabitants and the communication difficulties which still existed throughout most of the nineteenth century, it is a remarkable historical phenomenon that the country did not break up into smaller independent countries as occurred to the Spanish-American empire.

During the nineteenth century Brazil easily fitted into the world economic order dominated by Great Britain. The latter had become the nucleus of the industrial center of the world, exchanging its manufactured products for food and raw materials from the periphery. The latter consisted of countries whose economies were completely dependent on the exports of such products. Brazil became a typical example of such a country. Its economy was dependent on one major primary export product (coffee) and a few minor ones (sugar, cotton, cocoa); throughout most of the period its economy was open to foreign (mainly British) manufactured products, and foreign (mainly British) capital which flowed into the country and was designed to build a financial, commercial and transport infrastructure which would link the country more efficiently into the nineteenth century world economic order.

THE COFFEE CYCLE

Although coffee was introduced into Brazil in the early part of the eighteenth century, it was at first grown as a specialty item. It was consumed mainly domestically and in the coffee houses of major European cities. With the improvement of European and North American living standards, resulting from the progress brought about by the industrial revolution, coffee consumption expanded rapidly. By the fourth decade of the nineteenth century coffee was the principal export item of Brazil.[25]

The rapid growth of coffee exports in the nineteenth century is shown by the following data for decadal exports (1,000 bags, each of 60 kg):[26]

1821-30	3,178
1831-40	10,430
1841-50	18,367
1851-60	27,339
1861-70	29,103
1871-80	32,509
1881-90	51,631

In the decade 1821-30 coffee accounted for 19 percent of total exports and by 1891 this share had risen to about 63 percent.

Until 1880 the bulk of Brazil's coffee was grown to the north and west of Rio de Janeiro (mostly in the Paraiba valley) and also in the northeast (the Cantagalo region). The production techniques were rudimentary, based on black and mulatto slaves who lived mostly outside the money economy. The plantation was run by the owner, the *fazendeiro* who presided "...as a powerful patriarch over the social and political affairs of the immediate area, in addition to controlling the economic activities of the plantation itself."[27] In the pre-railroad days the coffee was shipped by mule train to the port of Rio de Janeiro. The handling of coffee between the *fazenda* and the export houses was conducted by commission agents (*comissarios*).[28]

As the good lands of the Paraiba valley were becoming exhausted around the 1880s, coffee production moved south to the state of São Paulo and then westward in that state. In the 1860s British capital and engineers built a railroad over the coastal escarpment separating the central plateau of São Paulo from the port of Santos, and in the next decades railroads were built deep into the São Paulo coffee zones.

São Paulo's coffee production grew rapidly in the 1880s
and 1890s. By 1890 the amount of coffee passing through
Santos was equal to that of Rio de Janeiro and by 1894 it
had become the world's most important coffee export center.[29]

The westward expansion in São Paulo resulted in the
development of large coffee estates since only a relatively
small number of persons had the economic and political
power necessary to establish and defend titles and to place
new lands into production. These employed an increasing
number of free laborers and even before the abolition of
slavery in 1888 they promoted European immigration. After
abolition there was a massive influx of immigrant labor,
mainly from southern and eastern Europe (especially from
Italy).[30]

There can be no doubt that coffee exports were the
engine of growth throughout most of the nineteenth century.
Also, as in the latter part of the nineteenth century the
coffee economy shifted to São Paulo, the economic center of
the country gradually shifted to that region, where it was
to remain until the present day. The secondary effects of
the São Paulo coffee economy--employment of free immigrant
labor, foreign investment in infrastructure, capital accumulation of coffee growers, and, as will be seen in a later
chapter, the derived growth of industry--were to deepen the
regional dualism between the center-south and the rest of
Brazil (especially taking into account the northeast).

Some students of Brazil's economic history, especially
Celso Furtado, have identified the backwardness of the
country vis-a-vis Europe and the United States as being
due to the privileged position of England as a supplier of
manufactured goods and to the lack of an important native
commercial class. Thus, political power was in the hands
of the land-owning classes whose interests were compatible
with the nineteenth century international division of labor.
Furtado emphasizes his points by comparing the Brazilian
and U. S. post-independence situation. The influence of
the small farming sector and the commercial classes and the
independence war against the supplier of manufactured goods
are taken by Furtado as important institutional factors ex-
plaining the nineteenth century progress in the U. S. in contrast to the socioeconomic stagnation of Brazil.[31]

In his discussion of the rise of the coffee economy
Furtado is very sensitive to non-economic phenomena. He
points to the differences between the formerly dominant
sugar estate owning classes and the newly emerging coffee

estate owners. In the heyday of sugar, commerce was a monopoly of the Portuguese. Thus, sugar estate owners, divorced
from commerce, never developed into outward-looking entrepreneurs. The coffee producers, however, were intimately
linked to the commercial end of their sector. They were
also much closer than the sugar owners to the capital of the
country. Thus, they were much more aware than other classes
of the potential role of the state in affecting their economic interests. This insight is of fundamental importance
in understanding the state support which the coffee sector
obtained in the twentieth century.[32]

OTHER EXPORTS

Although coffee was dominant throughout most of the
nineteenth century, other primary export products continued
to be present in the country's export list. Sugar production
expanded due mainly to a growing domestic market, since the
value of annual export growth was less than 1 percent. The
latter was due to the competition of beet sugar in protected
European markets, to the sugar production in the U. S. and
to the competition of more low cost Cuban sugar.[33]

Cotton exports did not fare much better than sugar;
their quantum rose by only 43 percent in the 1850-1900
period. High transportation costs from the interior to the
ports seem to have been one of the major causes for the
slow growth of these exports.[34] Tobacco exports from Bahia
appeared in the last decades of the nineteenth century.
These never became significant due to the poor production
practices which made Brazilian tobacco uncompetitive in the
international market. At the close of the nineteenth century
cacao exports from southern Bahia made their appearance.
After the introduction of a high-yielding variety of cacao
from Ceylon in 1907, plantations expanded rapidly and Brazil
became one of the world's leading exporters of the product.

A spectacular export boom began in the Amazon region
in the last decades of the nineteenth century. Since at
that time the region was the world's main source of rubber,
the rapidly growing demand for the product and rising prices
resulted in the rapid penetration and settlement of the area
by both domestic and foreign business groups. Much of the
labor to gather the sap of the scattered wild rubber trees
came from northeastern Brazil, especially from Ceará. The
calamitous drought of the 1870s had resulted in the availability of a large pool of labor ready to migrate to the
Amazon. Rubber exports rose from an annual average of

6,000 tons in the 1870s to 21,000 tons in the 1890s and
35,000 tons in the first decade of the twentieth century.
In the latter period Brazil was supplying 90 percent of the
world's rubber and by 1910 the product counted for 40 percent
of Brazil's exports.[35]

In the 1870s seeds of the rubber trees (*Hevea*) were
smuggled out of Brazil for experimentation in London's Kew
botanical gardens. By 1895 plantations were established in
Asia and by 1899 the first Asian rubber appeared in the
world market. The growth of the world rubber supply by the
second decade of the twentieth century caused prices to decline dramatically. By 1921 rubber prices were less than
one-sixth the 1910 level. Brazil could not compete with the
much cheaper Asian product and gradually lost its entire
share of the world market.

The net effects of the rubber boom on the Brazilian
economy were hardly discernible after its collapse. The
income generated was mostly spent on imports from abroad
and on wildly conspicuous consumption (as exemplified by
the famous opera house built in the jungle city of Manaus).

PUBLIC POLICIES IN THE NINETINTH CENTURY

In the decade and a half prior to independence the
Portuguese court "in exile" made efforts to diversify the
socio-cultural and economic life of Brazil, especially in
Rio and its vicinities. This was manifested in the founding
of the first Banco do Brasil in 1808, the first modern-style
bank in Latin America; the founding of a stock exchange in
Rio; the importation of the first printing press; the con-
tracting of technicians; and the assistance provided to
various types of industrial undertakings (like the development of metallurgical shops in Minas Gerais and São Paulo).[36]
As will be seen in the next chapter, many of the early industrialization efforts were nullified after independence
due to the open-door policies to industrial imports. Though
import duties existed throughout the period, they, along
with export duties, were the principal source of government
revenues and rarely had protectionist effects.

One of the principal government developmental measures
in the second half of the nineteenth century was the promotion of railroad construction. The main policy tools consisted of subsidies and guaranteed rates of return.[37] Unfortunately the railroad network developed was deficient in
many ways. Different lines were constructed with different

gauges, they linked plantations to the port, and there was
a tendency for many lines to meander instead of linking the
interior with the port in the most efficient way. The resulting transportation system did not link the country into
a more unified market. Table 1 shows the growth of Brazil's
railroad trackage.

TABLE 1
Growth of the Brazilian Railroad Lines, 1854-1934

Kilometers of track

1854	14
1864	474
1874	1,284
1884	3,302
1894	12,260
1904	16,306
1914	26,062
1924	30,306
1934	33,106

Source: *Anuário Estatístico do Brasil,* Ano V, p. 139.

Most of the railroads were constructed by British
firms. In 1870 four British companies owned 72 percent of
Brazil's railroad trackage. After the suspension of the
rate of return guarantees in 1901, most construction of
additional trackage was in the hands of the government,
which also gradually took over an increasing number of
foreign private lines.[38]

Throughout the nineteenth century the central government was intermittently active in promoting immigration and
colonization. Already prior to independence the Portuguese
crown attracted a group of Swiss colonizers by paying their
passage and providing the means for them to start a settlement.[39] The existence of slavery made the spread of such
schemes difficult, though some others were carried out in
southern Brazil in the 1820s and 1830s with German immigrants. Only with the end of slavery in the south did
large-scale immigration to that area begin. After abolition
in 1888 and the establishment of the republic in 1889
immigration reached large-scale proportions.[40]

Immigration was to have a positive effect on the economic development of Brazil, especially in the south, since

it provided the country with a large number of economically ambitious people. Also, "...the public subsidization
of immigration was, for the short-run, a reasonably effective substitute for investment in education as a means of
building up the quality of human resources in the economy."[41]

Towards the end of the century the government became
active in protecting Brazil's major export sectors. Government-guaranteed earnings and import tariff exemptions for
equipment were used as incentives for investments in heavily
capitalized central sugar mills *(usinas)*.[42] And in the first
decade of the twentieth century, as Brazil's coffee production was outstripping world demand, resulting in declining
prices, the state of São Paulo placed a ban for five years
on new coffee tree plantings, and in 1907 São Paulo (with
some cooperation from the states of Minas Gerais and Rio
de Janeiro) initiated the first of the valorization schemes
(although this was known as the Convênio de Taubaté, the
program was carried out almost single-handedly by the state
of São Paulo). Using at first proceeds from export taxes
and later foreign loans (which had central government
guarantees), São Paulo bought large amounts of coffee which
were withheld from the market in order to stabilize prices.[43]

ENDNOTES

1. William P. Glade, *The Latin American Economies: A Study of their Institutional Evolution.* New York: American Book-Van Nostrand, 1969, chapters III and IV.

2. Caio Prado Junior, *História Ecônomica do Brasil.* São Paulo: Editôra Brasiliense, 12a. ediçao, 1970, pp. 35-6.

3. Ibid., pp. 24-7; Mircea Buescu and Vicente Tapajós, *Historia Do Desenvolvimento Econômico Do Brasil.* Rio de Janeiro: A Casa do Livno, Ltda., 1969, pp. 29-31.

4. Before 1548 an annual average of two ships sufficed for the Brazilian colony's trade. Forty years later, the annual average had reached 45, and by 1620 the number stood at 200. Ronald Dennis Hussey, "Colonial Economic Life," in *Colonial Hispanic America,* Volume IV of Studies in *Hispanic American Affairs,* edited by A. Curtis Wilgus, 1935, p. 334.

5. Glade, op. cit., p. 156.

6. Ibid.; see also Buescu and Tapajos, op. cit., pp. 100-4.

7. The best known work describing this society is: Gilberto Freyre, *The Masters and the Slaves.* New York: Alfred A. Knopf, 1946. Freyre's description, however, is far from complete. For example, he ignores the free sugar cane growers who were somewhere between the "masters" and the "slaves." Freyre's Brazil more accurately describes the northeast of the nineteenth century (especially Pernamburo) than anything else.

8. Caio Prado Junior, op. cit., pp. 34-8; Buescu and Tapajós, op. cit., pp. 33-4.

9. Celso Furtado, *Formação Econômica do Brasil.* São Paulo: Companhia Editora Nacional, Décima Primeira Edição, 1972, pp. 30-1.

10. Ibid., pp. 45-6.

11. Ibid., pp. 50-52.

12. Ibid., p. 64; Buescu and Tapajos present some estimates of Brazil's cattle herd in the sixteenth and seventeenth centuries, op. cit., pp. 36-7.

13. Glade, op. cit., p. 162.

14. Ibid., pp. 163-31;for some quantitative estimates of sugar exports in selected years during the colonial period, see Buescu and Tapajós, op. cit., pp. 24-4 and p. 128.

15. Caio Prado Junior, op. cit., pp. 81-2.

16. In another book Caio Prado Junior gives a very negative appraisal of slavery in its influence on economic and social development: He states that "...the universal use of slaves in the different trades and occupations of economic and social life ended by influencing the attitude to work, which came to be regarded as con-

temptible and degrading." See his: *The Colonial Background of Modern Brazil.* Berkeley and Los Angeles: University of California Press, 1967, p. 325.

17. Glade, op. cit., p. 166; Buescu and Tapojós, op. cit., pp. 38–40.

18. Furtado, op. cit., p. 76; Glade, op. cit., p. 167.

19. Caio Prado Junior, *História*, pp. 50-9.

20. Caio Prado Junior gives succinct picture of the educational level of the colony

   ...no attempt was made to make up for the isolation in which the colony was compelled to exist by providing even an elementary system of education. The meager instruction given in the few official schools that existed in some of the colony's largest centers did not go much beyond the teaching of reading, writing, and arithmetic...Created after 1776, these schools were generally neglected and understaffed, the teachers badly paid, the pupils unruly, and the classes unorganized. The cultural level of the colony was extremely low and the crassest ignorance prevailed. The few scholars who distinguished themselves were in a world apart, ignored by a country utterly unable to understand them...

   in *The Colonial Background*, pp. 160-1.

21. Buescu and Tapajós, op. cit., pp. 110-1.

22. Caio Prado Junior, *História Econômica*, pp. 82-3.

23. Glade, op. cit., p. 171.

24. Caio Prado Junior, *História*, p. 346. Earlier estimates of Brazil's population were as follows:

1550 - 15,000	1690 - 300,000
1600 - 100,000	1776 - 1,900,000
1660 - 184,000	

25. Thomas H. Holloway, *The Brazilian Coffee Valorization of 1906: Regional Politics and Economic Dependence.* Madison, Wisconsin: The State Historical Society of Wisconsin for The Department of History, University of Wisconsin, 1975, p. 5.

26. Caio Prado Junior, *História*, p. 160.

27. Holloway, op. cit., p. 5; see also Stanley Stein, *Vassouras, A Brazilian Coffee County, 1850-1900.* Cambridge, Mass.: Harvard University Press, 1957.

28. Holloway, op. cit., p. 6.

29. Holloway, op. cit., pp. 7-9.

30. Ibid., pp. 15-7. From 1887 to 1906 around 1.2 million immigrants entered São Paulo, of whom more than 800,000 were from Italy.

31. Furtado, op. cit., pp. 111-3.

32. Furtado, op. cit., pp. 114-6.

33. David Denslow, "Exports and the Origins of Brazil's Regional Pattern of Industrialization," in *Dimensões Do Desenvolimento Brasileiro*, edited by Werner Baer, Pedro Geiger and Paulo Haddad, Rio de Janeiro: Editora Campus, 1978; and David Denslow, "As Origens da Desigualdade Regional no Brasil," in *Formação Econômica do Brasil: A Experiência da Industrialização*, edited by Flavio R. Versiani and José Roberto Mendonça de Barros. São Paulo: Edição Saraiva S.A., Série ANPEC De Leituras de Economia, 1977.

34. Denslow, "As Origens...", pp. 59-60.

35. Caio Prado Junior, *História*, pp. 236-41; Glade, op. cit., p. 297.

36. Glade, op. cit., p. 299; Werner Baer, *The Development of the Brazilian Steel Industry*, Nashville, Tennessee: Vanderbilt University Press, 1969, chapter 4.

37. Annibal V. Villela and Wilson Suzigan, *Política do Governo e Crescimento da Economia Brasileira, 1889-1945*, Rio de Janeiro: IPEA, Serie Monografica, No. 10, 2a. Edicao, 1975, pp. 378-83. Villela and Suzigan note that the system of railroad concessions was subject to abuse. They find that "...The concessions were often given as favors to influential persons, who sold these as a monopolistic privilege. Also, the guarantees of rates of return on invested capital did not lead to the most rational layout of lines. The latter were often longer than necessary and technically imperfect...", p. 381.

38. Villela and Suzigan, op. cit., pp. 383-4.

39. Glade, op. cit., p. 303.

40. Ibid, p. 306; Douglas H. Graham, "Migração Estrangeira e a Questão da Operta da Mão-de-Obra No Crescimento Econômico Brasileiro, 1880-1930," *Estudos Econômicos*, Vol. 3, No. 1, 1973, pp. 10-13.

41. Ibid., p. 306.

42. Glade, op. cit., p. 303.

43. Holloway, op. cit.

3

EARLY INDUSTRIAL GROWTH

PRE-WORLD WAR I PERIOD

The few attempts at promoting the production of manufactures in the last years of colonial Brazil were nullified by the open-door policies of the post-independence government. Most pronounced was the presence of British goods, which for many years had privileged access to the Brazilian market. Merchandise from other European countries and the United States also appeared after commercial treaties were negotiated in the 1820s.[2] The tariff of 1828, which set import duties at 15 percent, ushered in the most liberal trade period.

Tariffs were raised in the 1840s, reaching an average of over 30 percent ad valorem by 1844. Though the primary aim of increased import duties was the raising of government revenues, they had some protectionist side-effects, resulting in the establishment of a number of textile firms. The state also provided tariff exemptions for raw material and machinery imports used by national enterprises. The latter were also exempted from paying local excise taxes.[3] By 1852, 64 factories and workshops had benefitted from these privileges. They could be found in such fields as textiles, apparel, soap, beer, foundries, glassware, leather products, etc.

Under the pressure of coffee interests which favored cheaper imports, some of these tariff policies were revoked in 1857 and duties were lowered. In the 1860s tariffs were raised again for fiscal reasons to an average of 50 percent, and in the following two decades further measures of protection were occasionally introduced.

The few workshops which existed in the middle of the

nineteenth century were especially concentrated in the textile sector. A number of textile firms were founded in the mid-1840s, as a result of the above mentioned tariff of 1844 and the special privileges granted for importing machinery. A further expansion of the number of textile firms in operation occurred in the first half of the 1870s in the Rio de Janeiro and São Paulo areas. Although by 1885 a total of 48 textile firms were in existence, their total impact was minor, as evidenced by the fact that all firms together only employed a little over 3,000 workers.[4]

The available statistical evidence indicates that Brazilian industrial growth became significant during the 1880s and continued for the following three decades. For example, Table 2 shows a more than tenfold increase in cotton textile production between 1885 and 1905 and an almost doubling of output in the ten years thereafter. Just prior to 1914, output of textiles had already reached 85 percent of the country's apparent consumption. The output of clothing, shoes, beverages, and tobacco products in 1911 had attained about 40 percent of the 1929 production (see Tables 3 and 4). When one considers that in the late 1920s Brazilian textile mills produced nearly 90 percent of domestic consumption, the high output prior to 1914 suggests that even then a very large proportion of consumption was supplied by domestic producers.[5]

TABLE 2
Cotton Textile Industry Production, 1853-1948

Year	Number of mills	Workers	Production (1,000 meters)
1853	8	424	1,210
1866	9	795	3,586
1885	48	3,172	20,595
1905	110	39,159	242,087
1915	240	82,257	470,783
1921	242	108,960	552,446
1925	257	114,561	535,909
1929	359	123,470	477,995
1932	355	115,550	630,738
1948	409	224,252	1,119,738

Source: Stanley Stein, op. cit., p. 191.

TABLE 3

Indicators of Real Product, 1911-19
(1929 = 100)

Year	Textiles	Clothing, shoes and other textiles	Beverages	Tobacco	Total*
1911	75.4	41.7	37.2	38.2	60.9
1912	79.2	47.3	47.0	42.5	65.8
1913	76.5	46.8	53.8	46.6	65.3
1914	62.0	35.4	48.4	42.2	53.5
1915	91.9	38.9	38.6	40.9	70.8
1916	86.4	47.2	40.8	53.3	70.6
1917	100.9	52.2	38.6	41.3	78.5
1918	91.0	52.1	40.2	46.4	73.4
1919	105.6	54.0	48.8	65.0	85.4

Source: Annival V. Villela and Wilson Suzigan, op. cit., p. 432.

*1919 weight was used in calculating the index of this column.

Indicators of capital formation, shown in Table 5, which are available only from 1901 on, rose uninterruptedly until 1914. They reached very high levels in the half decade before World War I. Apparent consumption of cement increased 12-fold (from 37,300 tons in 1901 to 465,300 in 1913); steel consumption increased by more than 8-fold (from 69,300 tons to 589,000 tons); and the importation of capital goods almost quadrupled in the same period. The extent of industrial growth in the latter period is also evident in the 1920 census, whose data refer to the year 1919. Of 13,336 industrial establishments which existed in that year, 55.4 percent were founded prior to 1914; and the average size of these firms, as measured by number of employees or installed power capacity per worker, was larger than those established during World War I (see Table 6).

The industrial structure which developed in this early period of growth was dominated by light industries. Textiles, clothing, shoes, and the food industries accounted for over 57 percent of industrial output in 1907 and for over 64 percent in 1919.

The basic force behind this early industrial growth was the coffee boom based on free immigrant labor. Substan-

TABLE 4

Industrial Production Index, 1920-1939
(1929 = 100)

	1920	1921	1922	1923	1924	1925	1926	1927	1928	1929	1930	1931	1932	1933	1934	1935	1936	1937	1938	1939
Total	78.0	77.1	89.1	106.4	88.9	89.6	88.8	95.9	103.5	100.0	95.2	103.1	103.4	118.6	133.9	152.9	174.9	187.1	199.4	224.6
Mining	126.8	99.8	108.4	94.2	81.3	93.6	95.8	85.7	104.7	100.0	91.1	85.8	82.3	86.2	85.0	96.3	104.5	128.3	140.1	137.7
Manufacturing total	76.9	76.6	88.7	106.7	89.1	89.5	88.6	96.1	103.4	100.0	95.3	103.5	103.9	119.3	135.1	154.2	176.5	188.4	200.7	226.6
Nonmet. minerals	93.0	101.6	104.9	132.0	125.9	87.9	82.7	70.8	97.8	100.0	87.8	151.2	145.4	208.9	282.5	332.0	426.5	498.6	558.3	619.5
Metal products	43.7	46.2	47.5	59.7	51.7	62.7	56.1	53.1	78.0	100.0	81.9	71.9	90.2	130.5	155.3	172.2	202.0	225.3	274.1	397.7
Paper products	n.a.	n.a.	n.a.	n.a.	n.a.	n.a.	67.7	51.2	84.1	100.0	80.3	120.7	102.2	238.8	290.8	424.1	459.7	546.9	566.6	781.9
Leather products	n.a.	n.a.	n.a.	n.a.	n.a.	n.a.	n.a.	n.a.	106.8	100.0	121.0	118.7	107.8	137.2	146.1	172.8	152.8	175.3	160.1	161.0
Chemicals and pharmaceuticals	55.5	52.1	58.7	79.4	82.8	87.8	96.8	105.1	108.8	100.0	100.3	66.4	73.4	82.7	79.2	105.0	113.2	133.6	138.3	151.2
Perfumes, soap, and candles	47.5	46.5	62.6	72.6	84.0	73.0	73.1	97.1	112.9	100.0	77.9	77.0	95.6	107.8	153.7	157.0	285.9	221.0	255.9	259.2
Textiles	106.6	104.1	116.7	166.5	110.2	105.8	105.6	122.1	123.9	100.0	97.2	125.6	127.4	131.0	145.7	165.4	195.8	207.5	219.8	247.0
Clothing and shoes	61.7	55.0	63.6	65.6	77.8	76.2	72.9	86.6	95.5	100.0	70.8	75.0	67.3	71.2	74.6	94.7	110.9	121.0	113.8	124.8
Food products	63.2	66.7	86.2	77.8	79.2	86.7	88.3	90.2	93.4	100.0	107.9	102.3	99.3	111.6	116.9	128.6	132.4	120.9	125.5	124.9
Beverages	64.2	63.2	73.2	76.1	70.0	75.5	81.0	92.6	96.4	100.0	83.5	70.3	76.3	79.8	81.7	97.3	107.7	110.4	110.5	129.6
Tobacco	67.6	61.5	72.4	70.2	67.0	85.8	69.5	81.6	91.7	100.0	86.7	87.7	85.5	88.5	135.5	102.0	121.2	143.4	148.4	120.3

Source: Villela et al, "Aspectos do Crescimento..."; estimates are based on data in Instituto Brasileiro de Geografia e Estatística (IBGE), Anuário Estatístico do Brasil, 1939/40; IBGE, *Recenseamento Geral do Brasil for 1920 and 1940*; and Ministério da Agricultura, Serviço de Estatística da Produção.

Note: Indexes for each industry group are weighted according to the average of their proportion in the value added to manufacturing industry during the census years 1919 and 1939.

TABLE 5
Indicators of Capital Formation

Year	Apparent consumption of cement (1,000 tons)	Apparent consumption of steel (1,000 tons)	Quantum index of imports of capital goods (1939 = 100)
1901	37.3	69.3	56.8
1902	58.8	107.0	31.7
1903	63.8	111.2	38.0
1904	94.0	127.3	41.3
1905	129.6	170.6	62.3
1906	180.3	220.3	66.1
1907	179.9	295.0	93.0
1908	197.9	267.6	96.4
1909	201.8	304.5	102.9
1910	264.2	362.3	118.7
1911	268.7	369.2	153.6
1912	367.0	506.6	205.3
1913	465.3	589.3	152.6
1914	180.8	200.5	63.4
1915	144.9	95.2	25.2
1916	169.8	96.9	32.2
1917	98.6	87.0	32.0
1918	51.7	50.0	36.9
1919	198.4	155.1	64.6
1920	173.0	279.7	108.1
1921	156.9	200.7	125.8
1922	319.6	201.6	91.5
1923	223.4	219.4	119.4
1924	317.2	349.6	151.0
1925	336.5	373.5	209.2
1926	409.7	399.4	154.7
1927	496.6	435.8	124.3
1928	544.2	483.1	133.2
1929	631.5	514.3	184.7
1930	471.7	259.2	99.7
1931	281.4	143.9	33.6
1932	310.0	165.7	28.9
1933	339.4	277.0	47.4
1934	449.6	343.6	82.9
1935	480.4	345.4	123.7
1936	563.3	386.7	114.5
1937	646.3	505.4	143.2
1938	667.5	355.7	122.5
1939	732.6	429.8	100.0
1940	759.2	414.5	56.4
1941	776.8	368.3	86.5
1942	818.8	262.8	67.1
1943	753.4	325.5	176.1
1944	907.4	492.6	166.7
1945	1,025.5	465.6	82.7

Source: Villela and Suzigan, op. cit., p. 437; for steel, Ministerio da Agricultural, Serviço de Estatística da Produção (SEP); for cement, see Serviço de Estatística do Sindato Nacional da Industria do Cimento; for imports, Ministerio da Fazenda, Serviço de Estatística Econômica e Financeira (SEEF).

TABLE 6
Industrial Establishments
According to Date of Founding, 1920

Date founded	Establishments Number	Percentage	Number of workers per establishment	Horse-power per worker	Value of output (percentage)
Until 1884	388	2.91	76	1.01	8.7
1885-1889	248	1.86	98	1.48	8.3
1890-1894	452	3.39	68	1.08	9.3
1895-1899	472	3.54	29	1.05	4.7
1900-1904	1,080	8.10	18	1.01	7.5
1905-1909	1,358	10.18	25	1.17	12.3
1910-1914	3,135	23.51	17	1.15	21.3
1915-1919	5,936	44.51	11	1.02	26.3
Date unknown	267	2.00	16	1.77	1.6
Total	13,336	100.00	20[a]	1.13[a]	100.0

Source: *Recenseamento do Brasil,* Vol. 5, *Indústria* for 1919, p. 69.
[a] Weighted averages.

tial infrastructural investment to service the coffee sector (railroads, power stations, etc.), financed by planters and foreign capital,[6] provided the setting for greater local industrial output and gradually created a demand for locally produced spare parts. The large immigrant population employed in the coffee and coffee-related sectors provided a large market for cheap consumer goods. Thus, in describing events in São Paulo, Warren Dean noted that

> The very first products to be manufactured...were those whose weight-to-cost ratio was so high that even with the most rudimentary technique they cost less to produce than to buy from Europe...The most important activities employed local agricultural materials, notably cotton, leather, sugar, cereals, and lumber, or nonmetallic minerals, especially clay, sand, lime, and stone.[7]

Most of the early Brazilian industrialists were importers who at a certain stage in their activities found it worthwhile to produce goods domestically instead of importing them. This was especially the case with textiles. For instance, it has been found that of 13 textile firms started in the nineteenth century and still functioning in 1917, 11 were controlled by importers.[8] These enterprises were financed by both importers and coffee planters. The former also had special access to European creditors in financing the importation of machinery.

The inflationary credit expansion (known as the "encilhamento") in the 1890s has been mentioned by some analysts as a contributing element in the establishment of new industrial enterprises in that decade.[9] Others, however, have claimed that existing evidence does not sustain this hypothesis.[10]

The occasional attempts at tariff protection since the 1840s do not seem to have been an important contributory force to industrial growth.[11] The same could be said for direct government aid to certain sectors, which was authorized only infrequently. It is true, however, that for specific sectors (special concessions and/or subsidies to railroads, steel firms, etc.) direct government help was crucial. Finally, occasional devaluation of the Brazilian currency vis-a-vis the British pound, by raising the price of imported goods, accelerated industrial growth.[12]

Returning to our quantitative presentation, it is of interest to note the substantial increase in productive capacity in the eight years prior to World War I. It will be seen in Table 5 that all indicators of capital formation grew more rapidly in that period than at any time before. This substantial spurt was due in part to the increased import capacity of those years and also to the appreciation of the currency vis-a-vis the pound sterling in the period 1905-1913. This lowered the price of foreign goods and caused large increases in the importation of machinery. It should be noted in Table 6 that the firms founded in the period 1905-14 were more capital intensive (as measured by horsepower per worker and excepting the relatively few firms established during 1885-89) than firms founded either before that time or during World War I. Also, these firms produced a larger proportion of total output in 1920 than either the establishments founded in the 1885-1904 period or newer firms.[13]

WORLD WAR I

Until recently most students of the Brazilian economy claimed that World War I had a pronounced impact on both industrial output and the growth of industrial production

capacity.[14] A close examination of all available data,
however, will show that World War I was not a catalyst to
industrial growth, principally because the interruption of
shipping made it difficult to import the capital goods necessary to increase productive capacity, and within Brazil no
capital goods industry existed at the time.

The three investment indicators in Table 5 also give
evidence of substantial downward trends in the war years.
Apparent cement consumption fell from over 465,000 tons in
1913 to a low of 51,700 tons in 1918; apparent steel consumption fell from 589,000 tons to 50,000 tons in the same
period; and the index of capital goods imports declined
from 205.3 in 1912 to 32.0 in 1917. An analysis of changes
in Brazil's import structure for 1911-13 and 1914-18 in
Table 7 also reveals a much greater decline in the import
of capital goods than of other types of products.

TABLE 7
Index of Quantum Changes in Brazilian Imports

Period	Consumer goods	Raw materials	Fuels	Capital goods	Total
1911-13	100.0	100.0	100.0	100.0	100.0
1914-18	45.1	47.8	65.0	22.2	44.6

Source: Villela et al., "Aspectos...", Vol. 1, p. 174
Note: Index values based on average yearly imports.

Turning to the existing evidence on output, we see in
Table 3 a considerable increase in the production of textiles, clothing and shoes. Beverages and tobacco output
hardly changed. These sectors accounted for about 50 percent of value added in 1919. Not included in the table because of lack of yearly data is the food products industry
which, after textiles, constituted the most important sector
of industrial activity. It accounted for 19 percent of
value added in industry in 1907 and 20.5 percent in 1919.
This industry had its capacity greatly expanded in the half
decade before the war - especially sugar refining and meat
packing plants. The latter was stimulated by the almost
doubling of electric generating capacity during 1910-14.

The effect of World War I was not to expand and change
the industrial productive capacity of Brazil, but rather to
increase the utilization of the food and textile producing

capacity which had been created prior to the war. Increased output went mainly to supply the import-starved domestic economy, but some textiles were exported to Argentina and South Africa, and sugar and frozen meats were sent to various Latin American countries. The quantities of these exports, however, were very small, especially in comparison to the export achievements during World War II.

THE TWENTIES

The dynamism of the Brazilian economy in the twenties was based on a booming coffee export sector. Coffee's share in exports rose from 56 percent in 1919 to over 75 percent in 1924. In the same period exports as a proportion of GNP rose from 5.7 to 12.5 percent. The country's favorable balance of payments situation during the decade brought along a slight appreciation of the exchange rate, which, together with rising internal prices, decreased any protection domestic industries had from foreign competition.[15]

The 1920s, in general, constituted a period of relatively slow growth for the industrial sector. The average yearly growth rate of industrial output fell from 4.6 percent in the period 1911-20 to 3 percent in the period 1920-9. Especially noteworthy in Table 4 is the very slow growth of textile output. There was, however, a rapid rate of expansion of metal products, due basically to the appearance of new small steel plants and capital goods enterprises. Of course, the small base from which the metallurgical sector began in the early twenties also explains the high growth rates observed. The second half of the decade marked the beginning of domestic cement production. A firm established in 1924 began to produce two years later, and output rose from a little over 13,000 tons in 1926 to about 96,000 tons in 1929.[16]

It is of interest to contrast the growth of industrial production in Table 4 with the indicators of capital formation in Table 5. While production grew at relatively slow rates, the importation of capital goods rose dramatically in the twenties to average yearly levels above those of the pre-World War I years. Also noteworthy is the large expansion of apparent consumption of cement and steel, which are fairly reliable indicators of investment activities. We thus have a spurt of investment activities alongside only modest growth rates of yearly industrial production. This becomes especially evident when contrasting textile production in the twenties with the importation of textile machinery

(see Tables 2 and 8). While output actually declined in
the period 1921-29, imports of textile machinery rose to
pre-World War I levels.

TABLE 8
Textile Machinery Imports
(metric tons)

1913-	13,345	1921-	6,295	1928-	6,244
1915-	2,194	1922-	6,635	1929-	4,647
1916-	2,450	1923-	8,838	1930-	1,986
1917-	2,002	1924-	10,192	1933-	2,051
1918-	2,932	1925-	17,859	1934-	4,112
1919-	2,753	1926-	10,430	1935-	3,875
1920-	4,262	1927-	6,744		

Source: Stein, op. cit., p. 124.

The slow growth of industrial output is due only in
part to the inflow of cheaper and better quality foreign
goods. An examination of changes in the import structure
in Table 9 reveals a sharp decline in food products and
beverages over the war years and continuing into the 1920s.
On the other hand, there was some proportional recovery in
textiles, which could reflect the competition of textile
imports with domestic products. The most prominent increase
in the share of imports occurred in products associated with
capital formation.

The slow industrial growth can also be attributed,
especially in the case of textiles, to the spurt in production during the war years which, in a sense, anticipated the
growth of a market for domestically produced goods. In other
words, the increased wartime use of capacity to furnish
goods might have occurred over a longer period of time had
the war not taken place. Thus, the postwar growth was
slower, in part, because the "normal" increase in domestic
output, which would have occurred had there been no war,
was packed into the period 1914-19.

The substantial increase in productive capacity during
the twenties can also be attributed to World War I. First,
since wartime production grew through increasingly intensive use of capacity, without replacement investment, some
of the investments of the twenties can be accounted simply
as replacement and repair of existing equipment. Second,
the data suggest an accelerator relationship with a lag.

The growth of output, especially in textiles, created among producers an anticipation of further market growth of domestic products; thus they ordered equipment which was delivered only during the twenties.[17]

TABLE 9

Changes in Brazil's Import Structure, 1901-29
(average annual percentages)

Import Category	1901-10	1911-20	1920-29
Mining	6.2	8.8	5.5
Manufactures	83.6	78.7	80.8
Metal products	12.3	13.0	13.8
Machinery	4.8	4.7	7.4
Electrical equipment	1.0	1.8	3.0
Transport equipment	2.6	4.0	8.0
Chemicals	5.6	9.0	11.9
Textile products	15.1	10.9	12.1
Food products	19.4	12.8	8.9
Beverages	6.0	4.1	2.1
Nonindustrialized products (mainly wheat)	10.2	12.5	13.7
Total	100.0	100.0	100.0

Source: Villela et al, "Aspectos..." Vol I, p. 115.

THE GREAT DEPRESSION

The depression of the thirties had a severely negative effect on Brazil's exports, whose value fell from US$445.9 million in 1929 to US$180.6 million in 1932.

GENERAL IMPACT

The price of coffee in 1931 was at one-third of the average price in the years 1925-29 and the country's terms of trade had fallen by 50 percent. In addition to the decline of export receipts, the entrance of foreign capital had come to almost a complete halt by 1932. The decline of export earnings and the large amounts of foreign exchange needed to finance the country's external debt (which amounted to over US$1.3 billion in 1931), not counting the remittances

of the profits of private entities, forced the government
to take some drastic actions. In August of 1931 it suspen-
ded part of foreign debt payments and began negotiations
towards a debt consolidation agreement. Brazil was also the
first country in Latin American to introduce exchange and
other direct controls. Combined with a devaluation of the
currency, which increased the price of imports, these controls caused a decline in the value of imports from U.S.
$416.6 millions in 1929 to US$108.1 million in 1932.[18]

Since at the beginning of the depression coffee accounted for 71 percent of total exports and exports, in
turn, stood at about 10 percent of GNP, the government's
main concern was to support the coffee sector. The steep
decline of world demand for coffee brought along by the depression also coincided with a huge coffee output, which
was the result of plantings which had taken place in the
twenties.[19] In order to protect the coffee sector, and thus
the economy, from the full impact of the decline of world
coffee markets and prices, the coffee support program was
transferred from the states (mainly São Paulo) to the federal government. The National Coffee Council (Conselho
Nacional do Café-CNA) was founded in May of 1931. It bought
all coffee, destroying the large quantities which could not
be sold or stored. Government protection of the coffee
sector also included measures to help the debt-plagued
agricultural producers, especially in the state of São
Paulo, by having the government pay off the debt, thus
creating new money and enabling the debtor to postpone his
payments. This program, known as the "Readjustamento
Econômico" reduced the farmers' debts by 50 percent.[20]

Another factor acting as a partial shock-absorber of
the depression vis-a-vis Brazil's agriculture was the rapid
growth of cotton production, especially in the state of São
Paulo. In the twenties the government of São Paulo had promoted research on cotton growing, resulting in improvements
in the quality of fibers produced, and by the thirties the
state distributed large quantities of seeds. With state-
sponsored improvements in domestic and international marketing and with relative prices in the thirties favoring cotton,
output rose substantially. Prior to 1933 Brazil produced
less than 10,000 tons a year. By 1934 São Paulo harvested
90,000 tons. Between 1929 and 1940 Brazil's share of the
world areas devoted to cotton planting increased from 2 to
8.7 percent, and cotton's share of Brazil's exports increased from an annual average of 2.1 percent in the late
twenties to 18.6 percent during 1935-39.[21]

INDUSTRIAL GROWTH AND INDUSTRIALIZATION

The curtailment of imports and the continued domestic demand resulting from the income generated by the coffee support program caused shortages of manufactured goods and a consequent rise in their relative prices. This acted as a catalyst for a spurt of industrial production.

Examining Table 4 again, it will be noted that in 1931 industrial production had fully recovered from a decline which started in 1928, and in the following eight years it more than doubled. Especially noteworthy by 1939 was the rapid growth of production in such sectors as textiles (147 percent larger than in 1929); metal products (almost three times larger than output in 1929); and paper products (almost seven times greater than in 1929).

Turning to indicators of capital formation (Table 5), it will be noted that investment did not equal or surpass its level in the twenties until the latter half of the thirties. By 1932 imports of capital goods had fallen almost to the lowest level reached during World War I and rose thereafter only slowly, never fully attaining the peaks of the twenties. Both cement and steel consumption reached their troughs in 1931 (cement consumption having declined to less than 50 percent of its 1929 level), but both regained their previous peaks in 1937.

It can be concluded that, as in World War I, growth of industrial output in the first half of the thirties was based on a fuller utilization of existing capacity, much of which had been underutilized and a large portion of which had been built in the previous decade. By the second half of the thirties, growth of industrial production was accompanied by capacity expansion. Steel capacity grew with the appearance of numerous new small firms and especially with the opening of Belgo-Mineira's new plant at Monlevade.[22] Similarly, new cement firms appeared, and paper production capacity was expanded at a very rapid rate.

THE FURTADO THESIS

Celso Furtado was the first economist to view the coffee support policy as a type of Keynesian anti-cyclical program. He states that the coffee support program was financed by credit expansion.[23] Guaranteeing minimum prices, it was possible to maintain the employment level of the coffee sector and, indirectly, in related internal sectors.

As coffee output continued to rise, it was possible for the income of the sector to fall less than its prices.[24] Thus, in Furtado's words: "It is important to note that the value of the product which was destroyed was much smaller than the income which was created. We were, in fact, constructing the famous pyramids which much later were to be mentioned by Keynes. In this manner, the coffee support policy in the years of the great depression became the main stimulator for national income growth. Unconsciously Brazil undertook an anticyclical policy of larger relative proportions than had been practiced in industrialized countries until that time."[25] The money injected into the economy to acquire, and partially destroy excess coffee, and the resulting income creation, counterbalanced the decline of investment expenditures.[26]

Furtado argues that the maintenance of domestic income and purchasing power, the decline of imports and the consequent increase of relative industrial prices, caused the internal market to become the dynamic sector of the economy. With an excess capacity in the industrial sector and a small capital goods industry, the growing internal demand stimulated greater domestic industrial production which, in turn, also contributed to at first maintain and then to raise domestic income.

Furtado's severest critic, Carlos M. Pelaez, attempted to destroy these arguments in a number of ways.[27] He maintained that most of the funds for buying coffee stocks originated from export taxes on coffee. Thus the support program could not be considered a Keynesian anticyclical mechanism.

Also, since the government was following orthodox monetary policies, credits provided for the support of the program by the Banco do Brasil necessarily reflected a decline of credits to other sectors, hence there was little net credit creation. Finally, Peláez claims that the coffee support program was prejudicial to the industrialization of the country because it artificially distorted relative profitabilities.[28]

The recent empirical study by Simão Silber dealing with this debate has clarified many of these issues and has shown that Furtado's analysis was basically correct, although he does show that his presentation was far from complete.[29] Silber throws considerable doubt on many of Peláez's assertions. For instance, taking the period May 1931 to February 1933, he found that 65 percent of coffee purchases were financed by export taxes. However, by adding the period 1933-34, Silber found that only 48 percent of the purchases were financed by the export tax.[30] Also, since the export tax was not fully born by the coffee sector, but was shared by coffee consumers, (due to the low demand elasticity for coffee), the net effect of the tax on the coffee sector was smaller than Peláez claimed.[31]

Peláez also disregarded the importance of exchange devaluation in helping to support the money income of exporters and the fact that the existence of a coffee support program kept the terms of trade from falling more than they would have without the support program. Furthermore, Silber shows that monetary policy in the thirties was anything but orthodox, since monetary expansion in the decade was over 100 percent, while the government budget was frequently in deficit.[32] Finally, it is difficult to see how the defense of the coffee sector hurt industry in the thirties. It is likely that the higher aggregate demand resulting from the defense of the coffee sector drew more investment into the industrial sector than was attracted away by opportunities in the coffee sector.

WORLD WAR II

Like World War I and the first half of the depression decade, World War II represented for Brazil a time of increased output, but little expansion of productive capacity. This becomes obvious from the data in Table 10. Industrial production grew at an annual rate of 5.4 percent in the period 1939-45. Especially noteworthy are the yearly average growth rates of metal products (9.1 percent), textiles (6.2 percent), shoes (7.8 percent), and beverages and tobacco (7.6 percent), which were all industries whose imports were drastically curtailed. The decline of the transport materials sector was due to the fact that, without imports, domestic capacity could not fully function. Investment activities fell at first, but rose again in 1945 (see Table 5). This was mainly due to the capital equipment Brazil was allowed to import during the war to construct its first large integrated steel mill at Volta Redonda.[33]

Except for the steel and the cement industries, little capital formation took place during the war, and increased output was achieved only by a more intense utilization of existing equipment. Thus, by the end of the war a large portion of Brazil's industrial capacity was in a state of deterioration and obsolescence.[34]

TABLE 10
Yearly Average Growth Rates of Industrial Production
(1939-1945)

Mining	3.7
Manufacturing	5.2
Nonmetallic minerals	14.1
Metal products	9.1
Transport equipment	-11.0
Paper products	4.1
Rubber products	30.0
Leather products	- 2.5
Oil and vegetables	6.7
Textiles	6.2
Shoes	7.8
Food products	0.9
Beverages and tobacco	7.6
Printing and publishing	2.3
Construction	4.8
Electric power	7.4
Total	5.4

Source: G. F. Loeb, "Números Indices do Desenvolvimento Fisico da Produção Industrial, 1939-40," *Revista Brasileira de Economia*, Março de 1953.

During the war Brazil's exports of manufactured products grew rapidly; textiles at one point contributed 20 percent of total export receipts. Due to the reappearance of traditional sources of supplies after the war, however, and, in part, due to the poor performance of Brazilian exports (frequent delivery delays and inadequate quality control), manufactures practically disappeared from the export list by the end of the war.

EVALUATION OF BRAZIL'S EARLY INDUSTRIAL GROWTH: INDUSTRIAL GROWTH AND INDUSTRIALIZATION

We have seen that substantial industrial growth occurred in the three decades prior to World War I; that World War I acted only as a stimulus to production, since investment could not take place; that the twenties was a

period of relatively slow growth, but high investment due
to the effects of World War I on producers' expectations;
and that the great spurt of industrial production in the
thirties, induced by a drastic decline in the capacity to
import was, at first, based mainly on increased utilization
of existing capacity and subsequently on the addition of
new capacity.

It would not be accurate, however, to talk about a con-
tinuous process of industrialization starting in the 1890s.
It is necessary to differentiate between an era of industrial growth and a period of industrialization. The former
characterizes events until the end of the 1920s, during
which time the growth of industry depended mostly on agricultural exports, the leading sector. Also, despite the
rapid growth of some industries, such a period of industrial
growth is not accompanied by drastic structural changes in
the economy. Industrialization, on the other hand, is
present when industry becomes the leading growth sector of
the economy and causes pronounced structural changes.

The following data on the distribution of Brazil's
physical product gives some support to this classification.
Despite events which led to industrial growth until and
during World War I, industry contributed only 21 percent to
the total physical product in both 1907 and 1919, as compared to agriculture's 79 percent. By 1939, however, industry's share had grown to 43 percent.[35] Although there
was no census to measure industry's share in 1930, the
slower industrial growth of the twenties leads one to conclude that industry's share surged in the thirties. This
surprisingly high share was due, in part, to the lower
prices for agricultural products, especially coffee, which
had not fully recovered from their depression low points,
being 29 percent below the high level reached in 1930. Also,
relative prices of manufactured goods were probably higher
than at the beginning of the twenties. Even if all information for price changes were available, adjustments would
not lower the 1939 share of manufacturing enough to negate
the impression of a substantial structural change.

Estimated annual growth rates of agriculture and industry since 1920 indicate that only in the thirties does
industry become the leading sector, heavily influencing
general economic growth. The average annual growth rates
from 1920-29, 1933-39, and 1939-45, respectively, were:
agriculture - 4.1, 1.7, and 1.7 percent; industry - 2.8, 11.3
amd 5.4 percent; total - 3.9, 4.9, and 3.2 percent.[36]

The 1907 import coefficient for industrial goods (44.6 percent) shows a high dependence on imports. This proportion is probably too high for comparability with the proportions of 1919 (28.0 percent) and 1939 (20.0 percent), since the 1907 census only covered the output of larger firms.[37] The decline from 1907 to 1919 and from 1919 to 1939 reflects the import substitution which occurred, especially during World War I and the thirties.[38] It would seem that prior to World War I industrial growth was only mildly of an import substitutive nature. Industrial output grew to satisfy *new* needs (of immigrants and of the new infrastructure) rather than to substitute for formerly imported supplies. This situation changed just prior to and especially during World War I. This initial import substitution, however, did not lead to industrialization, as defined above. It became a process of industrialization only in the thirties.

A comparison of the industrial structures of 1919 and 1939 (Table 11) should help to clarify the difference between industrial growth and industrialization. The 1919 structure was dominated by light industries. Textiles, clothing, food products, beverages, and tobacco made up 70 percent of industrial output. By 1939 this group had shrunk to 58 percent, with metal products, machinery, and electrical products having made noticeable gains. The move toward a greater balance in the industrial sector contributed to the possibility of making industry the motive force in the economy, which is another way of characterizing the industrialization process.

Measurements performed by Huddle show the degree to which intensive industrialization had already taken place by the end of the thirties. Using the ratio of domestic supplies to total supplies, Brazil was close to self-sufficiency in consumer goods and supplied over 80 percent of its own intermediate goods and over 50 percent of its investment goods.[39]

A notable feature of Brazil's industrial sector is the small amount of labor it had absorbed since the early part of the century. For instance, the distribution of the economically active population changed in the following way between 1920 and 1940:[40]

	1920	1940
Primary sector	70%	66%
Secondary sector	14%	10%
Tertiary	16%	23%
Total	100%	100%

TABLE 11

Brazil's Industrial Structure in 1919 and 1939
(Percentage Distribution of Total Value Added)

	1919	1939
Nonmetallic minerals	5.7	5.2
Metal products	4.4	7.6
Machinery	0.1	3.8
Electrical equipment	-	1.2
Transport equipment	2.1	0.6
Wood products	4.8	3.2
Furniture	2.1	2.1
Paper products	1.3	1.5
Rubber products	0.1	0.7
Leather products	1.9	1.7
Chemicals	1.7*	*
Pharmaceuticals	1.2*	*
Perfumes, soap and candles	0.7*	*
Textiles	29.6	22.2
Clothing and shoes	8.7	4.9
Food products	20.6	24.2
Beverages	5.6	4.4
Tobacco	5.5	2.3
Printing and publishing	0.4	3.6
Miscellaneous	3.5	1.0
Total	100.0	100.0

Sources: Censuses of 1920 and 1940.
* The 1919 total percentage for these three categories
  was 3.6; for 1939 it was 9.8.

The proportion of the economically active population employed in industry actually declined. However, due to
different classifications used in the 1920 census, comparisons between it and later censuses are misleading. For example, the 1920 census included tailors and seamstresses in
the secondary sector; later censuses placed them in the
tertiary sector. Thus, the 1920 employment proportion for
industry would be much smaller had the 1940 classification
criteria been applied. Not enough information is available
to make adjustments.[41] Even if it were and the industrial
employment proportion for 1920 were adjusted downward, it
seems fairly probable that the growth of labor in the industrial sector in the 1920–40 period would be small.

EARLY ATTEMPTS AT PLANNING IN BRAZIL

Until the thirties there were few attempts by Brazil's governments to plan the economic development of the country, especially its industrial development. This does not mean that the government never had a conscious policy to support specific sectors of the economy. We saw in previous sections of this chapter that some degree of "planning" went into the formulation of coffee support policies. Also, the free trade policy of the nineteenth century represented a conscious program to maintain the economic structure prevalent at the time.

There were occasions in the late nineteenth and early twentieth centuries when individuals both within and outside government attempted to make systematic evaluations of the Brazilian economy with a view toward recommending policies to deal with balance of payments and other problems. One example can be found in the stabilization program of Joaquim Murtinho, the finance minister in the years 1898-1902.[42]

In the 1930s and 1940s systematic analyses and evaluations of Brazil's economic structure for purposes of influencing the direction of the country's development became more frequent. They were carried out by both foreigners and Brazilians. One of the first to appear in the 1930s was the *Niemeyer Report*, which was published in 1931. The report was named after Sir Otto Niemeyer, who had been invited by the Brazilian government to study ways for the country to overcome the economic crisis created by the depression. Niemeyer was the first to publicly state what many Brazilians were already aware of: that the principal weakness of the economy was its dependence on the exportation of one or two export crops. This explained why the world crisis had initially hit Brazil's economy more violently than that of industrialized nations. To criticize the country's overreliance on coffee at the time, however, was considered almost sacrilegious. The report was thus received without much enthusiasm.

Niemeyer advocated the diversification of Brazil's economic structure. By that, however, he meant agricultural diversification. He did not recommend a program of industrialization. He believed that diversification of agriculture would raise the income of that sector. The latter, combined with the savings of foreign exchange, would in the end generate the funds required for investing in new industries.[43]

Much of the rest of the Niemeyer report was devoted to a critique of Brazil's public finances and methods of restructuring them. Although the report had little influence and did not lead to any effort to consciously influence the economic development of Brazil, it represented the first effort of Brazilian authorities to have the economy examined as a whole, with the possibility of affecting the direction of its growth.

The next attempt at evaluating the Brazilian economy, recommending changes in its structure and means for achieving them, was made by the Cooke Mission. The latter consisted of a group of American technicians sponsored jointly by the Brazilian and U. S. governments. The mission visited the country in 1942 and 1943. It was conceived after both countries had entered the war for the purpose of establishing the type of contribution Brazil would be able to make to the war effort.

The Cooke Mission's work represented the first systematic analytical research work ever done on the Brazilian economy with a view towards formulating a program of action. For the first time the economy was analyzed from a regional point of view, dividing the country into three distinct regions (northeast/east, north/center, and south) whose economic characteristics were distinct enough to warrant substantially different development programs.[44] An important conclusion of the mission was that a major effort should be made to develop the south of the country, since that region had the best conditions for rapid economic growth. The assumption was that from a development nucleus in the south, growth would inevitably spread to other regions.

The mission pointed to a number of factors (now so familiar to development economists) which constituted obstacles to rapid growth, especially to further industrial growth: an inadequate transportation system, a backward system for distributing fuels, lack of funds for industrial investments, restrictions on foreign capital, restrictions on immigration, inadequate technical training facilities, an underdeveloped capacity to generate power, etc.

The Cooke Mission recommended the expansion of the steel industry, which would provide the basis for the development of a capital goods industry; the development of the wood and paper industries; and the further expansion of textile production facilities for both domestic consumption and for the export market.

The task of industrialization, according to the mission's report, should be left to the private sector, while the government should concentrate on general industrial planning, developing industrial credit facilities and providing technical education.

The net effect of the Cooke Mission was to clarify some of the development problems the country was facing at the time. It had little direct influence on immediate policies.

ENDNOTES

1. Many sections of this chapter appeared previously in: Werner Baer and Annibal V. Villela, "Industrial Growth and Industrialization: Revisions in the stages of Brazil's Economic Development," *The Journal of Developing Areas*, January 1973, pp. 217-34.
2. Glade, op. cit., p. 300; Nicia Vilela Luz, *A Luta Pela Industrializacão do Brasil, 1808 a 1930*, São Paulo: Difusão Européia Do Livro, 1961, p. 18.
3. Glade, op. cit., p. 301; Luz, op. cit., pp. 19-29; Flávio Rabelo Versiani and Maria Teresa R.O. Versiani, "A Industrialização Brasileira Antes de 1930: Uma Contribuição," in *Formação Econômica Do Brasil: A Experiência Da Industrialização*, edited by Flavio R. Versiani and José Roberto Mendonca de Barros. São Paulo: Edição Saraiva, Série ANPEC Leituras de Economia, 1977, p. 133.
4. Stanley Stein, *The Brazilian Cotton Manufacture: Textile Enterprise in an Underdeveloped Area, 1850-1950*. Cambridge, Mass.: Harvard University Press, 1957, p. 191.
5. Stanley Stein, op. cit., p. 127.
6. A recent study shows that planters and foreign capital were not alone in financing infrastructural development, but that native merchant capital was also present (especially in Rio de Janeiro). See Joseph Sweigert: "The Middlemen in Rio: A Collective Analysis of Credit and Investment in the Brazilian Coffee Economy, 1840-1910." Austin, The University of Texas, Doctoral Dissertation, 1979.
7. Warren Dean, *The Industrialization of São Paulo, 1880-1945*. Austin, Texas: The University of Texas Press, 1969, pp. 9-10.
8. Versiani and Versiani, op. cit., p. 126.
9. Albert Fishlow, "Origens e Consequências da Substituição de Importações no Brasil," in Versiani and Mondonça de Barros, editors, op. cit., p. 15.
10. Versiani and Versiani, op. cit., pp. 136-7.
11. Stein, op. cit., p. 15.
12. Villela et al, "Aspectos do Crescimento...", Vol. 1, pp. 287-9. Although most of my references are to this early mimeographed version of Villela's study, most of the materials can also be found in the published version: Annibal V. Villela and Wilson Suzigan, *Política do Governo e Crescimento da Economia Brasileira 1889-1945*. Rio de Janeiro: IPEA, Série Monografica No. 10, 1973.

13. The influence of exchange rate appreciation on investment is also supported by the findings of Versiani and Versiani, op. cit., p. 132. Although exchange rate appreciation cheapened imported machinery, it also decreased the protection of the domestic market. On the other hand, a depreciation increased domestic protection while raising the price of imported investment goods. It seems, given our present knowledge, that in the latter case the growing domestic market was a greater force than the higher costs of imported machinery in times of depreciation.

14. See, for example, Roberto Simonsen, *A Evolução Industrial do Brasil*. São Paulo: Empresa Grafica da Revista dos Tribunals, 1939; Caio Prado Junior, *Historia Econômica*, chapter 24; Nicia Vilela Luz, op. cit., p. 45; Werner Baer, *Industrialization and Economic Development in Brazil*. Homewood, Illinois: Richard D. Irwin, 1965, p. 16.

15. Simão Silber, "Análise da Política Econômica e do Comportamento da Economia Brasileira Durante a Período 1929/1939," in Versiani and Mendonça de Barros, editors, op. cit., p. 187.

16. Villela et al, "Aspectos", Vol I, pp. 243-6.

17. Stein, op. cit., pp. 108-13.

18. Werner Baer, *Industrialization and Economic Development in Brazil*. Homewood, Illinois: Richard D. Irwin, Inc., 1965, pp. 20-22; Villela and Suzigan, op. cit., chapter VI; Simão Silber, op. cit., pp. 199-201. Reynold E. Carlson, "Brazil's Role in International Trade," in T. Lynn Smith and Alexander Marchant, editors, *Brazil: Portrait of Half a Continent*. New York: The Dryden Press, 1951, pp. 274-81. The price of coffee fell from 15.75 cents per pound in 1929 to 8.06 in 1932 and 5.25 in 1938, while the coffee export quantum fell from 859 thousand long tons in 1929 to 718 thousand in 1932 and was up to 1,033 thousand in 1938. The Brazilian milreis depreciated from $0.118 in 1929 to 0.071 in 1932, rising to 0.087 in 1937.

19. Villela and Suzigan, op. cit. pp. 173-7.

20. Ibid., pp. 182-3.

21. Carlos M. Peláez, "A Balança Comercial, a Grande Depressao e a Industrialização Brasileira," *Revista Brasileira de Economia*, Março de 1968, p. 47; Villela and Suzigan, op. cit., pp. 184-7.

22. For details see: Werner Baer, *The Development of the Brazilian Steel Industry*. Nashville, Tennessee: Vanderbilt University Press, 1969.

23. Furtado, op. cit., p. 188.

24. Ibid., p. 190.

25. Ibid., p. 192.
26. Ibid., pp. 193–4.
27. Carlos M. Peláez, *História da Industrialização Brasileira*. Rio de Janeiro: APEC Editora S. A., 1972.
28. Ibid, p. 50 and p. 213.
29. Simao Silber, "Análise da Politica Econômica" in Versiani and Mendonça de Barros, editors, op. cit.
30. Ibid., pp. 192–5.
31. Fishlow, "Origens e Consequencias" in Versiani and Mendonça de Barros, editors, op. cit., pp. 26–8.
32. Silber, op. cit., pp. 197–200.
33. For details, see: Werner Baer, *The Development of the Brazilian Steel Industry*. Nashville, Tennessee: Vanderbilt University Press, 1969, chapter 4.
34. Villela et al, "Aspectos do Crescimento", Vol. I, p. 193.
35. Villela et al, "Aspectos do Crescimento," Vol. II, p. 156; data derived from value-added estimates on the basis of the economic censuses for 1920 and 1940 and on comparable available statistics for 1907.
36. Ibid., p. 128; rates secured from index of real output of agriculture and industry weighted by the average share of these sectors in the physical output (value added of agriculture plus industry) in 1919 and 1939.
37. Ibid., Vol. I, p. 268; coefficients represent value of imports of industrial products divided by value of total supply of industrial products; calculated from current cost, insurance and freight (c.i.f.) import figures of industrial products and data on the gross value of industrial output.
38. The decline of the import coefficient is somewhat exaggerated because of the way it is measured. During import-substitution industrialization periods, prices of new manufactured products are substantially higher than c.i.f. import because of protection. The numerator of our ratio is measured by using c.i.f. import prices, while the denominator consists of the sum of high-priced domestic goods plus low-priced imports. Thus the ratio tends to overstate the degree of import substitution. These remarks also apply to the analysis of import coefficients for the post-World War II period. Another reason that the data may overstate the degree of import-substitution is that they are based on gross value rather than value added, and first substitution is likely to be for industries in which VA/gross value is low.
39. Donald Huddle, "Postwar Brazilian Industrialization: Growth Patterns, Inflation and Sources of Stagnation," in *The Shaping of Modern Brazil*, edited by Eric N. Baklanoff. Baton Rouge: Louisiana State University Press, 1969, p. 96.

40. Villela and Suzigan, op. cit., p. 94.
41. For further discussion, see Villela et al, "Aspectos do Crescimento," Vol. II, pp. 71-2.
42. Villela and Suzigan, op. cit., pp. 87-8; Furtado, op. cit., p. 195.
43. Much of the material in these paragraphs is derived from the writings of Dorival Teixeira Vieira, especially his *O Desenvolvimento Economico do Brasil e a Inflaçao*, (São Paulo: Faculdade de Ciencias Economicas e Administrativas, Universidade de Sao Paulo, 1962), and a series of mimeographed lectures given at the Escola de administração de Empresas de São Paulo, Fundação Getúlio Vargas, entitled "Desenvolvimento Economico do Brasil."
44. For details, see: Fundação Getúlio Vargas, *A Missão Cooke*, Rio de Janeiro, 1949.

4

THE POST-WORLD WAR II INDUSTRIALIZATION DRIVE: 1946-61

Although the continuation of Brazil's industrialization process shortly after World War II was due to circumstances similar to those prevailing in the depression years, i.e. balance of payments difficulties, its ultimate characteristics were to be quite different from those of earlier times. By the 1950s industrialization was no longer a defensive reaction to external events. It had become the principal method for the government to modernize and raise the rate of growth of the economy. Policy-makers had become convinced that Brazil could no longer rely on the exportation of its primary products to attain its developmental ambitions. Since the justifications for policies followed in the decade-and-a-half after World War II were based on trends in world trade and Brazil's role in it, we shall begin this chapter with a brief review of trends in Brazil's foreign trade and its role in the economy during those years.

BRAZIL'S FOREIGN TRADE AND ITS ROLE IN THE ECONOMY

It will be noted in Table 12 that both before and after World War II Brazil's export commodity structure was concentrated on a small number of products: coffee, cocoa, sugar, cotton and tobacco. The principal markets for these goods were the U. S. and Western Europe. The commodity import structure was not as one-sided, each commodity group having a fairly substantial proportion of total imports. The notable decline of manufactured consumer goods and the rise of capital goods and fuels imports in the post-World War II period reflects the import substitution measures which will be discussed below.

The evidence that Brazil was heavily dependent on exports for its well-being at the end of the war is clear-cut.

TABLE 12

(a) Commodity Distribution of Exports
(percentages based on dollar figures)

	1925-9	1935-9	1945-9	1957-9	1962
Coffee	71.7	47.1	41.8	57.9	53.0
Cotton	2.1	18.6	13.3	2.7	9.2
Cocoa	3.5	4.5	4.3	5.6	2.0
Iron ore	-	-	-	3.3	5.7
Sugar	0.4	-	1.2	3.7	3.2
Tobacco	1.9	1.6	1.8	1.2	2.0
Sisal	-	-	-	1.1	1.9
Manganese	-	-	-	2.5	2.2
Rubber	2.9	1.1	1.0	-	-
Pinewood	0.4	1.0	3.5	3.9	3.2
Other	17.1	26.1	33.1	18.1	17.6
Total	100.0	100.0	100.0	100.0	100.0

(b) Geographic Distribution of Exports

	1925-9	1935-9	1945-9	1957-9	1962
United States	45.3	36.9	44.3	41.3	40.0
France	10.3	6.9	2.3	3.4	3.4
Germany	9.1	15.1	-	6.8	9.1
United Kingdom	4.4	9.7	9.1	6.7	4.4
Netherlands	5.7	3.7	2.7	4.2	6.1
Italy	5.2	2.5	2.7	2.7	2.9
Japan	-	4.1	-	3.0	2.4
Sweden	2.3	2.2	2.4	2.5	3.5
Argentina	6.0	4.8	9.0	6.6	4.0
Uruguay	2.7	-	1.7	2.1	-
Belgium-Luxemburg	2.7	3.2	4.1	-	2.5
Other	6.3	10.9	21.7	20.7	21.7
Total	100.0	100.0	100.0	100.0	100.0

(c) Commodity Distribution of Imports

	1938-9	1948-50	1961
Food Prods., beverages & tobacco	14.9	17.9	13.5
Fuels	13.1	12.8	18.8
Raw materials (except fuels)	30.0	23.8	26.3
Capital goods	29.9	35.2	39.8
Manufactured consumer goods	10.9	9.7	1.5
Other	1.2	0.6	0.1
Total	100.0	100.0	100.0

Sources: Helio Schlittler Silva, "Comercio Exterior do Brasil
e Desenvolvimento Econômico," *Revista Brasileira de
Ciencias Sociais,* Março de 1962; Conselho Nacional
de Economia, *Exposição Geral da Situação Econômica do
Brasil, 1961,* (Rio de Janeiro, 1962); Banco do Brasil,
Relatorio, 1962.

In the late 1940s the largest share of the GNP was occupied by the agricultural sector (almost 28 percent) and in 1950 over 60 percent of the economically active population was employed in that sector. Table 13 shows the share of agricultural exports in the national income and in total agricultural output. The proportions in the early postwar years were of such magnitudes that changes in the earnings of the country's principal exports had strong positive or negative effects on the entire economy. The subsequent decline of these proportions was due to both the decline of earnings from the principal exports and the internal growth of the economy based on import-substitution industrialization, which will be discussed below.[1]

TABLE 13

(a) Share of Agricultural Exports in Domestic Income

In Current Prices				In 1953 Prices			
1947	10.5%	1955	8.1%	1947	14.9%	1955	6.7%
1948	10.2	1956	6.8	1948	14.1	1956	7.2
1949	9.1	1957	5.4	1949	11.8	1957	6.2
1950	9.9	1958	4.2	1950	9.3	1958	5.5
1951	10.6	1959	5.5	1951	9.4	1959	6.3
1952	7.7	1960	5.7	1952	7.5	1960	6.1
1953	7.9			1953	7.9		
1954	8.5			1954	8.2		

(b) Share of Agricultural Exports in Total Agricultural Output

In Current Prices				In 1953 Prices			
1947	39.0%	1955	27.1%	1947	43.0%	1955	23.4%
1948	36.3	1956	25.1	1948	41.3	1956	25.9
1949	32.6	1957	19.5	1949	35.6	1957	21.8
1950	34.6	1958	16.5	1950	30.4	1958	20.6
1951	38.2	1959	20.3	1951	32.5	1959	23.8
1952	26.5	1960	20.3	1952	24.4	1960	23.2
1953	27.1			1953	27.1		
1954	28.6			1954	21.6		

Sources: Calculated from data in *Revista Brasileira de Economia,* Março de 1962; IBGE, *O Brasil em Numeros,* Rio de Janeiro, 1960.

THE WORLD MARKET
FOR BRAZIL'S TRADITIONAL EXPORTS IN THE FIFTIES

Postwar policy-makers were pessimistic about the future markets for Brazil's traditional exports. From the late forties to the early sixties the highest yearly rates of growth of world exports for the type of products Brazil was exporting could be found in sugar (3.8%) and the lowest was coffee (2.2%), while world exports of manufactured products was expanding at a yearly rate of 6.6%.[2] It was difficult at the time to imagine how the country could hope to achieve high rates of growth while relying principally on the exportation of primary products. To this bleak picture should be added the decline of Brazil's share of the world market for its principal export commodities. One of the main reasons for this decline was the maintenance of high coffee prices in the early postwar period, when Brazil dominated the world market. This encouraged the production of competitors in other countries.[3]

The fate of Brazil's exports was part of a general worldwide unfavorable trend in the market for primary products, especially food and raw materials. It is clear from Table 13 that this had been a long-run trend. Part (b) of the table indicates that world imports and imports of industrial countries from nonindustrial countries had been shrinking considerably, much of this being due to the decline of the share of Latin America. It should be noted that this decline would have been even greater had petroleum and petroleum products been excluded. Further evidence for the dim outlook for the exports of primary producing countries at the time was available in a number of surveys. For example, the United Nations obtained the following estimates for the income elasticity of demand for imports of industrially advanced countries from developing areas:[4]

Commodity Group	Income Elasticity
Foodstuffs (SITC groups 0 to 1)	0.76
Raw materials (SITC 2 to 4)	0.60
Fuels (SITC 3)	1.40
Manufactured products (SITC 5 to 8)	1.24

Another statistical analysis which is even closer to the Brazilian case is concerned with the income and price elasticity of demand for coffee in the United States. It was shown that an increase of 10 percent in the price of coffee caused consumers to reduce their consumption of coffee by $2\frac{1}{2}$ percent, while a 10 percent increase in real per capita

TABLE 14

Changes in the Structure of World Trade: 1913-1961

(a) World Exports of Merchandise (% distribution at
current prices)

	World			World- Excl. Socialist Econ.	
	1913	1929	1937	1913	1953
Food	29.0	26.1	24.8	27.0	22.6
Agric. raw mats.	21.1	20.0	19.5	20.7	13.9
Minerals	14.0	15.8	19.5	14.7	19.8
Manufactures	35.9	38.1	36.2	37.6	43.7
	100.0	100.0	100.0	100.0	100.0

	1948	1953	1958
Primary goods	55.5	51.0	48.2
Manufactured goods	44.5	49.0	51.8
	100.0	100.0	100.0

Sources: L. P. Yates, *Forty Years of Foreign Trade.* (London:
George Allen & Unwin, Ltd., 1959). Joseph D. Coppock,
*International Economic Instability: The Experience
after World War II.* (New York: McGraw-Hill Book
Co., 1962).

(b) World Imports by Geographical Areas (percentage distribution).

Imports from To	Non-Industrial Areas			Latin America		
	1953	1960	1961	1953	1960	1961
Industrial areas*	37.4	28.3	27.1	12.9	8.7	8.0
World	31.5	24.8	24.3	9.8	6.8	6.5

Source: GATT, *International Trade,* 1961.
*Excluding Eastern Europe, including Japan.

income usually led to an increase of 2½ percent in the consumption of coffee.[5]

Finally, it was also noted at the time that consumption of raw materials by industries in advanced countries tended to increase at a slower rate than their production because of more efficient techniques of production which resulted in a decline of raw material input per unit of output. It was noted, for instance, that the percentage of raw material consumption to gross national product in the U. S. declined from 22.6 percent in 1904-13 to 12.5 percent in 1944-50.[6]

The evidence seemed to indicate to Brazil's policy makers that the country found itself not only among the group of nations whose exports steadily lost in the share of world trade, but also among those countries whose exports had little chance of regaining their former pre-eminence. It is in this context that one should view the gradual decision of the Brazilian government to change the structure of the economy through the promotion of import substitution industrialization.

IMMEDIATE POSTWAR YEARS

The drastic decline of imports during World War II and the boom of exports resulted in a substantial increase of the country's foreign exchange reserves, from US$71 million prior to the outbreak of the war to US$708 million in 1945. In February 1945 the government established a foreign exchange regime without restrictions, except for some limitation in the remittance of profits. There existed no quantitative restrictions on imports and foreign exchange was freely available for most capital transactions. The cruzeiro was kept at its prewar value of Cr$18.50 per dollar and did not change until 1953, while prices rose 285 percent from 1945 to 1953.[7] Even in 1945 the exchange rate had been overvalued in terms of dollars since in the 1937-45 period Brazil's prices had risen by 80 percent more than in the U.S.[8]

The continued overvaluation of the cruzeiro can be attributed to a number of government policy goals. First, policy-makers were anxious to spend the wartime accumulated foreign exchange reserves in order to meet the pent-up demand for imports. Second, since inflation was of primary concern, a balance of payments deficit financed by past foreign exchange accumulation to keep prices down was deemed justified. There was also a fear of the additional

inflationary impact of devaluation. It has been observed
that these policies "...illustrate the conservative nature
of the...government..." since they "...favored the traditional land-owning interests rather than growth of newer urban
industrial sectors..."[9]

· Within one year, however, most of the accumulated wartime foreign exchange reserves had vanished as a result of
the import spree. Table 15 shows how the import quantum
increased by 40 percent and the dollar value of imports by
80 percent, while the export quantum decreased and its value
rose by only 17 percent. It is not certain whether the
sharp drop in the real rate of growth of output was due to
the sudden flood of imports, but it will be noticed that
the real growth rate rose again in 1948, after reserves had
been exhausted and remained at a high level for the rest of
the decade.

TABLE 15
Imports, Exports, and Real Output, 1944-50
(yearly % growth rates)

	Exports		Imports		
	Quantum	Value	Quantum	Value	Real GDP
1944-45	6	16	5	6	1
1945-46	21	49	-17	50	8
1946-47	-5	17	40	80	2
1947-48	3	3	-10	-8	7
1948-49	-11	-8	16	-1	5
1949-50	-13	24	22	-2	6

Sources: Comissão Mista Brasil-Estados Unidos para Desenvolvimento Econômico,*Relatorio Geral*, 1 Tomo (Rio de
Janeiro, 1954); and *Conjuntura Economica*.

The balance of payments shown in Table 16 seems to con-
tradict the above assertion that by 1947 most of the foreign
exchange reserves had been exhausted. It will be noted that
in 1946 the current account balance was still positive and
only turned negative the following year, though not enough
to eat up most accumulated reserves. This contradiction
can be resolved by considering that the current account surpluses of the war years were especially due to surpluses
with European countries; in the same years Brazil had deficits with the U. S. Since European currencies were in-
convertible in the early postwar years, a substantial part
of Brazil's reserves in those currencies could not be used
to cover the growing deficit with the U.S.[10]

TABLE 16

Brazil's Balance of Payments 1939–47
(in millions of US$)

	1939	1940	1941	1942	1943	1944	1945	1946	1947
Commercial balance	87.6	56.3	127.6	208.2	205.4	230.7	277.7	371.5	11.3
Goods and services balance	34.1	-7.4	74.1	175.4	154.2	143.3	200.3	193.5	-161.3
Official capital movements	-0.03	-22.4	-32.4	-26.5	43.9	18.4	-11.2	-5.5	26.0
Official compensatory finance	0.8	-4.4	-60.4	-149.6	-252.8	-157.4	-61.8	-80.9	80.1

Source: Same as Table 15; Brazilian balance of payments data have been collected since 1947. The earlier data in this table were estimated by the International Monetary Fund.

EXCHANGE CONTROLS: 1946-1953

The post-World War II industrialization spurt was initially the consequence of measures taken for coping with balance of payments difficulties. Only gradually, mainly in the fifties, did these measures become conscious instruments for the promotion of an industrial complex. Foreign exchange control was one of the principal tools for the promotion of the country's industrialization.

In June 1947 exchange controls were reintroduced; these were to last until January 1953. Throughout the period the cruzeiro became increasingly overvalued. As this encouraged imports, which were also spurred on by the outbreak of the Korean War in 1950, a system of import licensing was used to keep demand in check.[11] Foreign exchange was made available according to a five category system of priorities which was determined by the Export-Import Department of the Banco do Brasil (CEXIM), which was in charge of operating the licensing system. Essential goods, such as drugs, insecticides, and fertilizers were allowed to be freely imported, while fuels, essential foodstuffs, cement, paper and printing equipment, and machinery received priority in the licensing system. At the other extreme were consumer goods, considered to be superfluous, which were discouraged by long waiting lists for the obtainment of licenses.[12] Additionally, annual capital repatriation was limited to 20 percent and the remittance of earnings to 8 percent of registered capital.

In the years 1948-1950 the government exercised enough control to equilibrate the balance of payments. One might claim that the sacrifices in terms of growth which were entailed were not all necessary. For example, a less rigid attitude on maintaining a fixed and overvalued exchange rate would have made the burden of the controls more equitable and might have spurred exports to a greater extent. The criterion for distributing import licenses was tradition. Each importer was given the right to a certain quota of foreign exchange proportional to the volume of his transactions before the introduction of the licensing system. This was a very static policy, which did not take into account the development and needs of new industries. The latter depended on supplies from abroad in the initial phase of their operation.

With the mounting pressure of excess demand for foreign exchange, the licensing system was beset by long delays, and many irregularities became evident in its operation. Since importers who received licenses made huge windfall profits "...it is hardly surprising that there were increasing allegations of corruption in the system's administration. Alternatively, the system was simply bypassed by smuggling."[13]

In 1951 CEXIM relaxed its controls mainly as a result of the belief that the Korean war would grow into a world conflict which would bring along a general shortage of supplies from abroad. As a result imports, which had averaged US$950 million a year in the years 1948–50, rose to an average of US$1.7 billion a year in 1951–52. Over 55 percent of increased imports was in capital goods and 28 percent in other producer goods. This reflected the deliberate industrialization policy which was becoming the principal concern of Brazil's government in the fifties. Some of the increase of imports was compensated by a rise in the value of exports, due mainly to the substantial increase in the price of coffee. A large share of the surging imports, however, had to be financed by commercial arrears and official compensatory finance. The latter amounted to US$291 and 615 million in 1951 and 1952 respectively.

Although Brazil operated at an overvalued fixed exchange rate during this period, there was a way in which this inflexibility could be circumvented through the use of compensatory deals (operações vinculadas). Exporters of certain products could sell their foreign exchange earnings directly at a premium. This "...amounted to a kind of 'ad hoc' devaluation of the cruzeiro, and it reached large proportions in the last years of the licensing period."14 This system worked quite well at first, the CEXIM authorities keeping a firm control over these operations, seeing to it that the exports concerned were of a basic nature (i.e., worth promoting) and that imports were of an essential nature. At the end of the period, however, this system weakened because of the appearance of many abuses.

This system also acted as a stimulus to the remittance of profits and to an outflow of foreign capital, while it discouraged the inflow of new capital. Between 1949 and 1952 US$173 million of profits were remitted abroad, while net direct investment inflow amounted to only US$13 million. All this occurred despite the above-mentioned restrictions on capital flows.

THE MULTIPLE EXCHANGE RATE SYSTEM: 1953-57

In January 1953 a new policy was adopted leading towards a more flexible exchange rate system. Law 1807 created a limited free exchange market in which were allowed the inflow and outflow of capital and its earnings, and the buying and selling of foreign exchange for tourism. Imports and most exports were retained in the official market (18.72 cruzeiros to the dollar) and controlled by CEXIM, and so were capital dealings considered of importance to the country. Certain exports which the government wanted to stimulate were partially or totally allowed into the free market. Controls on capital earnings were kept to the extent that outflow of interest would not exceed 8 percent and of profits 10 percent per year.

Since the dollar in the free market was quoted high above the official rate, the authorities made use of Law 1807 to give a stimulus to certain types of exports. Thus, in February 1953 Instruction 48 of SUMOC (Superintendency of Money and Credit) divided exports into three categories: one category in which 15 percent of exchange receipts could be sold on the free market; a second one where 30 percent could be sold there; and a third category where 50 percent could be sold in that market. Many instructions followed which increased the list of essential exports, and after a while all these products were placed in the third category.

The earnings of traditional exports (coffee, cocoa and cotton) were supposed to be exchanged at the official rate. Exceptions were made, however, through the system of "minimum lists"; exporters were supposed to sell in the official market only exchange corresponding to certain minimum prices, anything above being allowed to enter the free market. These maneuvers were used to both increase and diversify exports. The full effect of this policy was never felt since the government tried to contain the free rate by selling exchange received in the official market. Though this was done for political and psychological reasons, it lessened the stimulus to exports and to capital inflows, while it created an unhealthy incentive to tourism and profit remittances.

In October 1953 a basic reform was instituted in the Brazilian exchange system. Instruction 70 of SUMOC and Law 2145 established a multiple exchange rate system. The latter eliminated direct quantitative controls and created an auction for obtaining foreign exchange. Imports were classified into five categories according to their degree of essentiality. The monetary authority (SUMOC) allocated foreign exchange among the categories and the import rates for each category were set in auctions.[15]

Some imports were considered too essential to be subject to the auction system. These included petroleum and derivatives, printing paper, wheat and equipment considered essential for the development of the country. The rate for

these products was the average export rate plus some sur-
taxes determined by the monetary authorities. These goods
accounted for approximately one-third of the total value of
imports.

On the export side, the Banco do Brasil regained its
monopoly position in buying foreign exchange, paying the
official rate (18.72) plus a sum of 5 cruzeiros per dollar
for coffee and 10 cruzeiros per dollar for other products.
Remittance of profits, interest and amortization payments
which were considered essential for the development of the
country could be exchanged at the official rate, plus an
additional tax determined by the monetary authorities.

Over the years of its operation the system underwent a
number of changes. Many imports were reclassified according
to categories, minimum "agios" were established for auctions
and raised over time to keep up with inflation, and on the
export side a number of changes occurred which finally resulted in four export categories being created in January
1955. The system became so complicated that at one time
more than a dozen official rates were in existence.

This multiple exchange rate system represented some
progress in the direction of currency devaluation in the
face of continued inflation. Also, it "...established a
market mechanism for equating foreign exchange supply and
demand. Moreover, it siphoned off to the government the
windfall profits from imports and eliminated the pressures
for administrative corruption in the issuance of licenses."[16]
The system seemed to be more flexible on the import than on
the export side. The flexibility on the import side presented advantages over a tariff system, which could be adjusted
only by a change in the law, whereas exchange classifications
could be changed by executive decision.

The system favored most capital goods, current inputs
to agriculture, and some selected industries. Next came
producer goods, and last came finished consumer goods. The
application of the system acted as a great disincentive for
exports. The government let export rates lag behind for a
number of reasons: it was interested in the additional
revenues it could gain from such a system; it was under the
impression that a lower export rate counteracted the downward trends in the terms of trade; and, finally, policy-
makers thought that a lagging export rate would be a method
to keep the prices of exportable products from rising
domestically.[17]

CHANGES IN EXCHANGE CONTROLS: 1957-1961

In August 1957 Brazil's exchange system once again underwent a basic change with the passage of Law 3244. Ad valorem tariffs were introduced, rising to 150 percent. The exchange rate categories were reduced from 5 to 2. A "general category" included the imports of raw materials, capital goods and certain essential consumer goods, while the other "specific category" included all goods not considered essential. An especially low exchange rate was maintained for the importation of wheat, petroleum and derivatives, printing paper, fertilizers, equipment considered to be of high priority, and interest and amortization payments for loans considered essential to the development of the country. This exchange rate was called "cambio de custo" and could not be below the average rate paid to exporters. Exchange rates for exports and financial transfers continued under the old rules.

In the mid-fifties the character of the exchange system changed. It was no longer regarded merely as an instrument to cope with balance-of-payments difficulties but more as a tool for the promotion of industrialization. By that time Brazilian policy-makers were convinced that high rates of economic growth and modernization could only be obtained through the type of structural changes which industrialization could bring about. The best evidence of this new attitude can be found in a number of complementary policies which were followed in that decade.

The principal novelty was the already mentioned Tariff Law of 1957 which gave newly stimulated industries adequate protection.[18] Another measure, introduced in early 1955, was SUMOC Instruction 113. It was principally designed to attract foreign direct investments. The instruction enabled the latter to import capital equipment without the need for exchange cover. It stated that a foreign investor was allowed to import machinery under the condition that "...he agreed to accept payment, not in the form of cash or deferred debt, but by assuming instead a cruzeiro capital participation in the enterprise by which the equipment was to be used."[19] Approval was to be given only where the investment was deemed to be desirable for the development of the country. This was to be decided by CACEX (the foreign trade department of the Banco do Brasil), which had replaced CEXIM.

A good was considered desirable if it fell into the first three categories of the import control mechanism which had been in operation until 1957. Most goods, however, fell

into the other categories. In order to determine their
desirability, CACEX had to consult with the monetary authorities, other interested official agencies and some non-
governmental bodies (like the National Confederation of Industries) prior to granting the Instruction 113 privileges.
The latter were given mainly to complete sets of manufacturing equipment and to some existing industrial units for
completion of the modernization of the plant. Companies receiving the privileges of Instruction 113 were not allowed
to sell the acquired machinery during its normal economic
life and were forbidden to make direct payments abroad which
corresponded to the value of the imported equipment.[20]

Instruction 113 was obviously advantageous to the
foreign investor. Without it, he would have had to send
dollars to Brazil at the free market rate and with the
cruzeiros bought he would have had to repurchase dollars in
the auction market at a higher price. The degree of benefit
could be measured by the difference between the cost of
foreign exchange in the relevant auction market category and
the free market rate. This difference was large for dollar
imports, but much smaller for non-dollar imports. This
difference disappeared, however, after currency convert-
ibility was achieved by most of the major exporting countries
at the end of 1958.

The Tariff Law of 1957 expanded and solidified the protection offered to domestic industry. In many cases tariffs
were as high as 60, 80 and 150 percent. Goods which were
already adequately supplied by domestic industry could be
imported only via the "special category," where the price
of foreign exchange would rise to two or three times as
much as in other categories. Favored industries and essential raw materials, however, could be imported at the "cambio
de custo," which was a strongly subsidized rate.

Over the following years a number of difficulties arose
in the administration of the system of exchange. The "cambio
de custo" for preferential imports was kept at low levels
for long periods of time (at Cr$53 to the dollar until
October 1958, Cr$80 until January 1959, when it was changed
to Cr$100) in the face of continuing inflation. The author-
ities had the dubious notion that such rigidity in readjustment would be an effective anti-inflationary tool. This
policy, however, encouraged distortions in the import
structure and in the general resource allocation pattern.

In the second half of the 1950s the government had to
deal increasingly with the overproduction of coffee. It

bought huge quantities of surpluses and remunerated coffee exporters with a rate fifty percent smaller than import rates. The difference between the rate paid to exporters and the one at which foreign currencies were sold to importers generated an extra revenue for the government which was used to finance both the domestic coffee support program and some other government activities.

In January 1959 the monetary authorities transferred manufactured exports to the free market, and in December of that year this was done for all other exports, with the exception of coffee, crude mineral oil, mamona and cocoa. In April 1959 freight payments for imports were also transferred to the free rate.

From 1958 until March 1961 the dollar in the free market was constantly below the rate in the "general category." This meant that foreign enterprises remitting profits and Brazilians traveling abroad received a more favorable rate than the importers of essential goods. During the last years of the system the government extracted forced loans from exporters and importers. The latter had to pay the agio in the auction market, but could only receive foreign exchange six months thereafter. Exporters received only a fraction of the cruzeiro prices of foreign exchange, the balance being investment in six month bills of the Banco do Brasil.

EXCHANGE REFORM: 1961-63

In early 1961 a new exchange policy was instituted with SUMOC Instruction 204. The "cambio de custo" was increased from Cr$100 to 200 per dollar; the general category imports were placed on the free market; all exports, except coffee, were also placed on the free market; and the forced loans imposed on importers were replaced by a system of "letras de importação." The latter consisted of having importers deposit the cruzeiro value of foreign exchange bought for a period of 150 days in exchange for notes of the Banco do Brazil.

Other SUMOC instructions which followed transferred exchange earned from coffee exports to the free market, requiring exporters to deliver 22 dollars per bag so as to enable the government, with the equivalent in cruzeiros, to finance the support of excess production. Another instruction did away with the "cambio de custo" system, transferring all imports to the free market. On the whole, these measures brought greater unity to the foreign exchange system.

The years 1962 and 1963 were dominated by political crises, by nationalist pressures which resulted in the passage of a severe profit remittance act in the latter part of 1962,[21] a continuing decline of foreign exchange earnings from exports, and by acceleration of the rate of inflation. Throughout most of this time the setting of the official "free rate" lagged substantially behind internal inflation, which did little to stimulate newer types of exports.

THE LAW OF SIMILARS

The reason for this long review of foreign exchange policy is that it was used as one of the principal policy instruments to stimulate the import-substitution industrialization drive of the 1950s. The above reviewed policies were supplemented by a rigorous application of the Law of Similars.

In the last decade of the nineteenth century tariff protection became generalized in what was referred to as the Law of Similars. In 1911 the "Register of Similar Products" was created. Brazilian producers who desired protection could apply for the registration of the goods they were producing or intended to produce. In the post-World War II period, and especially in the 1950s, the registration of a product as a similar became the basis for tariff protection and for classification of a product in a high foreign exchange category. The exact definition of "sufficient quality and quantity" for a product to warrant protection was flexible by the law and was subject to the discretion of the authorities.

The law was applied in such a way as to encourage a substantial amount of verticle integration as the industrialization process continued, i.e. vertical integration either within firms or within the country by the emergency of supplying firms. According to a study of American companies operating in Brazil

> ...the operation of the law of similars has been a most powerful incentive for foreign investors to move from importing into assembly, or from assembly into full-fledged manufacturing. The essential feature of this incentive has been fear of outright exclusion from the market rather than hope for preferential treatment in relation to competitors. In many cases, the mere report that some

Brazilian or competing foreign firm was contem-
plating manufacture, with the implication that
imports of similar goods would henceforth be
ruled out, was the critical factor impelling
U. S. companies to move to preserve their market position by building local plants...[22]

This law, however, also stimulated many local groups
to establish supplying firms. Thus, even though the initial
protective devices of the government stimulated industries
of a "non-essential" nature (at first light consumer goods
were kept out of the country), complementary policies provided substantial incentives for vertical integration and
thus for the ultimate growth of a heavy capital goods industry.

SPECIAL PLANS AND PROGRAMS

It was shown previously how in the 1930s and during the
second World War attempts were made to assess Brazil's resources in order to plan for their efficient utilization.
Such attempts continued in the postwar period and occasionally resulted in public investment programs which acted as
complements to the various stimuli given to the private
sector.

The first postwar attempt at planning occurred with
the introduction of the SALTE plan (the name being an anagram
containing the first letters of the Portuguese words for
health, food, transportation, and energy). It was not a
full-scale economic plan, but a five-year public expenditure
program in the four fields,[23] which was to run from 1950 to
1954. Total expenditures for that period were supposed to
be Cr$19.9 billion, of which Cr$2.6 billion were destined
for the improvement of health services, Cr$2.7 billion for
modernization of food production and supply, Cr$11.4 billion
for the modernization of the transportation system, and
Cr$3.2 billion for increasing the energy capacity of the
country.

The plan did not last more than one year because of
implementation problems and especially because of financing
difficulties. Since the plan contained not only special
development projects, but also projects which appeared in
the regular government budget, it "...had the effect of
carving out from the normal budget statement some of the
expenditure which was assumed to be of a developmental
nature, and was thus a step in the direction of 'functional'

budgeting."24   Thus the plan did not call for additional
expenditures equivalent to the value of all programs contained therein, since 30 percent was already covered by
activities included in the normal budget.   There were difficulties in obtaining financing for the 70 percent not covered.   Some of the new resources needed were supposed to be
obtained from taxation of the additional income resulting
from the plan itself, some through the sale of foreign
currencies held by the Banco do Brasil, and another amount
was supposed to come from a readjustment of customs duties
to a more realistic ad valorem basis.   This left a sum of
about seven billion cruzeiros for which there was no cover.
It was decided that this amount would have to come from
borrowing operations.

The plan's discontinuance after one year was due to
overoptimistic estimates of revenues and borrowing possi-
bilities.   The planners did not reckon with the possibility
of balance of payments difficulties which would reduce the
prospects for financing the plan from the sale of reserves,
with increasing inflation, and with the budget deficits,
which made borrowing more difficult.   After the plan's discontinuance in 1951, some of the planned public works projects were transferred to various government departments,
to be continued as resources became available.

The SALTE plan was not really global in nature.   It did
not contain targets·for the private sector or programs to
influence the latter.   It was basically a public expenditure
program covering a five-year period.   It did, however, draw
attention to other sectors of the economy which were lagging
behind industry and thus might hamper further growth.

The work of the Joint Brazil-United States Economic
Commission in the period 1951 to 1953 constituted a much
more ambitious and thorough attempt at planning.   Its large
Brazilian and American technical staff made one of the most
complete surveys of the Brazilian economy which had ever
been undertaken and formulated a series of infrastructure
projects.   The proposed expenditures amounted to US$387.3
million in foreign exchange and 14 billion cruzeiros, which
were to be divided among the following projects:

	Investment in Foreign currency	Investment in domestic currency
Railroads	38%	55%
Road building	2	–
Harbor construction	9	5
Coastal shipping	7	3

Electric energy	34	33
Other	10	4
Total	100%	100%

Source: BNDE, op. cit. in footnote 23.

More concretely, these categories involved projects to modernize various railroad lines, harbors, and coastal shipping, and the expansion of installed power producing capacity; the "other" category included the importation of agricultural equipment, the construction of silos, and the construction or expansion of some industrial plants. The commission also made recommendations in the fields of technical training, diversification of exports, measures to overcome the noticeable regional disparities in income (see chapter 9), and ways to achieve monetary stability.

Foreign exchange resources were expected to come from international agencies and direct loans from foreign governments, while domestic resources were to come from a "forced loan" collected as an addition to the income tax, and also from loans of insurance companies, social security institutes, etc.

Although the plan of the joint commission was never formally adopted, it had a number of beneficial effects. It led to the establishment of the National Bank for Economic Development (BNDE) whose purpose it was to help plan, analyze and finance infrastructure and a number of industrial projects. Many of the studies of the commission were subsequently used to prepare projects financed by BNDE and by international lending agencies. The commission's work was more successful than the SALTE plan in giving impetus to projects in sectors of the economy which had been lagging behind and which might soon develop into bottleneck areas.

Between 1953 and 1955 technicians of the BNDE and the Economic Commission for Latin American (ECLA) of the UN cooperated in an effort at systematic overall planning.[25] The work consisted principally in observing aggregate relationships in the economy between 1939 and 1953 and making projections under alternative hypotheses about changes in the rate of savings, terms of trade, etc., for a seven-year period. It seems that the group's principal function was to call the attention of Brazilian policy-makers to the key variables (such as the savings ratio, capital/output ratio, foreign capital influx, etc.) which determine the rate of growth of the economy and which could be influenced

by various types of policy actions. The raising of the
rate of growth of the economy had become of prime importance
to the government because of the high growth rate of the
population in the 1950s (which had reached a rate above 3
percent per year).[26]

These postwar series of development plans and the intense discussions surrounding them "...spread a sort of
political mystique of development - what came to be called
as 'desenvolvimentismo' - among the leaders of Brazilian
public and political opinion."[27] This concern with develop-
ment--i.e., the attainment of high rates of growth within a
relatively short period of time--and the government's role
in influencing it substantially, became the hallmark of
the administration of president Juscelino Kubitschek (1956-
61). The day after his inauguration a National Development
Council was created which formulated the *Programa de Metas*
(Program of Targets).

This program was not a global development plan. It
did not include all areas of public investment or basic industries, and it did not attempt to reconcile over a five-
year period the resource needs of thirty basic sectors which
were covered by the plan with the needs of fields not included. Targets were supposed to be set for both government and the private sector. Five general areas were
covered: energy, transportation, food supply, basic industries, and education (especially the training of technical
personnel). Infrastructure investment was mainly concerned
with the elimination of bottlenecks. Groundwork for the
latter had already been done by the joint commission. In
many cases detailed targets were drawn up, including many
individual projects, while other targets were formulated
in only broad terms.

The targets for basic industries concerned the growth
of steel, aluminum, cement, cellulose, automotive, heavy
machinery, and chemicals. These were considered as "growing
points" industries which would set the pace for further
rapid industrialization. A special project included in
Kubitschek's program was the construction of the new interior capital of Brasília. Since this project did not
immediately contribute to increasing the productive capacity
of the economy, a substantial amount of controversy developed
over the merit of its undertaking, given the limited resources available for the other programs. Many would later
argue that the longer-run benefits outweighed the initial
costs of the capital, since its construction led to the
opening of vast new agricultural lands which have contributed

to the foreign exchange earning capacity of the country in
the 1970s.

Investments programmed for the five-year period 1957-
61 were 236.7 billion in cruzeiros and 2.3 billion in U.S.
dollars. This was to be distributed among the main sectors
in the following manner:[28]

	Goods and Services Produced in Brazil	Goods and Services Imported
Energy	46%	37%
Transportation	32	25
Food production	2	6
Basic industries	15	32
Education	5	–
Total	100%	100%

Financing in domestic currency was supposed to come from
government budgets (39.7% federal, 10.4% state), from private firms or mixed enterprises (35.4%), and from public
entities (14.5%). Foreign exchange finance came from both
loans of international agencies (much of it administered by
the development bank) and from the inflow of private foreign
capital attracted by the numerous inducements discussed
above.

During the Kubitschek administration considerable
progress was made towards fulfilling many of the targets,
especially in industry and in some of the planned infrastructure.

SPECIAL INCENTIVES PROGRAMS

Lastly in this survey of policies which contributed to
the industrialization spurt in the fifties should be mentioned a number of specific programs established under the
Kubitschek administration to promote such industries as
automobile and utility vehicle construction, naval construction, and heavy machinery. These programs were organized
through the development bank (BNDE). The favored industries
were given special treatment for importing manufacturing
equipment, raw materials, components, etc. for specific
periods of time.

The most successful of these programs was the one
designed to promote the automobile industry. It was directed

by GEIA (executive group for the automotive industry). It offered substantial benefits for the importation of manu-facturing equipment and automotive components for a limited number of years. In return, the firms committed themselves to a policy of progressive replacement of imports by com-ponents made in Brazil. GEIA was also instrumental in per-suading Brazilian companies to get into the automotive parts industry and in making arrangements for them to negotiate technical assistance agreements with foreign firms. In general, "...encouragement was given to arrangements for intensive recourse to external Brazilian suppliers and sub-contractors for reproduction of specialized parts. It was intended by these means to build a large Brazilian industry of noncaptive component makers."[29] Finally, automotive firms were classified as "basic industries," enabling them to receive financial assistance from the BNDE.

The guidance provided by GEIA not only led to rapid vertical integration of automotive production within the country, but it was also responsible for bringing about what was thought to be a correct mix of vehicles. By the end of the Kubitschek administration only half of the out-put consisted of passenger cars, while the rest consisted of utility vehicles and trucks. Other executive groups made similar efforts in the creation of shipbuilding, heavy machinery, tractor, and automatic telephone equipment in-dustries.

EFFECTS OF INDUSTRIALIZATION POLICIES

The industrialization process in the post-World War II period resulted in very high rates of economic growth. The average yearly growth rate of the economy in the period 1947-62 was over 6 percent; and in the most intensive indus-trialization period, 1956-62, the average yearly growth rate of the real product was 7.8 percent. While the real product increased by 128 percent from 1947 to 1961, the real agri-cultural product increased by only 87 percent; the indus-trial product, however, increased by 262 percent. For the absolute increase of gross domestic product between 1947 and 1961, agriculture was responsible for only 18 percent, while the non-agricultural sector contributed the rest. The key element was the direct and indirect effects of the more than tripling of the industrial sector. It should be noted that the fixed investment proportion was low during the entire period under review (Table 17), averaging 15 percent, which implies a low incremental capital/output ratio.

TABLE 17

Real Growth Rates, Investment Coefficient and Foreign Financing

	Real Growth Rates			Gross Capital Formation	Net Inflow of Capital (millions of 1953 dollars)
	Total	Industry	Agriculture		
1947	7.4	11.3	6.9	17	33
1948	6.6	10.2	4.5	16	20
1949	6.5	11.3	1.5	15	37
1950	5.9	6.4	0.7	13	31
1951	3.7	5.0	9.1	16	35
1952	2.5	8.7	0.2	16	57
1953	10.1	8.7	7.9	13	91
1954	6.9	10.6	7.7	17	128
1955	3.2	6.9	-2.4	14	168
1956	8.1	5.7	9.3	13	413
1957	7.7	16.2	2.0	13	574
1958	5.6	11.9	5.3	14	675
1959	9.7	9.6	4.9	16	850
1960	10.3	10.6	7.6	15	625
1961	5.3	7.8	5.5		878
1962	1.5	0.2	1.0		534
1963					358

Sources: Fundação Getúlio Vargas, *Conjuntura Econômica*; Raouf Kahil, *Inflation and Economic Development in Brazil, 1946-1963* (Clarendon Press, Oxford, 1973) pp. 198 and 336.

Because of the high import content of investments, the overall investment proportion was correlated with balance of payments deficits. This was especially the case during the latter part of the period examined, when the investment coefficient was maintained by substantial inflows of private capital.

One indication of the transformation of the economy is the change in the sectoral distribution of the GDP, which is shown in Table 18. The latter contain estimates in current and in constant 1953 prices. Once again, it is clear that industry was the dynamic sector of the economy, for its share climbed steadily, bypassing agriculture in the second half of the fifties.

TABLE 18
Changes in the Sectoral Shares of Gross Domestic Product
(percentage distribution)

	1939	1947	1953	1957	1960	1966
In Current Prices						
Agriculture	25.8	27.6	26.1	22.8	22.6	19.1
Industry	19.4	19.8	23.7	24.4	25.2	27.2
Other sectors	54.8	52.6	50.2	52.8	52.2	53.7
	100.0	100.0	100.0	100.0	100.0	100.0
In 1953 Prices						
Agriculture		30.0	26.1	24.6	22.2	21.9
Industry		20.6	23.7	24.5	28.0	28.8
Other sectors		49.4	50.2	50.9	49.8	49.3
		100.0	100.0	100.0	100.0	100.0

Source: Calculated from Fundação Getúlio Vargas, Centro de Contas Nacionais and Conjuntura Econômica.

An examination of changes in the structure of the manufacturing sector should begin with a brief review of changes in the import structure. In doing so, one should not overlook the downward trend in the ratio of imports to GDP. Table 19, which shows the changes in the commodity structure of imports, reveals a decline in the share of processed goods from 81 to 68 percent between 1949 and 1962. A large share of the increased proportion of raw materials imported represents goods not available in sufficient quantities in Brazil

TABLE 19
Changes in Brazil's Commodity Import Structure*
(percentage distribution)

Commodity Groups	1949	1962	% Change of imports in 1949 US$- 1949 to 1962
Food, beverages, tobacco	4.58	3.13	+245; +25**
Textiles	3.99	0.13	-89
Clothing and footwear	0.05	0.00	n.a.
Wood products	0.18	0.04	n.a.
Paper and paper products	2.36	2.58	+55
Printing and publishing	0.31	0.47	+320
Leather products	0.27	0.01	n.a.
Rubber products	0.12	0.07	n.a.
Chemical, petroleum, coal products	19.55	18.02	+5; -43; -42; -14§
Nonmetallic mineral pdts	2.04	1.33	-1
Basic metal and metal pdts	11.48	11.62	
(Iron and steel)	(3.71)	(3.43)	(+27)
(Nonferrous metals)	(3.02)	(3.97)	(+108)
(Others)	(4.75)	(4.22)	(n.a.)
Machinery	14.21	12.99	
(Metal working machinery)	(7.06)	(7.64)	(+63)
(Others)	(7.15)	(5.35)	(-29)
Electrical Machinery	6.61	6.27	+46
Transport equipment	14.30	10.17	
(Motor vehicles)	(9.58)	(2.44)	(-60)
(Others)	(4.72)	(7.73)	(+112)
Other manufactures	1.92	1.95	
Total manufactures	81.97	68.78	+45
Non processed raw materials	18.03	31.22	
Total	100.00	100.00	
Change in industrial production			+213
Change in real GNP			+105

*The original data used were those expressed in current dollars.
**Food +245; beverages +25.
§Chemicals (proper) +5, products of petroleum and coal -43; fertilizers -14; medicinal and pharmaceutical preparations -42.

Sources: Serviço de Estatística Econômica e Financeira, *Comercio Exterior do Brasil*, several years. The basic data from this source were retabulated to make them comparable to the industrial census classification.
n.a. - not available.

(such as petroleum and coal), but which were very important
to the functioning of the new industries.

The new industries represented not only activities in
the last stages of production, but also at other levels of
the production process. The newly emerging industrial
structure was fairly well balanced both from a horizontal
and vertical point of view. Import substitution in sectors
can be noticed in Table 20 from both a decline in their
share of total imports and from their decline in real terms
in relation to the average imports of 1949-50 (see column 3).
Import substitution also took place in sectors whose share
did not change or even increased and whose real amounts of
imports rose because these increases were substantially less
than the increase of industrial production, which more than
tripled. This impression is reinforced by noting that in
only three categories did imports rise by more than real
GDP, which doubled in this period.

A more accurate measure of import substitution is the
change which occurred in imports as a proportion of total
domestic supplies.[30] This is shown in Table 20. It will
be noted that in 1949 substantial amounts of import substitution had already taken place in consumer and intermediate goods industries, while 59 percent of capital goods
were still supplied from abroad. The policies maximizing
vertical linkages, especially backward linkages, were responsible for the drastic decline in the latter proportion. Although import substitution was the principal motive force for
the period as a whole, its major impact seems to have been in
the middle and late fifties when the greatest declines occurred in the import-total supply ratios of capital and consumer goods. The intermediate goods ratio had been falling
drastically since the late forties.[31]

TABLE 20
Imports as a Percentage of Total Supply

	1949	1955	1960	1962	1965	1966
Capital goods	59.0	43.2	23.4	12.9	8.2	13.7
Intermediate goods	25.9	17.9	11.9	8.9	6.3	6.8
Consumer goods	10.0	12.2	4.5	1.1	1.2	1.6

Source: "A Industrialização Brasileira: Diagnostico e
Perspectivas," in *Programa Estrategico de Desenvol-
vimento, 1968-70,* Estudo Especial (Rio de Janeiro:
Ministerio do Planejamento e Coordenação Geral,
Janeuro de 1969).

Another way of observing changes in Brazil's economic structure is to examine trends in the distribution of gross value added and employment in the manufacturing sector. This is done in Table 21. It will be noted that the traditional industries (textiles, food products, clothing) suffered declines in their relative position, while the most pronounced growth took place in such key import-substitution industries as transport equipment, machinery, electric machinery and appliances, and chemicals. It is interesting to note that in the traditional industries there was a greater relative decline of gross value added than of employment, while for many new industries the increase in gross value added was greater than the increase of employment.

IMBALANCES AND BOTTLENECKS

The import substitution industrialization strategy of the fifties left a legacy of problems with which policy-makers of the sixties would have to struggle in order to insure continued growth and development. Although these problems will be dealt with separately in the second part of the book, we shall briefly summarize them here for the sake of perspective.

Although the agricultural sector was neglected throughout most of the post-World War II period,[32] its expansion at a yearly rate of 4.5 percent would seem satisfactory in relation to a yearly population growth rate of 3.1 percent. A more disaggregative examination, however, reveals actual and potential problems which were emerging at the time.

While the growth of the population was smaller than the growth of the food supply, there was another factor which threw a shadow on this favorable picture. There occurred an intensive rural-urban migration, resulting in an urban population growth rate of about 5.4 percent per year in the fifties. Most of the increase of food production was due to new lands placed under cultivation rather than increased productivity of older agricultural areas. Since the rapidly rising demand for food in urban centers had to be supplied from increasingly distant areas, there was an increasing strain on the country's precarious rural-urban transportation network and on the agricultural marketing system. (It was estimated at the time that the loss of agricultural products due to a backward marketing system was as high as 20 percent.) It was generally recognized by the early sixties that further industrial growth would be severely hampered if no breakthrough were made in agricultural productivity near the

TABLE 21

(a) Changes in Brazil's Industrial Structure
1939-1963: Gross Value Added

	1939	1949	1953	1958	1963
Nonmetallic minerals	5.2	7.4	7.4	6.7	5.2
Metal products	7.6	9.4	9.6	11.5	12.0
Machinery	3.8	2.2	2.4	3.0	3.2
Electrical equipment	1.2	1.7	3.0	4.3	6.1
Transport equipment	0.6	2.3	2.0	7.0	10.5
Wood products	5.3	6.1	6.6	5.4	4.0
Paper products	1.5	2.1	2.7	2.4	2.9
Rubber products	0.7	2.0	2.2	1.9	1.9
Leather products	1.7	1.3	1.3	1.2	0.7
Chemicals, pharmaceuticals, plastics, perfumes, etc.	9.8	9.4	11.0	13.1	15.5
Textiles	22.2	20.1	17.6	13.4	11.6
Clothing and shoes	4.9	4.3	4.9	4.0	3.6
Food products	24.2	19.7	17.6	15.8	14.1
Beverages	4.4	4.3	3.5	2.8	3.2
Tobacco	2.3	1.6	2.3	1.6	1.6
Printing and publishing	3.6	4.2	3.5	3.3	2.5
Miscellaneous	1.0	1.9	2.4	2.6	1.4
Total	100.0%	100.0%	100.0%	100.0%	100.0%

Source: IBGE, *Recenseamento Geral do Brasil.*

(b) Changes in Brazil's Industrial Employment Structure

	1950	1960
Nonmetallic minerals	9.7%	9.7%
Metal products	7.9	10.2
Machinery	1.9	3.3
Electrical equipment	1.1	3.0
Transport equipment	1.3	4.3
Wood products	4.9	5.0
Furniture	2.8	3.6
Paper products	1.9	2.4
Rubber products	0.8	1.0
Leather products	1.5	1.5
Chemicals	3.7	4.1
Pharmaceuticals	1.1	0.9
Perfumes, soap, candles	0.8	0.7
Plastic products	0.2	0.5
Textiles	27.4	20.6
Clothing, shoes	5.6	5.8
Food products	18.5	15.3
Beverages	2.9	2.1
Tobacco	1.3	0.9
Printing and publishing	3.0	3.0
Miscellaneous	1.7	2.1
Total	100.0%	100.0%

Source: IBGE, *Recenseamento Geral do Brasil, 1960, Censo Industrial.*

principal consuming centers. The rise of relative food prices would not only increase inflationary pressures, but would also lead to rising social tensions.

A second major problem was the rising rate of inflation. Although, as will be discussed in a separate chapter, inflation might, for a while, have played a positive role in the reallocation of resources to support the industrialization drive, its rates attained such levels by the early sixties that any contribution to growth from a forced savings mechanism was overwhelmed by the effects of inflation-induced distortions.

A third major problem was that industrial growth brought along an accentuation of inequalities--the unequal distribution of the benefits from growth on a regional, sectoral and income group basis--which was producing increasing socio-political pressures for remedial actions. There was also pressure to deal with the long-neglected and backward education system, both to supply better trained manpower for the modern industrial sector and to provide greater social mobility, and thus access to the fruits of industrialization to a larger proportion of the population.

Finally, there were mounting balance of payments pressures resulting from the fact that the growth in the fifties, especially in the second half of the fifties, was financed by a substantial influx of foreign capital, both in the form of direct investments and in the form of loans. By the beginning of the sixties Brazil's foreign debt already amounted to more than two billion dollars. A large proportion of the latter was short-term, and both the interest and amortization payments, combined with profit remittances of foreign firms, produced increasing balance of payments difficulties. The fact that import substitution policies had been one-sided, i.e., that export promotion and diversification had been completely neglected, was now coming to be a major problem.

ENDNOTES

1. In quantum terms, the share of principal exports in the
    total output of each product in 1950 was as follows:
    coffee - 95%; cocoa - 88%; cotton - 12%; rubber - 14%;
    tobacco - 27%; iron ore - 46%. See: W. Baer,
    Industrialization and Economic Development in Brazil.
    Homewood, Illinois: Richard D. Irwin, Inc., 1965, p. 38.
2. Baer, *Industrialization*, p. 40.
3. One might argue that had the country been more reason-
    able in its price policies in the early postwar period,
    it would have had a better chance to maintain its share
    of the world market. Due to balance of payments diffi-
    culties at the time, however, the policy-makers were
    under pressure to maximize export earnings in the
    short-run. In addition, one should also consider that
    Brazil was the first country to dominate the world
    coffee market. One cannot expect a first-comer to
    always maintain its original market share. It was
    only natural for many of the newly independent countries
    in the post-World War II years, which had natural con-
    ditions to produce coffee, to enter the market (just
    as it was only natural to have the world's first auto-
    mobile producing nation lose its share of the world
    market as other nations with the requisite resources
    also became automobile producers.) For greater detail
    on coffee policies, see: A. Delfim Netto, *O Problema
    do Café no Brasil*, (São Paulo: Universidade de São
    Paulo, 1959); and A. Delfim Netto and Carlos Alberto de
    Andrade, "Uma Tentativa de Avaliação da Política
    Cafeeira," in Versiani and Mendonça de Barros,
    editors, op. cit., pp. 223-238.
4. United Nations, *World Economic Survey*, 1962, Part 1,
    "The Developing Countries in World Trade," p. 6, where
    it is stated that "These estimates were derived from
    regression of gross domestic product of the industrially
    developed countries on imports of each commodity group
    from the developing countries. The sample covers the
    period 1953-60."
5. Rex F. Daly, "Coffee Consumption and Prices in the
    United States," *Agricultural Economics Research*,
    July 1958.
6. T. Schultz, "Economic Prospects of Primary Products,"
    in H. Ellis and H. Wallich, editors, *Economic Develop-
    ment for Latin America*. New York: St. Martin's Press,
    Inc., 1961, p. 313.
7. Joel Bergman, *Brazil: Industrialization and Trade
    Policies*. London: Oxford University Press, 1970,
    pp. 27-8.

8. Donald Huddle, "Balanço de Pagamentos e Controle de Cambio no Brasil," *Revista Brasileira de Economia,* Março de 1964, p. 8; see also continuation of Huddle article in Junho de 1964 issue.
9. Bergman, op. cit., p. 28.
10. Baer, *Industrialization,* p. 48; Joseph A. Kershaw, "Postwar Brazilian Economic Problems," *The American Economic Review,* June 1948, pp. 333-4.
11. Much of the material used in this section is based on two monographs: Mario H. Simonsen, *Os Controles de Preços na Economia Brasileira* (Rio de Janeiro, CONSULTEC, 1961); Lincoln Gordon and Engelbert L. Grommers, *United States Manufacturing Investment in Brazil: The Impact of Brazilian Government Policies 1946-1960* (Boston: Division of Research, Graduate School of Business Administration, Harvard University, 1962.) The overvalued exchange rate not only discouraged exports and encouraged imports, but it was also a barrier to the inflow of capital and a stimulus to increasing profit remittances. It also resulted in a black foreign exchange market, where foreign currencies were quoted at rates substantially above the official values.
12. For greater details, see: Bergsman, op. cit.; Huddle, op. cit.
13. Gordon and Grommers, op. cit., p. 16.
14. Ibid.
15. For a more detailed description and analysis of this system, see: A. Kafka, "The Brazilian Exchange Auction System," *The Review of Economics and Statistics,* August 1956, pp. 308-22.
16. Gordon and Grommers, op. cit., p. 17.
17. For more additional quantitative details, see Bergsman, op. cit., pp. 31-2.
18. For a more thorough discussion of the tariff system, see Bergsman, op. cit., pp. 32-54.
19. Gordon and Grommers, op. cit., p. 19.
20. Ibid., p. 20.
21. For detailed description of the political events of the time, see: Thomas E. Skidmore, *Politics in Brazil, 1930-64: An Experiment in Democracy.* New York: Oxford University Press, 1967.
22. Gordon and Grommers, op. cit., pp. 23-4.
23. Sources for the paragraphs on the SALTE plan are: BNDE, *XI Exposição Sôbre o Programa de Reaparelhamento Econômico,* Exercício de 1962, Rio de Janeiro, pp. 3-6; H. W. Singer, "The Brazilian SALTE Plan," *Economic Development and Cultural Change,* February 1953; Dorival Teixeira Vieira, *O Desenvolvimento Econômico do Brasil e a Inflação.* Sao Paulo: Faculdade de Ciencias Economicas e Administrativas, Universidade de São Paulo, 1962.

24. Singer, op. cit., p. 342.
25. See: United Nations, *The Economic Development of Brazil*, Analyses and Projection of Economic Development, II. New York, 1956.
26. It was, of course, only known in the early sixties that the actual population growth rate had exceeded 3 percent. The previous demographic growth rate for the 1940-50 period had been about 2.5 percent.
27. Gordon and Grommers, op. cit., p. 123.
28. BNDE, op. cit., p. 14.
29. Gordon and Grommers, op. cit., p. 51.
30. For more sophisticated measurements of import substitution see: S. Morley and G. W. Smith, "On the Measurement of Import Substitution," *American Economic Review*, September 1970.
31. Huddle has minutely examined various subperiods in the post-World War II era and found that import-substitution industrialization was mainly concentrated in the middle and late fifties; see: Donald Huddle, "Postwar Brazilian Industrialization: Growth Patterns, Inflation and Sources of Stagnation," in *The Shaping of Modern Brazil*, edited by Eric N. Baklanoff. Baton Rouge: Louisiana State University Press, 1969, pp. 91-7.
32. Agriculture had not been completely neglected. However, investments in marketing facilities and extension services were not widespread and occurred only sporadically. See, Julian Chacel, "The Principal Characteristics of the Agrarian Structure and Agricultural Production in Brazil," and Gordon W. Smith, "Brazilian Agricultural Policy, 1950-1967," both in Howard Ellis (editor), *The Economy of Brazil*. Berkeley and Los Angeles: The University of California Press, 1969.

5

STAGNATION AND BOOM: BRAZIL IN THE SIXTIES AND SEVENTIES

INTRODUCTION

In the early sixties the Brazilian economy lost its dynamism. After the growth rate of the real GDP reached a peak of 10.3 percent in 1961, it fell to 5.3, 1.5 and 2.4 percent in 1962, 1963 and 1964 respectively.

The immediate cause of the stagnation which set in after 1961 seems to have been the continuing political crisis which the country experienced after the resignation of Janio Quadros from the presidency in August 1961. Quadros had been elected with a broad backing of the Brazilian population. His short-lived administration tried to cope with some of the economy's imbalances. A determined effort was made to deal with inflation. The multiple exchange rate system was simplified and the inflationary subsidies on essential imports, such as wheat and petroleum, were substantially lowered. Although this raised the prices of such consumer items as bread and bus fares, it helped the government to cut its budgetary deficit. In addition, the Quadros government imposed credit tightening and a wage freeze and began a harsh program of streamlining government operations. By the middle of 1961 some evidence had already developed that the growth of inflation was being slowed and Brazil's foreign creditors were beginning to look at the country in a more sympathetic way. An element which played a role in the latter was also the fact that the first years of the sixties were the beginning of Kennedy's Alliance for Progress which was supposed to favor reformist governments. It seems probable that efforts at structural reforms and the vigorous stabilization effort were among the principal causes for the formidable pressures on Quadros which brought his early resignation.[1]

The turbulent years from Quadros's resignation in late
August 1961 until the overthrow of the Goulart government
in April 1964 were devoid of any consistent line of economic
policy. This was owing to the lack of leadership shown by
President Goulart. In the first half of his tenure this
was caused by circumstances not directly of his making.
Goulart was allowed to take over the presidency only after
it was agreed that he would share power with a newly created
parliamentary form of government. This muddled the lines
of authority and no other clear leadership emerged. After
a plebiscite in 1963 which restored full power to the presidency, however, Goulart proved to be a weak man overwhelmed
by pressures from many opposing quarters. There were half-
hearted attempts at stabilization which were soon abandoned
when Goulart could not resist the demand of labor leaders
for rapid wage adjustments, the demand of the business com-
munity to refrain from painful credit restrictions, the
pressure from many quarters not to abandon inflationary subsidy exchange rates for the importation of petroleum and
wheat, or the pressure not to readjust public utility and
transportation rates in accordance with over-all price increases. The latter created further inflationary pressures
through increased public budgetary deficits.[2]

During the Goulart tenure, groups clamoring for basic
institutional reforms and for more nationalist policies
vis-a-vis foreign capital became increasingly vociferous
and had substantial influence over the president. Agitation
for land and tax reform grew, institutional change in the
country's educational structure and a greater control over
foreign capital's activities (and in some cases expropriation)
were demanded. Goulart sympathized with these groups clamoring for reforms, used their arguments in his pronouncements,
but failed to implement concrete programs.

Some actions were taken at the time, such as a severe
profit remittance control law passed by the congress in
October 1962, and a Three-Year Plan was formulated in 1963
which was to control inflation drastically and systemat-
ically deal with the economy's principal imbalances. This
plan was soon shelved when it became obvious that the government had neither the means nor the will to impose its
stabilization and reform measures. The lack of political
control, the continued agitation for reforms and the lip
service which Goulart paid to the latter, and the denunci-
ation of foreign capital, resulted in increasingly severe
economic problems. Budget deficits increased and the rate
of inflation grew to levels of 50 percent and finally to
yearly rates of more than 100 percent in 1964. With

political uncertainties, foreign and domestic investment declined and the growth rate of the economy steadily declined from its 1961 peak.

TWO VIEWS OF THE STAGNATION OF THE SIXTIES

It became fashionable during the sixties to speculate about the aftermath of Import Substitution Industrialization (ISI) in developing countries. Most analysts were pessimistic. They had doubts about the possibility of high rates of economic growth once the dynamism of ISI had vanished. Orthodox critics of the ISI process itself felt that the inefficient industrial structure resulting in the production of high-priced goods, which could not be sold in large quantities domestically or abroad, would severely limit the prospects of industrial growth. They also believed that the failure to diversify exports during the period of ISI would lead to stagnation based on import constraints. Thus, they felt that the post-ISI hopes of high rates of growth would lie primarily in developing the agricultural export sector and the rationalization of industry (i.e., weeding out industries with no present or prospective comparative advantage).

Nonorthodox (sometimes called "structural") critics felt that since ISI had not solved some of the underlying socio-economic problems which were present even before the process had started--e.g., the backwardness of the agricultural sector, the unequal distribution of income, etc.-- economic stagnation was bound to return once the inherent dynamism of ISI had spent itself. Some structural critics have even pointed to the evidence showing that ISI aggravated existing socio-economic problems. In Brazil and in a number of other developing countries undergoing ISI, income has become more concentrated than before and the new industries have not created sufficient employment for the rapidly growing urban population.[3]

Brazil's stagnation lasted until 1967; it was followed by a remarkable economic boom which lasted from 1968 to 1974. The defenders of the regime spent their time analyzing the favorable results of the policies in the post-1964 governments, while the critics worried about the distribution of the benefits and the distribution of growth among sectors. In fact, the debate during the boom implicitly centered on the question whether Brazil's growth also represented development.

ECONOMIC POLICIES SINCE 1964

It was the vision of the new regime established in 1964 that the path to economic recovery lay in the control of inflation, the elimination of price distortions which had accumulated during the past, the modernization of capital markets which would lead to an increased accumulation of savings, the creation of a system of incentives which would direct investments into areas and sectors deemed essential by the government, the attraction of foreign capital (both private and official) to finance the expansion of the country's productive capacity, and the use of public investments in infrastructural projects and in certain government-owned heavy industries.

In the first years after the 1964 change of government, policy-makers emphasized stabilization and structural reforms in the financial markets. The former consisted of classic stabilization measures - curtailment of government expenditures in a number of sectors, increased tax revenues as a result of improvements in the tax-collection mechanism, tightening of credit, and a squeeze on the wage sector.[4] The stabilization program also included measures to eliminate the price distortions which had worsened during the previous decade of inflation. For instance, public utility rates (which are government controlled and which had lagged behind the general price increase) were raised sharply. Although this had an additional short-run inflationary impact (this being what is known as "corrective inflation"), such measures led to the gradual elimination of deficits in various sectors (for example, transportation), reducing the necessity for government subsidies.[5]

These policy actions resulted in a steady decline in the government budget deficit. In 1963 the deficit amounted to 4.3 percent of the GDP; by 1971 this proportion had declined to 0.3 percent. The inflation rate was brought down gradually to about 20 percent, where it hovered in the boom years 1968-74.

The modernization and strengthening of capital markets was also deemed essential for sustained economic growth. The indexing of financial instruments was instituted - i.e., a system was set up whereby the principal and interest on debt instruments were readjusted in accordance with the rate of inflation.[6] It was initially applied to government bonds, making it possible for the government to rely increasingly on noninflationary financing of the budget deficit. Over the years it was extended to other financial instruments. For example, the newly created housing bank (BNH) was allowed to issue indexed bonds and to index its loans. Indexing was extended to savings deposits, savings and loan associations and corporate debts, and a mechanism was developed for periodic revaluation of the capital of firms in accordance with price changes.

A capital market law, instituted in 1965, provided an institutional setting for strengthening and increasing the use of the stock market and encouraged the establishment of investment banks to underwrite new issues. New credit mechanisms were gradually developed to increase the demand of investors and consumers for the output of Brazil's growing industrial capacity. Many special funds were created, functioning as adjuncts of the government development bank (BNDE), to finance, for example, the sales of small and medium-size Brazilian firms or finance the acquisition of capital goods.[7]

A large proportion of the resources for these official credit institutions was provided by a system of forced savings whose burden was borne to a large extent by the working classes. Since the late 1960s a number of social security and retirement funds have provided an increasing proportion of national savings, comprising the bulk of the funds borrowed by the national treasury, the housing bank, and resources used by the BNDE and the official savings banks (Caixas Econômicas). These savings, of course, were all indexed.[8]

Over the decade 1964-74 the Brazilian government made increasing use of tax incentives to influence the allocation of resources among regions and sectors. For instance, heavy use was made of an already existing tax-incentive mechanism connected with SUDENE (the development agency for the northeast region of Brazil) to attract investors to that backward region; the mechanism was subsequently extended to the Amazon area. Among other tax measures were incentives to stimulate exports, tourism, reforestation, and the stock market.[9]

Government investment expenditures were never cut back during the vigorous stabilization years after 1964, as existing infrastructure projects were continued. Also, while the financial reforms and stabilization programs mentioned above were being carried out, the government engaged in some basic sectoral studies (in collaboration with the U. S. Agency for International Development, the World Bank, and the Inter-American Development Bank) designed to guide the expansion of the country's power supply, transportation

system, urban infrastructure, and heavy industries--
especially steel, mining, and petrochemicals--which were
dominated by government enterprises. The time-lag between
these studies, negotiations to finance investment, and
actual investment activities, came to three or four years
and only in the late 1960s were the results of such planning
activities felt.[10]

Finally, foreign economic trade policy was considered
of central importance by post-1964 regimes. The rapid
growth and diversification of exports was deemed essential
to the recovery and long-term health of the Brazilian economy.[11] To achieve these goals the government adopted a
number of policies over the years, including the abolition
of state export taxes, simplification of administrative
procedures for exporters, and the introduction of tax incentives and subsidized credit. At least as important was
the adoption in 1968 of a more realistic exchange rate
policy, consisting of frequent (but unpredictable) small devaluations of the cruzeiro. It was hoped that in this way
the cruzeiro could be kept from become overvalued as inflation continued, while keeping speculation against the
currency at a minimum and keeping the exchange rate from
becoming a political issue.

ACHIEVEMENTS OF THE POST-1964 GOVERNMENTS

The stagnation evident in the Brazilian economy by
1962 continued after the change of regime in 1964 and lasted
until 1968. It can be attributed to a combination of factors: the effects of the stabilization measures applied in
those years; the time-lag involved before the effects of the
institutional reforms in the financial system could be felt
and before the numerous studies and plans for the expansion
of the country's infrastructure and heavy industries could
result in actual construction activities; and, finally, the
time-lag involved in convincing the domestic and foreign
private and official investors of the new regime's stability
and control over the economy.

The Brazilian economy entered its remarkable seven-year
boom in 1968. Annual real growth of the GDP, which averaged
only 3.7 percent in the period 1962-67, surged to yearly
rates averaging 11.3 percent in the years 1968-74. As will
be noted from Table 22, industry was the leading sector,
expanding at yearly rates of 12.6 percent. Within manufacturing, one observes (Table 23) that the highest growth
rates were achieved by such sectors as transport equipment,

TABLE 22
Yearly Growth Rates of Real GDP, Per Capita GDP, Industry and Agriculture (percent)

Years	Real GDP	Per Capita real GDP	Industry	Agriculture
1956-62*	7.8	4.0	10.3	5.7
1962-67*	3.7	1.3	3.9	4.0
1968	11.2	8.1	13.3	4.4
1969	9.0	6.8	12.1	3.7
1970	8.8	5.8	10.3	1.0
1971	13.3	10.2	14.3	11.4
1972	11.7	8.7	13.3	4.1
1973	14.0	10.8	15.0	3.5
1974	9.8	6.8	9.9	8.5
1975	5.6	2.8	6.2	3.4
1976	9.2	6.3	12.9	4.2
1977	4.7	2.0	2.3	9.6

* Yearly average.

Source: Calculated from data of Centro de Contas Nacionais, Fundaçâo Getulio Vargas. Published in *Conjuntura Economica* (Various issues).

machinery, and electrical equipment, while traditional sectors like textiles, clothing, and food products experienced much slower rates of growth. In other words, much of the manufacturing growth was concentrated in consumer durables and chemicals. The expansion of the Brazilian economy can be illustrated more graphically by mention of a few numbers of actual output in both basic industries and consumer goods industries: steel output grew from 2.8 million tons in 1964 to 9.2 million in 1976; installed electric power capacity expanded from 6,840,000 megawatts to 21,796,000 in the same period; cement from 5.6 to 19.1 million tons; motor vehicales from 184,000 to 986,000 and passenger cars from 98,000 to 527,000; paper from 0.6 to 1.9 million tons; by 1976 television set production had reached 1,872,000 and production of refrigerators 1,276,000. The average yearly growth rate of road construction increased from 12 percent in the period 1964-67 to 25 percent in 1968-72 and the rate of growth of paving from 6 percent to 33 percent.

A notable feature of Brazil's growth in the fifties

TABLE 23
Average Annual Growth Rates of Individual Sectors
(percent)

	1967-1970*	1971	1972	1973	1974	1975	1976	197
Nonmetallic minerals	17.3	11.1	13.7	16.3	14.8	9.0	12.0	8.
Metal products	14.4	5.6	12.1	9.4	5.2	9.2	13.5	7.
Machinery	22.7	3.6						
			18.9	28.2	10.9	7.2	11.6	
Electrical equipment	13.4	21.3						
Transport equipment	32.6	19.0	22.5	27.6	18.9	0.5	7.2	-2.
Paper and paper prds.	9.1	6.3	7.0	9.4	4.3	-14.6	20.8	2.
Rubber products	15.3	11.8	13.0	22.3	18.2	4.7	11.2	-2.
Chemicals	15.6	13.6	16.3	22.1	8.4	3.0	17.8	6.
Textiles	7.4	8.8						
			4.1	8.4	-2.8	3.4	7.2	
Clothing, shoes, etc.	1.7	-1.8						
Food products	8.3	3.6						
			13.3	10.6	6.5	1.4	12.0	
Beverages	8.2	4.8						
Tobacco	9.6	5.7						
Total manufacturing	14.2	11.6	13.6	15.8	7.8	3.8	10.5	
Construction	14.4	8.4	13.0	15.4	11.2	3.8	12.8	
Public utilities	12.2		11.1	12.5	12.0	10.2	10.1	

* Yearly average.

Source: Same as Table 22 and Anuario Estatistico do Brasil (IBGI 1976.

and sixties was the relatively low capital coefficient. According to revised national accounts, gross capital formation as a proportion of GNP rose from about 14 percent in 1949 to 19 percent in 1959, while it averaged 22 percent in the early seventies (see Table 24). While at this writing no revised national accounts exist for the sixties, the old series[12] shows the capital coefficient to have hovered around 16.5 percent from the mid-fifties until the end of the sixties. Even if revisions should raise this average, it is probable that they would not show a rising trend. The constancy of the capital coefficient, i.e., gross capital formation as a percentage of GDP, has been attributed to the substantial amount of excess capacity which existed throughout the sixties, thus

TABLE 24

Gross Capital Formation and Taxes as a Percentage of GDP

Year	Gross capital formation Total	Fixed	Direct taxes	Indirect taxes
1949	13.9	12.9	4.7	9.2
1959	20.7	18.5	5.2	12.8
1970	23.5	22.2	8.6	15.3
1971	25.3	22.9	9.0	15.0
1972	25.5	22.9	10.1	14.8
1973	27.3	23.0	10.5	14.7
1974	31.6	24.2	10.8	14.2
1975	25.3	25.3	11.7	13.2
1976		24.2		
1977		22.6		

Source: Calculated from *Conjuntura Economica,* July 1977 and February 1978.

TABLE 25

Sectoral Composition of Net Domestic Product, at Current Prices (%)

Year	Agriculture	Industry	Other	Total
1949	26.0	26.0	48.0	100.0
1959	19.2	32.6	48.2	100.0
1970	10.2	36.3	53.5	100.0
1974	11.2	39.8	49.0	100.0
1975	10.5	39.4	50.1	100.0
1976	10.7	38.6	50.7	100.0
1977	12.2	37.0	50.8	100.0

Source: Same as Table 24.

enabling many sectors to expand output without the need for much investment expenditures. One study found that in the 1962-67 stagnation idle capacity in industry reached nearly 25 percent and that in the subsequent boom period capital stock was growing at 8.3 percent per year while the manufacturing growth rate was 14.5 percent. The latter "...was only possible due to the existence of a substantial amount of idle capacity...The result was an increase in the degree of capacity utilization from 75% in 1967 to 100% in 1972, an annual average of nearly 6%."[13]

The higher capital coefficient in the seventies was thus due in large measure to the full use of capacity which induced many firms to make new investments. It was also due to the growing dominance of government investments, in both infrastructure projects and heavy industries, which are characterized by high capital/output ratios.

The efforts of the post-1964 governments to raise tax collection resulted in a notable increase of both direct and indirect taxes as a proportion of GNP (Table 24). It is probable that had it not been for the above mentioned tax-incentive schemes, the direct tax/GNP ratio would have risen even more. It has been estimated that in the early seventies these incentives amounted to 50 percent of total direct taxes.

Table 25 shows that in the period 1959 to 1973 the decline of the share of agriculture in the Net Domestic Product accelerated, while the growth of the shares of industry and services was about evenly divided.

Table 26 and Tables 29 and 30 in chapter 6 summarize Brazil's foreign trade position. External trade grew at rates substantially higher than those of the growth of the economy as a whole. In the years 1970-73 the average yearly growth rate of exports was 14.7 percent and of imports 21 percent. The trade deficit resulting from the higher import growth was increased still further by a rising deficit in the service balance. Until 1974, however, this was more than covered by a massive inflow of official and private capital. The net inflow of direct investment grew from a yearly average of US$84 million in the period 1965-69 to a yearly average of US$1 billion in the period 1973-76. Even more notable were net foreign loans, which increased from a yearly average of US$604 million in 1965-69 to an average of US$6.5 billion in 1973-76. Foreign financing substantially exceeded the deficit of the current account until 1973, resulting in an increase in Brazil's foreign exchange

TABLE 26

Balance of Payments Position and Foreign Debt, 1960-1976
(US$ billions - current prices)

	1960-64*	1965-69*	1969	1970	1971	1972	1973	1974	1975	1976
Exports	1.34	1.84	2.31	2.74	2.90	3.99	6.20	7.95	8.66	10.13
Imports	1.25	1.51	1.99	2.51	3.25	4.23	6.19	12.63	12.17	12.28
Trade balance	0.91	0.33	0.32	0.23	-0.35	-0.24	0.01	-4.68	-3.51	-2.15
Service balance	-0.34	-0.51	-0.64	-0.82	-0.98	-1.25	-1.72	-2.31	-3.56	-3.86
Net foreign direct inv.	0.07	0.08	0.14	0.12	0.17	0.38	0.98	0.94	0.97	1.01
Loans (net)	0.35	0.61	1.05	1.44	2.52	4.30	4.50	6.89	6.53	8.97
Foreign debt	2.90	-	4.40	5.30	6.60	10.20	12.60	17.40	22.00	29.00
Reserves	-	0.40	0.65	1.19	1.72	3.90	6.80	5.70	4.00	6.50

* Yearly average.

Source: Boletim to Banco Central do Brasil.

reserves from an average of US$400 million in the period 1965-9 to US$6.8 billion in 1973.

It should be noted (Table 30 of chapter 6) that in these years Brazil succeeded in diversifying its commodity export structure. The portion of the value of exports accounted for by coffee declined from an average of 42 percent in the mid-1960s to 12.6 percent in 1974; manufacturers increased from 7.2 to 27.7 percent in the 1965-74 period; soybeans were not a part of Brazil's export structure in the mid-1960s and stood at 7.4 percent in 1974. The import commodity structure was noted for the growth of capital goods, whose portion of total imports rose from about 31 percent in the mid-1960's to about 40 percent in the mid-1970s. And with the world oil crisis, petroleum imports rose from 11.5 percent of imports in 1973 to about 25 percent in 1975.

The post-1964 policies clearly opened the economy to foreign trade. Whereas the import substitution policies of the fifties decreased the import coefficient (that is, the import/GDP ratio) from 16 percent in 1947-49 to 5.4 percent in 1964, the opposite occurred as a result of the post-1964 policies, making the coefficient rise to 14 percent in 1974.

THE GOVERNMENT SECTOR

One aspect of Brazil's economic growth which is only beginning to receive attention is the large and growing involvement of the state in the economy.[14] Government expenditures (all levels of government) as a proportion of GDP have grown from 17.1 percent in 1947 to 22.5 percent in 1973. State enterprises dominate in steel, mining and petrochemicals. They control over 80 percent of power-generating capacity and most of the public utilities. It has been estimated that in 1974, for the 100 largest firms (in value of assets), 74 percent of the combined assets belonged to state enterprises; while for the 5,113 largest firms 37 percent of the assets belonged to state enterprises. Similarly state banks play a dominant role in the financial system. Of the fifty largest banks (in terms of deposits), state banks accounted for about 56 percent of total deposits in 1974 and about 65 percent of loans to the private sector.

There exists substantial evidence that much of the growth since 1968 is due to the impact of government programs,[15] and that, given the elaborate control mechanisms of the state, the allocation of resources is more the result of government policies than of market forces.

ISSUES SURROUNDING THE POST-1964 GROWTH EXPERIENCE

It has been generally recognized that the fruits of the rapid expansion of the Brazilian economy have been unevenly distributed. This became apparent with the publication of the 1970 demographic census which revealed an increase in the concentration of the distribution of income.

THE EQUITY QUESTION

As can be seen from Table 27, the share of the national income of the lowest 40 percent of the income recipients declined from 11.2 percent in 1960 to 9 percent in 1970; the share of the next 40 percent fell from 34.4 to 27.8 percent, while the top 5 percent increased their share from 27.4 to 36.3 percent. There is also considerable evidence that the real wages declined at first in the second half of the 1960s and then rose at a rate substantially smaller than the rate of productivity increases.[16]

TABLE 27
Changes in Income Distribution

			Per capita income in US$	
	1960	1970	1960	1970
Lower 40%	11.2	9.0	84	90
Next 40%	34.3	27.8	257	278
Next 15%	27.0	27.0	540	720
Top 5%	27.4	36.3	1,645	2,940
Total	100.0	100.0	300	400

Source: Calculated from IBGE, *Censo Demográfico*, 1970.

Although Table 28 shows minimum rather than average wages, one should take into account that in the states of Rio de Janeiro and São Paulo over 25 percent of the 1973 work force in manufacturing earned one minimum salary or less and over 30 percent of workers in commerce earned one minimum salary or less, while workers earning two minimum salary or less amounted to 65 and 70 percent in the respec-

TABLE 28

Minimum Wages in 1965 Cruzeiros
(Cr$ per month)

	1966	1967	1968	1969	1970	1971	1972	1973	1974	1975	1976
Rio de Janeiro	53.9	53.1	52.9	51.2	50.8	51.9	54.2	55.3	49.9	53.8	51.0
São Paulo	50.9	50.8	50.0	49.1	50.2	50.2	50.9	51.8	47.1	51.5	51.9
Porto Alegre	49.2	50.4	51.2	51.5	50.6	51.7	52.3	49.9	47.1	49.1	50.5

Note: All numbers refer to December of each year.

Source: Boletim do Banco Central do Brasil, Maio de 1977.

tive sectors; the situation was much worse in the northeast.[17] Sample surveys in 1972 revealed that fewer than 40
percent of Brazil's urban households had access to a general
water supply system, fewer than 43 percent were connected
with a general sewage system or had septic tanks, only 53
percent had electricity, and only 5 percent had telephones.
Moreover, there were huge variations among regions.[18]

The first question that is raised by this distributional
situation is whether the situation will ultimately lead to
stagnation, inasmuch as the small proportion of the population will not constitute a large enough market to sustain
a high rate of economic growth (see Table 27). But for two
reasons the stagnation argument might not apply to Brazil.
First, there is the size of the government sector that, if
correctly managed, can keep growth going. Second, there is
the absolute size of Brazil's population. Even if 20 percent of the population receives over 63 percent of the
country's income, this represents about twenty-two million
people, which is a large market. It remains to be seen,
however, how economic growth could expand rapidly beyond
the import substitution industrialization period. This
raises another question. Has a new dualism emerged in
Brazil, in which two socioeconomic groups will perpetuate
themselves side-by-side? This has been described by some
as the "Belgium in India" situation - that is, a population
of about twenty-two million with per capital income of about
US$1,200 while eighty-five million receive incomes below
US$300. Is this dualism permanent? Or assuming no drastic
income redistribution policies by decree, would the dynamism
inherent in a market serving twenty-two million people
gradually draw an increasingly larger number of the eighty-
five million into the higher income society?[19]

Even though the increasingly unequal distribution
of income might not lead to long-term stagnation, the issue
has been central to the debate between the defenders and the
critics of the regime. The basic reason for its centrality
was that a system producing high rates of growth of a product
distributed in a blatantly unequal fashion seemed in the long
run to be both morally and politically unjustifiable. The
defenders of the regime argued, however, that the very
success of the Brazilian growth experience of the late 1960s
and early 1970s had produced an increase in the concentration
of income, because the high growth rates increased the demand
for skilled manpower, which was in short supply. Market
forces thus caused an immense rise in the relative income of
skilled laborers, technicians and managers, which meant that
a large proportion of the increment in the real income was
captured by groups with large amounts of scarce human capital.[20]

In the view of the defenders the solution to the problem lies in increased investment in education, which would gradually improve the country's income distribution by raising the supply of skilled labor relative to demand and thus cause a decrease in the difference between the remuneration for different kinds of labor.[21] Simonsen and Campos believe that the government has chosen the most adequate way for reconciling maximum growth with an improvement in the distribution of income. The improvement in distribution is being achieved in an indirect manner "through an extension of free education, an improvement in the educational pyramid, credit facilities for low income housing, small businesses and small rural establishments, retirement benefits for rural workers and the creation of the retirement funds for industrial and government workers and the program for social integration."[22]

Critics have viewed this kind of analysis as being incomplete at best and as an apology for the policies of post-1964 government at worst. If the basic explanation of the rise in the concentration of income in the 1960s were related to the scarcity of skilled labor, of course little direct blame could be placed on the specific government policies since 1964. But many of the critics have argued that in fact the "education" explanation was of minor importance, and a number have blamed the increase in the concentration of income on the wage policies which were instituted after 1964.[23] There is substantial evidence that real minimum wages and average industrial wages declined during the stabilization years. John Wells has shown that even after real wages began to rise again in the late 1960s, they lagged substantially behind productivity increases, thus contributing to continuing deterioration in the distribution of income between labor and capital.[24]

Other elements contributing to the income concentration have been cited by various critics, and one of them is technology. Over time Brazil's industries have become increasingly capital-intensive. Thus, with industry as the leading sector--having a capital/labor ratio that is much higher than the ratio in the traditional sectors--increased concentration in the distribution of income is bound to occur, all other things being equal. This will be the case even though labor in the capital-intensive industries receives higher real wages than in other sectors, inasmuch as total labor used is small relative to capital and other nonlabor inputs. A second factor, besides technology, was the widespread use of tax incentives to allocate resources, which has inevitably favored the higher income groups. These groups were in a position to make use of the incentives, contributing to the increased concentration in income.

WHO SAVES?

One traditional justification for a concentration in the distribution of income has been that the upper income groups have a greater propensity to save than the lower income groups. Thus, to increase investment and future productive capacity, income concentration must be tolerated for a while. Simonsen and Campos, for instance, have stated that "the so-called 'Brazilian Miracle' must be credited to the sacrifices which were endured during the Castello Branco administration. (It was rooted in the) orthodox recognition that any type of developmental process has to be based on savings and market considerations: the first requirement for rapid and sustained growth is a high rate of savings."[25]

Brazilian savings have experienced a remarkable growth since the late 1950s and early 1960s. Revised national accounts data show that domestic savings as a proportion of GDP stood at 17.5 percent in 1959; by 1973 the figure had risen to 21 percent. According to these data, however, most of the increment in savings came from the government sector - the government saving /GDP ratio having risen from 5.1 percent in 1959 to 8.4 percent in 1973.[26]

An estimate shows the sum of the various social programs funds representing forced savings (the unemployment fund FGTS, PIS, and PASEP, which did not exist in 1959) at 14 percent of total domestic savings for 1973. With government savings for that year they account for 52 percent of total savings. By 1976 the rapid growth of the unemployment and retirement funds resulted in the rise of their proportion of total domestic savings to 15.3 percent.

These data lead to some skepticism about the alleged link between the distribution of income and the economy's savings behavior. In addition, the rapid rise of consumer durable consumption of the more favored income groups would seem to indicate that the system (that is, consumer credit and the availability of an increasing variety of consumer goods) encourages them to consume rather than to save.[27] A recent study suggests that a large portion of the indexed credit of the housing bank, whose funds are drawn from the retirement funds mentioned above, have been used to finance middle and upper income housing, other urban construction, and urban infrastructure, rather than housing for the poor.[28]

This would be an additional instance of forced savings by lower income groups financing projects for the more favored income groups.

DEMAND AND PRODUCTION PROFILES

Increased concentration of income raises a further problem, rarely discussed until recently; increased investment in a society with concentrated incomes produces a production capacity profile which is unlikely to be adequate for a more egalitarian society. This problem is closely related to the arguments developed by Furtado in his recent critiques of the Brazilian model. He argues that the profile of the productive structure that has evolved in Brazil over the last decades mirrors the demand profile of the population which, in turn, is influenced by the distribution of income:

> The concentration in the distribution of income of Brazil resulted in a demand profile in which the goods of technologically advanced industries are heavily represented. This is also reflected in the country's productive structure. Thus, the continued dynamism of technologically advanced industries depends on the maintenance or even on an increase in the concentration of income.[29]

The tax incentive programs, the emergent financial structure characterized by increasing amounts of credit institutions catering to the financing of consumer durables, and the growth of an absolutely large (though proportionally small) class of managers and skilled laborers with high incomes, has been crucial to maintain the "correct" demand profile.

It has also been suggested (without further elaboration) that the large presence of multinational firms and the sophistication of the financial system have contributed to influence the consumption pattern of the population. Through advertising by the multinationals and through developments in the credit mechanism, new demand has been created for many consumer durables. Some economists have claimed that this has "distorted" the demand profile of the lower income groups, inducing them to buy goods they would normally not purchase, given their income level.[30]

Most of these arguments remain to be tested empirically. Of course, the much faster growth of output in consumer durable industries than in the traditional industries (see

Table 23) gives some support to Furtado's analysis. It would be interesting to test the degree of rigidity of the production capacity profile when changes occur in the demand profile. The more rigid it is, the weaker becomes the defense of a temporary increase in the concentration of income, while the more flexible it is, the stronger is the defense.

A large proportion of Brazil's capital formation in the late 1960's and the first half of the 1970s consisted of public investments and investment activities in government enterprises (in 1969 this amounted to as much as 60 percent of total capital formation). The productive profile resulting from these investments does not necessarily imply the need for a demand profile weighted in favor of a minority of wealthier people - increased steel production capacity, petrochemicals, iron ore mining, power generating capacity, urban rapid transit systems, and so on, would all be necessary regardless of the income distribution. One may, however, question the wisdom of the huge government investments in road building, which supported the capacity expansion of the automobile industry and made the country increasingly dependent on the consumption of petroleum, 80 percent of which is imported.

OTHER DISTRIBUTIONAL PROBLEMS

Although the post-1964 governments have attempted to come to grips with Brazil's age-old problem of regional imbalances, they have made few inroads into the dramatic maldistribution between the southeast-south and the northeast (this is discussed in greater detail in chapter 9). It was mentioned above that this problem was dealt with mainly through the well-known tax incentive program of SUDENE. This resulted in some notable industrial growth in the northeast, but most of that growth was concentrated in the cities of Salvador and Recife, and most industries were so capital-intensive that they provided few employment opportunities.[31] By 1970, although the northeast still contained 30.3 percent of the population, it accounted for only 12.2 percent of the national income and only 5.6 percent of industrial output; the southeast, however, with 42.7 percent of the population, accounted for 64.5 percent of the national income and 80.6 percent of industrial output. The 1972 sample survey of PNAD, moreover, revealed dramatic regional differences in social well-being. In São Paulo, for instance, 85 percent of the households had electricity, while in the northeast this proportion was only 25 percent; 73 percent of São Paulo households were linked to a sewage system or had septic tanks, but only 15 percent of the northeastern households had this provision.[32]

The most publicized attempt at a new regional policy
was the Transamazon highway project announced by President
Medici in September 1970. Huge sums were poured into this
project designed for simultaneous road construction and
colonization. In addition to the policy makers' desire to
increase the population of a huge empty territory--a territory assuming increasing strategic importance in the eyes
of Brazil's military--it was also hoped that a massive migration of population would be a relatively efficient way
of resolving the socioeconomic problems of such areas as
the northeast. Unfortunately, the Transamazon project was
carried out without adequate preliminary planning so that
it created more problems than it solved, and by the mid-
1970s the project seemed to have fallen to a very low priority among the government's economic policies.[33]

DEPARTURE FROM POST-1964 ORTHODOXY

Many of the rules and institutions established by the
first post-1964 government helped to produce the high growth
rates in the 1968-74 period without the distortions that
occurred during the import substitution industrialization
boom of the 1950s. It is of interest to note how the suc-
cessor governments, especially in the 1970s, have begun to
deviate from some of these rules as a result of internally
generated pressures.

One example is the indexing system. The post-1964
governments had enough force to keep the wage sector out of
indexing. Also, from the beginning, the agricultural sector
was exempt: loans to agriculture always carried an interest
rate substantially below the rate of inflation. Loans for
agricultural inputs, for instance, cost only 7 percent at a
time when inflation was running three times that rate. This
has amounted to a deliberate subsidy to the agricultural
sector (the credit most often going to the more privileged
farming units).

Subsidization by index exemption has grown in the 1970s.
As the many debtors of the housing bank could not keep up
their real payments (probably as a result of the lag in
money wage increases and the faster increase of the prices
of goods other than rent) there was the danger of widespread
default. The government consequently had to find ways to
ease the debt burden through such means as lengthening re-
payment periods and even lowering the interest rate.

Pressure for exemption from indexing also came from the

industrial sector. The public criticisms voiced in 1974-75 against the growth of government and multinational enterprises to the detriment of the Brazilian private sector resulted in the reduction of the index burden of loans by the government development bank (BNDE). This amounted, in effect, to massive subsidy through indexation exemption.

The increased exemptions from indexation of borrowing groups have raised uneasy questions about their effects on creditor groups. A large portion of the latter are composed of workers whose savings are invested in pension and social security funds. Should these workers be the ones to subsidize the borrowers or should the burden be borne by the taxpayers in general? According to a policy decision made in 1975, it would seem that the creditors bear much of the burden. Evidence for this was provided by the introduction of a new price index for the purpose of indexing: the index is "cleansed" of "accidental phenomena"--such as droughts--on the price level (in Portuguese this has been called the *indice de preços expurgados*). Naturally, the increase of this index has been much slower than the increase in the regular cost-of-living index.[34]

Another violation of the post-1964 rules came in the way the exchange rate policy instituted in 1968 was used in the mid-1970s. As the mini-devaluations proceeded, the total yearly devaluations amounted to less than the total rate of inflation minus the inflation of Brazil's trading partners. The resulting overvaluation of the cruzeiro did not matter, however, inasmuch as export incentives (tax incentives and subsidized credits) more than compensated for the overvaluation. By the mid-1970s, however, the total yearly devaluations of the cruzeiro had fallen behind the rate of inflation to such an extent that the competitiveness of Brazil's exports was threatened.

The pressures against devaluation came from two sources. First, there was concern about resurging inflationary forces rekindled by the world oil crisis: too much devaluation was seen as an added source of inflation. Second, during the boom years many Brazilian firms had obtained large amounts of credit from foreign banks: rapid devaluation of the cruzeiro would substantially increase the cost of the debt in cruzeiro terms and thus increase the financial burden on sectors the government had relied upon to continue high levels of investment and production activities.

These two examples indicate that although the Brazilian government has the power to enforce economic decisions on the

distribution of resource in accordance with rules originally developed in the mid-1960s, it has found it increasingly
difficult to live within those rules as it has been sub-
jected to market pressures beyond its control.

ENDNOTES

1. For further details on the political situation of the period, see Thomas E. Skidmore, *Politics in Brazil 1930-64, An Experiment in Democracy*. New York: Oxford University Press, 1967, chapter VI.
2. Werner Baer, Isaac Kerstenetzky, and Mario H. Simonsen, "Transportation and Inflation: A Study of Irrational Policy-Making in Brazil," *Economic Development and Cultural Change*, January 1965.
3. The first group's arguments can be found in such works as: Mario H. Simonsen, *Brasil 2001* (Rio de Janeiro: APEC Editôra S.A., 1969), and Mario H. Simonsen, "Brazilian Inflation: Postwar Experience and Outcome of the 1964 Reforms," in *Economic Development Issues: Latin America* (New York: Committee for Economic Development, Supplementary Paper No. 21, August 1967). The second group's thoughts are well represented in such works as: Celso Furtado, *Um Projeto Para O Brasil* (Rio de Janeiro: Editora Saga S.A., 1968), and Maria da Conceição Tavares, *Da Substituição de Importações ao Capitalismo Financeiro* (Rio de Janeiro: Zahar Editores, 1972). Some of these issues are also discussed in the general Latin American context in: Werner Baer, "Import Substitution Industrialization in Latin America: Experiences and Interpretations," *Latin American Research Review*, Spring 1972.
4. More detailed discussions of these policies can be found in the following articles: Albert Fishlow, "Some Reflections on Post-1964 Brazilian Economic Policy," in *Authoritarian Brazil*, edited by A. Stepan (New Haven: Yale University Press, 1973); Harley H. Hinrichs and Dennis J. Mahar, "Fiscal Change as National Policy: Anatomy of a Tax Reform," in *Contemporary Brazil: Issues in Economic and Political Development*, edited by H. Jon Rosenbaum and William G. Tyler (New York: Praeger Publishers, 1972) pp. 191-208; Fundação Getúlio Vargas, "Políticas Econômicas: Registros de Um Quarto de Século," *Conjuntura Econômica*, Novembro de 1972; W. Baer and I. Kerstenetzky, "The Economy of Brazil," in *Brazil in the Sixties*, edited by Riordan Roett (Nashville: Vanderbilt University Press, 1972), pp. 105-146.
5. A more detailed analysis of Brazil's inflation can be found in chapter 8.
6. For details, see chapter 8 and Werner Baer and Paul Beckerman, "Indexing in Brazil," *World Development*, December 1974; Albert Fishlow, "Indexing Brazilian Style: Inflation Without Tears," *Brookings Papers on Economic Activity*, 1974:1.

7. For more details, see: M. H. Simonsen and R. Campos, *A Nova Economia Brasileira* (Rio de Janeiro: Livraria José Olympio Editôra, 1974), chapter 6; Walter L. Ness, Jr., "Financial Markets Innovation as a Development Strategy: Initial Results from the Brazilian Experience," *Economic Development and Cultural Change,* April 1974.

8. For a detailed description of how these funds were organized, see Julian Chacel, M. H. Simonsen, and Arnoldo Wald, *A Correcão Monetária* (Rio de Janeiro: APEC Editôra S. A., 1970.

9. Simonsen and Campos, op. cit., pp. 137-50.

10. Further details can be found in Donald E. Syvrud, *Foundations of Brazilian Economic Growth,* AEI-Hoover Research Publications 1 (Stanford, California: Hoover Institution Press, 1974), chapter 6.

11. Brazil's foreign trade is discussed in greater detail in chapter 6.

12. Fundação Getúlio Vargas, *Conjuntura Econômica,* September 1971, and February and August 1972.

13. Pedro S. Malan and Regis Bonelli, "The Brazilian Economy in the Seventires: Old and New Developments," *World Development,* January-February 1977, p. 28.

14. A more extensive treatment can be found in chapter 7.

15. Werner Baer, "The Brazilian Boom, 1968-72: An Explanation and Interpretation," *World Development,* August 1973.

16. John Wells, "Distribution of Earnings, Growth and the Structure of Demand in Brazil during the Sixties," *World Development,* January 1974, p. 10; Edmar L. Bacha, "Issues and Evidence on Recent Brazilian Economic Growth," *World Development,* January/February 1977, pp. 53-56.

17. These numbers were calculated from data in Programa Nacional de Amostragem de Domicílios (PNAD), *População, Mão de Obra, Salário, Instrução, Domicílio, 4th trimestre* 1973 (IPGE). The minimum salary, decreed by the government, is that salary which enterprises must pay their workers like the U. S. minimum wage.

18. Data calculated from PNAD survey, IBGE, 1972.

19. For more formal analyses of an emerging dualist society, see: E. Bacha and L. Taylor, "The Unequalizing Spiral: A First Growth Model for Belindia," *The Quarterly Journal of Economics,* May 1976.

20. Carlos G. Langoni, *Distribuição de Renda e Desenvolvimento Econômico do Brasil* (Rio de Janeiro: Editora Expressão e Cultura, 1973), chapter 5; Mario H. Simonsen and Roberts Campos, *A Nova Economia Brasileira* (Rio de Janeiro: Livrana José Olympio Editora, 1974) pp. 185-87.

21. Langoni, op. cit., chapter 19.

22. Simonsen and Campos, op. cit., p. 187.

23. Ricardo Tolipan and Arthur Carlos Tirelly (editors), *A Controvérsia Sobre Distribuição de Renda e Desenvolvimento* (Rio de Janeiro: Zahar Editores, 1975), especially articles by Fishlow and Hoffman; also Bacha in *World Development,* Jan.–Feb. 1977.

24. John Wells, op. cit.

25. Simonsen and Campos, op. cit., p. 10.

26. Data from Fundação Getúlio Vargas, Centro de Contas Nacionais, *Sistema de Contas Nacionais, Novas Estimativas* (Rio de Janeiro, September 1974).

27. Wells came to the same conclusion after examining the few consumer budget surveys available. See Wells, op. cit., pp. 20–24.

28. Clark W. Reynolds and Robert T. Carpenter, "Housing Finance in Brazil: Toward a New Distribution of Wealth," in Wayne A. Cornelius and Felicity M. Trueblood (editors), *Latin American Urban Research,* Vol. 5 (Beverly Hills: SAGE Publications, 1975) pp. 147–74.

29. Celso Furtado, *O Mito Do Desenvolvimento Econômico* (Rio de Janeiro: Editora Paz e Terra, 1974).

30. Ibid; also, Maria da Conceição Travares, *Da Substituição de Importações ao Capitalismo Financeiro* (Rio de Janeiro: Zahar Editores, 1972.

31. David E. Goodman and Roberto Cavalcanti de Albuquerque, *Incentivos a Industrialização e Desenvolvimento do Nordeste* (Rio de Janeiro: IPEA, Coleção Relatórios de Pesquisa, No. 20, 1974).

32. Data calculated from IBGE, PNAD sample surveys (Rio de Janeiro, 1972).

33. For further details on the Amazon region, see: Dennis Mahar, "Development Policies for Amazonia: Past and Present," in *Dimensões do Desenvolvimento Brasileiro,* edited by Werner Baer, Pedro P. Geiger and Paulo Haddad (Rio de Janeiro: Editora Campus, 1978).

34. For a description of the new index see *Conjuntura Econômica,* November 1975, p. 101.

PART II
CONTEMPORARY
ISSUES

6

THE EXTERNAL SECTOR: TRADE AND FOREIGN INVESTMENTS

The international economic policies of Brazil since the second World War can be divided into two distinct periods. From the late forties until the early sixties import substitution industrialization (ISI) was the dominant concern of governments and foreign economic policies were shaped in such a manner as to help maximize this process. From 1964 until 1974 policy-makers emphasized the rationalization of the economy, i.e., remedying some of the imbalances or distortions which had arisen during the period of intense ISI. This, as we saw in the previous chapter, also included foreign economic policies which became more outward-oriented than previously. Since 1974, when the effects of the oil crisis began to make themselves felt, a renewed emphasis on ISI and a search for secure supplies of raw materials became the dominant theme of Brazil's foreign economic policies, opening a new era in the country's international economic relations.

INTERNATIONAL ECONOMIC POLICIES IN THE ISI PERIOD

Brazil emerged from World War II with a substantial accumulation of foreign exchange reserves. Since the government which took control in 1945 was dominated by traditional free-traders and by individuals concerned with controlling inflationary forces, all trade and exchange barriers were lifted; at the same time the exchange rate remained at the pre-war level (from 1937 to 1952 the official exchange rate remained fixed at 18.50 old cruzeiros per US$). This resulted in an import spree which left the country without adequate reserves within about a year and in 1947 led to a reimposition of trade and payments restrictions. The "real" exchange rate in 1952 was almost half that of 1946. The

* This chapter is based on an earlier article written with Carlos Von Doellinger, "Determinants of Brazil's Foreign Economic Policy," in Joseph Grunwald (editor).

protective measures of the late forties, thought designed
mainly as a defense of the country's balance of payments,
acted as a stimulus to the continuation of the industrialization process, mostly of consumer goods, which had started
in the thirties.[1]

We have already seen how the Brazilian government
adopted ISI in the fifties as its principal development
strategy and how the protective measures of the late forties
were now deliberately employed as ISI promotional tools instead of being used primarily for balance of payments protection. The emphasis was on developing a domestic productive capacity for as many formerly imported manufactured
products as possible. Special attention was given to the
internal production of more sophisticated consumer durable
goods, basic inputs, energy, etc. We have seen that to
this end various types of exchange rate control systems and
tariffs were applied. The latter resulted in a structure of
effective tariffs which was over 250 percent for manufactured
products.[2] Policies towards foreign capital were extremely
favorable. Not only was there the attraction of a large
and highly protected market, but other policies favoring
firms establishing productive facilities in Brazil were
developed (see chapter 4).

These unorthodox ISI policies did not make it possible
to obtain much financing from such international institutions
as the World Bank or the United States aid agencies, and
most of the financing came from the international private
sector.

The overall development approach in the fifties was
"inward oriented." ISI was supposed to make Brazil's growth
less dependent on the traditional industrial centers of the
world, i.e., the "engine of growth" would reside increasingly within the newly developing industrial sector. Hence the
success indicator of the period was considered to be the
rapidity with which the import coefficient was being reduced.

During the entire period exports were neglected. In
fact, Brazil's ISI policies worked to the detriment of the
export sector. Long periods of exchange rate overvaluation
were thought by many analysts to have acted as a restraint
on the expansion of both traditional and new exports. As
a result of their neglect, the commodity structure of exports hardly changed in the fifties while a profound transformation had taken place in the structure of the economy.
In the early sixties traditional primary exports still

accounted for over 90 percent of total exports, while manufactured products amounted to only 2 percent in 1960.

By the sixties it had become evident that the neglect of international trade during the ISI years was placing the country in a precarious position. A limit to the compression of the import coefficient had been reached as the growing industrial sector necessitated inputs of primary materials, intermediate goods and capital goods which could not be obtained domestically. The continued neglect of exports was placing the country in a dangerous balance of payments position, since a decline in export earnings necessitating a reduction of imports could lead to industrial stagnation. The result was a massive accumulation of current account deficits, and since financing was hard to obtain, Brazil accumulated a substantial amount of "forced indebtedness," mainly in the form of suppliers' credits. By 1964 it had become clear that this policy could not be continued.

THE "OUTWARD LOOKING" POLICIES OF THE 1964-74 PERIOD

The formulators of economic policies after the 1964 change of regime acted on the assumption that high rates of growth in Brazil's post-ISI era could only be achieved in a more open economic setting than in the fifties. In order to increase the rate of growth and diversification of exports the government undertook a series of measures: it abolished state export taxes, simplified administrative procedures for exporters, and introduced a program of export tax incentives and of subsidized credits to exporters.[3] These policies were directed not only towards a more rapid growth of total exports, but also to an increase in the share of manufactured goods. This would lead to a reduction of the country's dependence on the exports of primary goods, especially coffee.

In the area of exchange rate policies the post-1964 governments only gradually developed an approach which was consistent with its export diversification aims. Although a number of large devaluations occurred which substantially eliminated the cruzeiro's overvaluation, the long periods between devaluations resulted in recurrent periods of overvaluation and speculation against the cruzeiro. In 1968 the government adopted a system of minidevaluations. This consisted in frequent, but unpredictable, small devaluations. It was expected that this system would prevent the cruzeiro from becoming overvalued as inflation continued, that it would keep speculation against the currency at a minimum, and that it would avoid having the exchange rate become a political issue.[4]

The outward orientation of policies on the import side consisted principally of a tariff reform in 1966 which resulted in a lowering of nominal tariffs from an average of 54 percent in 1964-66 to 39 percent in 1967. Subsequent changes led again to a rise in the rates, but not to the pre-reform levels. There is evidence that nominal tariffs were higher than the actual ones due to the frequency of exemptions and special reductions for imports of goods for priority projects.

Real protection was also reduced in the late sixties and early seventies by the fact that the rate of devaluation of the cruzeiro was smaller than the rate of inflation.

The post-1964 policies with regard to foreign capital were to encourage the inflow of both official and private loan capital and of direct private investment. Without doubt the political stability and the general orthodox orientation of the post-1964 governments provided a favorable climate for foreign investments. As will be seen in the next section, however, it took a number of years for massive inflows of foreign capital to materialize. The economic stagnation which lasted until 1968 and the considerable amount of excess capacity of the manufacturing sector in the early years of the 1968-74 boom explain in large part why substantial increases of foreign direct investments occurred only after 1971. Before that time financial capital inflows were dominant. These had grown noticeably only in the late sixties. Two reasons seem important to explain this lag. First, there was a long gestation period involved in making feasibility studies for large projects and in negotiating loans from such entities as the World Bank, the Inter-American Development Bank, and the United States Agency for International Development. The second reason was that foreign private investors waited for some time until they were convinced of the stability of the regime and its commitments to the new policy orientation.

Domestic financial policies were also responsible for large inflows of private loan capital in the seventies. For instance, the rate of devaluation of the cruzeiro was substantially less than the domestic inflation rate, and the monetary correction applied to financial instruments was greater than the exchange rate devaluation. This made borrowing from foreign sources especially attractive for Brazilian firms. The massive inflow of capital, due to a

large extent to the international oversupply of money, increased foreign exchange reserves and also contributed to
inflationary pressures. This forced the government to
gradually impose a minimum time requirement for foreign
funds from the end of 1972 on.[6]

STATISTICAL SUMMARY OF BRAZIL'S FOREIGN POSITION

During the period of ISI Brazil's trade dependence as
measured by both the export/GNP and the import/GNP ratios
declined from 9 percent each in 1949 to 5 and 8 percent
respectively in 1959. During the "outward looking" policies
of the post-1964 period these ratios increased again, rising
steeply in the aftermath of the oil crisis, reaching 8 and
13 percent respectively in 1974.

One can get an impression of the overall international
position of Brazil by an examination of the balance of payments which is presented in Table 29. Although the current
account balance has been negative in almost every year since
the fifties, the trade balance was generally positive until
1971. Despite the high rates of growth of exports resulting
from the government's incentive programs, the high internal
growth (especially the investment growth from 1970 onward),
combined with import liberalization, provoked an import expansion which was greater than that of exports. Also, the
continuing internal boom resulted in many industries attaining full capacity production prior to satisfying internal
demand. This resulted in increased reliance on imports -
as was the case, for instance, with steel products. Of
course, the appearance of the giant trade deficits in 1974
was the result, to a large extent, of the huge petroleum
price increases. In addition, however, the ambitious investment programs of the government and multinational enterprises also accounted for continuously rising imports of
capital goods and raw materials.

The service balance of Brazil has always been negative,
the heaviest burden being capital payments, followed by
transportation costs. As can be observed in Table 29, the
rate of growth of these payments has been very rapid in the
seventies, reflecting the increased indebtedness of Brazil,
the greater reliance on foreign direct investments with its
concommitant profit remittances, and the increased usage
of foreign shipping which accompanied the rapid increase
of imports.

The growing current account deficit and amortization

TABLE 29

Balance of Payments, Foreign Debt and International Reserves (US$ millions)

	1959	1960	1963	1966	1969	1970	1971	1972	1973	1974	1975	1976
Balance of trade	72	-23	112	438	318	232	-341	-244	7	-4,690	-3,499	-2,152
Exports (FOB)	1,282	1,270	1,406	1,741	2,311	2,739	2,904	3,991	6,199	7,951	8,670	10,126
Imports (FOB)	-1,210	-1,293	-1,294	-1,303	-1,993	-2,507	-3,245	-4,235	-6,192	-12,641	-12,169	-12,278
Service balance	-373	-459	-269	-463	-630	-815	-980	-1,250	-1,722	-2,433	-3,213	-3,860
Travel (net)	-31	-48	-14	-31	-89	-130	-135	-178	-205	-250	-328	-400
Transportation (net)	-87	-78	-87	-48	-135	-185	-277	-338	-618	-1,066	-903	-850
Capital payments	-116	-155	-87	-197	-263	-353	-420	-520	-712	-901	-1,700	-1,850
(net interest)	(-91)	(-115)	(-87)	(-155)	(-182)	(-234)	(-302)	(-359)	(-514)	(-653)	(-1,463)	(-1,520)
(net profits)	(-25)	(-40)	(0)	(-42)	(-81)	(-119)	(-118)	(-161)	(-198)	(-248)	(-235)	(-330)
Other services	-139	-178	-81	-187	-143	-147	-148	-214	-187	-216	-132	-220
Unilateral transf.	-10	4	43	79	31	21	14	5	27	0.5	0.1	4
Direct investments	124	99	30	74	189	146	189	337	977	945	1,006	1,010
Loans	439	348	250	508	1,201	1,510	2,523	4,300	4,495	6,891	6,530	8,971
Amortization	-377	-417	-364	-350	-493	-672	-850	-1,202	-1,673	-1,920	-2,120	-2,888
International reserves	367	345	219	425	656	1,187	1,746	4,183	6,417	5,252	4,041	5,122

Source: Banco Central do Brasil, *Boletim.*

payments were more than offset by capital inflows, especially from the late sixties to 1973. This enabled Brazil to accumulate foreign exchange reserves, reaching US$6.4 billion in 1973. It will be noted that the largest proportion of the capital inflow consisted of loans, although from 1972 on there was a large jump in the yearly inflow of direct investments.[7]

The massive inflow of capital continued after the oil crisis, increasing the country's indebtedness from US$10.2 billion in 1972 to about US$40 billion in early 1978. These inflows, however, were not enough to cover the huge negative current account and amortization payments and the country's foreign exchange reserves declined to about US$4 billion in 1975, reaching US$3.5 billion in May of 1976. As a result of the country's indebtedness, the proportion of debt service (interest and amortization payments) to total exports reached 40% in 1975. This constituted a heavy burden on the country's balance of payments.

BRAZIL'S TIES WITH THE OUTSIDE WORLD

Besides achieving high rates of overall export growth since the late sixties, Brazil also managed to diversify the commodity and geographic structure of its exports.

TRADE

Table 30 shows the dramatic decline of coffee (the rise in 1976 was due to the soaring international price of coffee resulting from the 1975 Brazilian frosts; it seemed unlikely that this price and hence this proportion would last more than two or three years), and the growth of nontraditional primary exports like soybeans and iron ore, and the expansion of the share of manufactured exports from 5 percent in 1964 to 36 percent in 1975. By the mid-seventies Brazil had achieved a much greater geographic balance in its exports than one or two decades prior to that time. Whereas the United States had accounted for 41.3 percent of Brazil's exports, this percentage declined to 15.4 percent by 1975, while Western Europe and Japan greatly increased their relative position as customers of Brazil. It is notable, however, that exports to LAFTA countries grew very little.

On the import side (see Table 30b) one observes an increasing importance of capital and intermediate goods. Special note should be taken of the growth in the share of

TABLE 30

(a) Commodity Structure of Exports
(percentage distribution)

	1955	1960	1964	1971	1973	1974	1975	1976
Coffee	59	56	53	27	22	13	11	21
Sugar	3	5	2	5	9	16	11	3
Soybeans and derivatives	-	-	-	1	15	11	13	17
Iron ore	2	4	6	8	6	7	11	10
Manufactures - semi processed					7	8	7	8
	1	2	5	22				
Manufactures - processed					22	28	29	26
Other primary products	35	33	34	37	19	17	18	15
Total	100	100	100	100	100	100	100	100

Source: Banco Central do Brasil, *Boletim.*

(b) Commodity Structure of Imports
(percentage distribution)

	1948-50	1960-62	1967	1971	1972
Capital goods	38.0	29.0	31.9	38.9	42.2
Intermediate goods	28.0	31.0	52.6	45.3	42.7
Consumer durables	8.0	2.0	3.8	6.3	6.6
Consumer non-durables	7.0	7.0	10.4	8.8	7.7
Other	19.0	31.0	1.3	0.7	0.8
Total	100.0	100.0	100.0	100.0	100.0

	1968-72	1973	1974	1975	1976
Machinery & equipment	37.6	34.6	24.8	32.3	28.7
Crude oil & derivatives	10.0	11.5	22.0	25.2	31.2
Pig iron & steel	6.2	8.0	12.2	10.4	5.0
Non-ferrous metals	5.0	4.6	4.8	3.0	3.4
Organic chemicals	5.3	6.0	5.1	4.3	5.8
Other	35.9	35.3	31.1	24.8	25.9
Total	100.0	100.0	100.0	100.0	100.0

Sources: Joel Bergsman, *Brazil: Industrialization and Trade Policies,* Oxford University Press, 1970; Carlos Von Doellinger, "Foreign Trade Policy and Its Effects," *IPEA Brazilian Economic Studies No. 1,* 1975; Banco Central do Brasil, *Boletim* and *Relatorio Anual.*

TABLE 31
(a) Exports: Geographical Distribution
(percentage distribution)

	1945-49	1957-59	1967	1970	1974	1975	1976
United States	44.3	41.3	33.1	24.7	21.8	15.4	18.2
Canada			1.0	1.5	1.2	1.6	1.4
LAFTA			9.7	11.1	11.5	13.8	11.9
Western Europe	23.3	26.3	39.8	40.3	35.2	31.4	34.9
COMECON			5.9	4.5	5.0	8.8	9.0
Japan		3.0	3.4	5.3	7.0	7.8	6.3
Other	32.4	29.4	7.1	12.6	18.3	21.2	18.3
(Middle East)			(0.9)	(0.6)	(4.2)	(5.2)	(2.7)
Total	100.0	100.0	100.0	100.0	100.0	100.0	100.0

(b) Imports: Geographical Distribution
(percentage distribution)

	1967	1970	1974	1975	1976
United States	35.4	32.9	24.2	25.3	23.1
Canada	1.1	2.4	3.3	1.7	2.5
LAFTA	13.0	10.5	7.1	5.9	9.5
Western Europe	31.3	35.1	30.4	31.1	24.5
COMECON	4.8	2.1	1.3	1.7	1.8
Japan	3.1	6.4	8.8	9.1	7.2
Other	11.3	10.6	24.9	25.2	31.4
(Middle East)	(7.1)	(5.5)	(17.1)	(19.0)	(24.8)
Total	100.0	100.0	100.0	100.0	100.0

Source: Banco Central do Brasil, *Boletim.*

petroleum and derivatives from 10 percent of total imports in 1968-72 to 31.2 percent in 1976. As in the case of exports, there was a steady decline in the reliance on the U. S. as a source of supply, and a rapid growth in the share of Japan and the Middle East. Finally, one observes a striking decline of imports from Latin American countries.

FOREIGN CAPITAL

Geographical diversification is also notable in the origin of foreign investments in Brazil. While in the early sixties 50 percent of foreign capital was U. S. owned, this had declined to 32 percent in 1976, with West Germany,

Switzerland, some other European countries, and Japan having substantially increased their shares (see Table 32). Three quarters of foreign investments were in manufacturing, concentrated especially in the capital goods, transportation, and chemicals sectors, which were among the most dynamic in the 1968-74 boom. The role of large multinational firms, American and European, became crucial to Brazilian industrial growth from the mid-sixties on.

FOREIGN INDEBTEDNESS

The foreign debt of Brazil, which reached US$40 billion in 1978, was mainly owed to private entities (see Table 33). Almost half of the debt in 1975 had maturities of 5 years or more. Most of this capital inflow was demanded by state firms and by multinationals to finance their investment programs, and by private Brazilian firms for their working-capital needs. This demand for foreign financing was due to a large extent to the weakness of the domestic capital market.[8]

CURRENT AND FUTURE DETERMINANTS OF BRAZIL'S EXTERNAL ECONOMIC POLICIES

Until the petroleum crisis of the seventies Brazil's trade policies and general trade position were fairly consistent with its internal growth objectives.

TRADE

The effects of the petroleum crisis has been to force Brazil to redouble its efforts at export promotion and to change its import strategy. A key to the former is the continuation of Brazil's export incentive program which, on occasion, has come under severe criticism in both the U. S. and Europe. Another important factor in determining the growth of exports is the rate of growth of the industrial economies which are the importers of Brazil's manufactured goods and industrial raw materials.

As a reaction to the world petroleum crisis which has drastically worsened its balance of payments, Brazil has made various attempts to control its imports and to once again turn towards an intensive import-substitution strategy. Massive investment programs in steel, metal products, capital goods, and petrochemicals and derivatives have been planned to substantially decrease the country's renewed dependence on imports for its industrial growth.

TABLE 32
Foreign Direct Investment: June 1976
(percentage distribution)

(a) Sectoral Distribution

Mining	3
Manufacturing	76
Non-met. min.	3
Metal products	8
Machinery	8
Electrical machinery	9
Transport equipment	13
Paper, cellulose	3
Rubber	2
Chemicals	14
Pharmaceuticals	4
Textiles	3
Food products & beverages	5
Tobacco	2
Other manufactures	2
Public utilities	3
Services	16
Other	2
Total	100

(b) Origin

United States	32
W. Germany	12
Switzerland	10
Sweden	2
United Kingdom	5
Netherlands	3
France	4
Japan	12
Luxemburg	2
Other	18
Total	100

Source: Banco Central do Brasil, *Boletim.*

    Brazil's policy-makers have not been able to use their minidevaluation scheme with as much liberty as was expected. On the one hand, there are pressures to devalue the cruzeiro at a more rapid rate than in the past. The rate of devaluation, especially after 1973, has consistently lagged behind the domestic inflation rate (even subtracting the inflation rate of its main trading partners), which was growing again after the steady decline of annual price increases in the period 1967-73. In the 1968-73 years the export incentive program more than compensated the negative effects of an overvalued cruzeiro. This was not the case in the midseventies. The reluctance to devalue has been due to the fear that this measure might add substantial fuel to the resurgence of inflation since the oil crisis. Also, since

TABLE 33
Brazil's Foreign Debt

(a) Distribution by origin of creditors (%) Sept. 1976

U. S. Government	5
World Bank	5
IDB	2
IFC	0.6
U.S. Export/Import Bank	3
Japan Export/Import Bank	0.5
German Gov. Dev. Bank	1
Private	82.9
Total	100.0

(b) Maturity structure (%) June 1975

Less than 1 year	5%
1 year	11
2 years	12
3 years	13
4 years	12
5 years	9
6-10 years	27
11-20 years	6
21 years and over	5
Total	100

Source: Same as Table 32.

there is a substantial dependency of Brazilian businesses on foreign loans, every devaluation substantially increases the cruzeiro cost of the debt. This pushes up internal interest rates and thus discourages new investments and hence the rate of growth of the economy.

TRADE AND THE MULTINATIONALS

Although Brazil's trade strategy provides an element of strength in its foreign economic relations, which was absent in the fifties, it has also provided a new type of dependency. Through multinationals and/or through joint ventures of Brazilian companies with multinationals, a large portion of Brazil's trade has become involved in a vertical international division of labor. For example, the Ford Motor Company produces engines for its Pinto car in Brazil; Volkswagen of Brazil sends components to its plants in other parts of the world; there are plans for joint ventures to produce semi-finished steel products in Brazil, etc. It remains to be seen how much decision-making autonomy is thus sacrificed within Brazil. The level of production of internationally vertically integrated firms depends on the decision of multinationals concerning their world production scheme (i.e., the distribution of their production plans throughout their plants around the world), on the pressure of labor unions in the home country of multinationals, etc. International bargaining for the share of production in such a system is still in its infancy, but it is certain that the Brazilian government will sooner or later be drawn into it.

THE SEARCH FOR SOURCES OF ENERGY AND RAW MATERIALS

In the mid-seventies Brazil was only able to provide 20 percent of its petroleum needs. It depended on imported coal for its steel industry, and it had to import such raw materials as copper, tin, zinc, chemicals, etc. Thus many of its foreign economic policy moves were motivated by either a desire for self-sufficiency in these raw materials or for insuring secure supplies of these vital inputs. In October 1975 the country made an unprecedented move away from the exclusive preservation of petroleum exploration for the state company Petrobras by allowing "risk contracts," i.e., foreign companies were allowed to prospect for petroleum in designated areas of the country and if the prospecting should bring results, the findings would be split between the foreign company and Petrobras. It was hoped in this way to bring in foreign capital for costly exploration activities and to develop Brazil's capacity to produce petroleum more rapidly.

The drive to increase economic ties with Paraguay and with Bolivia is also motivated by energy considerations. The building of the world's largest hydroelectric dam at Itaipu as a joint venture between Paraguay and Brazil, will make Paraguay the world's largest exporter of electric energy and contribute substantially to the energy needs of Brazil's Center-South. No doubt, this will make Paraguay's economy very dependent on Brazil. Similarly, Brazil's large-scale investments in Bolivia are designed to bring that country's abundant natural gas and other raw materials to the industrial center of Brazil.

To assure itself of petroleum supplies, a subsidiary of Petrobras, Braspetro, has made technical assistance and prospecting contracts with Middle Eastern, African and South American countries. There has been an increase in bilateral trade with socialist countries for the same reason.

THE PRESENCE OF MULTINATIONALS

Although multinationals represent only 10 percent of total investments, their importance is much greater due to their dominance in some of the most dynamic sectors of the

country and their key position in the country's present
and future foreign trade relations. We have already
mentioned the potential problems which may arise through the
vertical division of labor with which these companies have
been associated. There are additional problems which will
make themselves felt over the next decade. Brazilian offi-
cials who are increasingly aware of the cost of technology,
are getting to be more sophisticated in bargaining for more
adequate transfer-of-technology contracts and in pressuring
multinationals to adapt and to locally develop technology.

A recent trend, which may result in a different role
for multinationals in Brazil, is the rise of joint ventures
between Brazilian state companies and private multinationals.
A number of joint ventures were created in the seventies -
e.g., the petrochemical complex in Camaçari, Bahia, which
involves Petrobras' subsidiary Petroquisa, and big mining
projects in the Amazon area under the leadership of the
state company Companhia Vale do Rio Doce. There are advantages to both Brazil and the multinationals in such arrangements. First, the majority state-owned company will be less
exposed to nationalistic pressures than the full-owned multinational subsidiary. Second, Brazilians may have more of a
say in the behavior pattern of such a firm with regard to
technology, transfer pricing, etc.

THE IMPLICATIONS OF INTERNATIONAL INDEBTEDNESS

Though Brazil's indebtedness places it in a weak position, the debt also has elements of strength. It weakens
the country for a number of reasons: as already mentioned,
high indebtedness results in large amounts of foreign exchange earnings being used to service the debt; it raises
the price of new debts abroad; to the extent that refinancing
is needed, it places the country at a bargaining disadvantage
with the major creditor countries; the latter implies a certain amount of interference in domestic policy formulation -
e.g., new loans being tied to desired internal credit policies; and, finally, increased indebtedness could result in
pressure by the creditor countries for more lenient treatment of multinationals operating in the country and even in
pressure for an increasing share of foreign capital in in-
debted Brazilian firms.

On the positive side, the large indebtedness of a
country as big and as important as Brazil gives the authorities some bargaining strength. Since multinational companies have large investments and thus an important stake in

the well-being of the country and since some of the major
private financial institutions have huge loans tied up in
. the country's total debt, there is an interest by these
companies and creditors to keep the economy growing and to
have it achieve a strong balance of payments position. This
could be used by the Brazilian government to get favorable
considerations in expanding its trade and in obtaining new
credits.

COMPLEMENTARITY VERSUS COMPETITIVENESS IN BRAZIL'S RELATIONS WITH THE INDUSTRIALIZED WORLD

Brazil's strategy of ISI for its economic development
was both a success and a failure. It resulted in the industrialization of the country, but it did not reduce its
external dependence. It only changed the nature of the
latter. The ISI strategy made the country more dependent on
imported inputs to run its industrial park. Although this
was an inevitable result when viewed in retrospect, given
the lack of a number of basic raw materials, one could argue
that the ISI strategy stressing the automobile industry as
one of the main elements in industrial growth and as the key
element in developing the country's transportation system
(neglecting railroads), made the country unnecessarily vul-
nerable and dependent in the post-1973 era. Dependence on
foreign capital and multinationals also increased, and the
bargaining power of these firms grew as they became crucial
to the continued high economic growth performance of the
country.[9]

Dependence was also increased by developing industries
which are vertically integrated into the world industrial
system and developing exports (like iron ore) which depend
on the performance of the industrialized countries. A more
realistic expression might be "interdependence." Most of
the major economies of the world have become increasingly
interdependent. The degree to which Brazil can profit from
this development will largely depend on the skills of its
policy-makers and economic diplomats. Its trade diversification and the diversification of its sources of investments
gives considerable room for maneuver.

There is also a degree of competitiveness in Brazil's
economic system with regard to its trading partners. First,
there is competitiveness in complementarity to the extent
that the Brazilian subsidiaries of multinationals are competing with the production facilities of these companies in
other areas of the world. Second, there is competitiveness

in the exportation of final products. This is the case
with the exportation of various types of consumer goods--
shoes, textiles, automobiles, etc., in which Brazil and its
competitors will have to come to some agreement as to the
market shares or as to the redistribution of the world
division of labor--e.g., a reduction in the productive
capacity of the American shoe industry to make room for
Brazilian producers, while the U. S. specializes in other
products for which there is a market in Brazil.

Finally, there are opportunities and potential con-
flicts in the diversification of Brazil's agricultural exports. The appearance of Brazil as the second largest world
exporter of soybeans and its products, the continued growth
of iron ore exports, and the potential of the country as a
meat exporter, present both opportunities for increased
trade and conflict with competitive economies.

ENDNOTES

1. We already described these policies in greater detail in chapter 4; see also, Joel Bergsman, op. cit., chapter 3; Donald Huddle, op. cit.; Carlos Von Doellinger, Leonardo C. Cacalcanti, and Flavio Castelo Branco, *Política E Estrutura Das Importacões Brasileiras* (Rio de Janeiro: IPEA, 1977).
2. Bergsman, op. cit., p. 42.
3. Carlos Von Doellinger, *A Política Brasileira de Comércio Exterior e Seus Efeitos: 1967-73* (Rio de Janeiro: IPEA, Coleção Relatórios de Pesquisa, No. 22, 1974), pp. 23-47; William G. Tyler, *Manufactured Export Expansion and Industrialization in Brazil* (Tübingen: J.C.B. Mohr, 1976).
4. Eduardo Matarazzo Suplicy, *Os Efeitos Das Minidesvalorizações Na Economia Brasileira* (Rio de Janeiro: Fundação Getúlio Vargas, 1976); Von Doellinger, Cavancanti and Castelo Branco, op. cit.
5. Carlos Von Doellinger, "Foreign Trade Policy and Its Effects," *Brazilian Economic Studies - 1*, (Rio de Janeiro: IPEA, 1975), p. 91
6. Carlos Von Doellinger, "Considerações Sôbre o Recolhimento Compulsório dos Emprestimos Externos," in *Pesquisa e Planejamento Econômico*, Dezembro de 1973.
7. As was noted before, the massive world supply of capital in the form of Eurodollars in the late sixties and early seventies made it easy for Brazil to obtain so much private finance capital.
8. José Eduardo C. Pereira, *Financiamento Externos e Crescimento Economico do Brasil, 1966/73*, (Rio de Janeiro: IPEA, Coleção Relatorios de Pesquisa, No. 27, 1974).
9. Brazil is not as important to the multinationals as they are to the country. For some additional information concerning this point see: Carlos Von Doellinger et al, *Empresas Multinacionais na Industria Brasileira* (Rio de Janeiro: IPEA, Coleção Relatorios de Pesquisa, No. 29, 1975.)

BRAZIL'S EXTENDED PUBLIC SECTOR

The development of Brazil's economic institutions over
the last half century has produced an economic system which
has yet to be completely understood. One important feature
differentiating it from the type of Western industrial market economy upon which so much contemporary economic theory
is based is the expanded role of the state in the economy.

The present dominance of the state over the Brazilian
economy has not resulted from a carefully conceived scheme.
It is largely the result of a number of circumstances which,
in most cases, forced the government increasingly to inter-
vene in the country's economic system. These circumstances
include: reactions to international economic crises; the
desire to control the activities of foreign capital, especially in the public utility sector and in the exploitation
of natural resources; and the ambition to rapidly industrialize a backward economy.

STAGES IN THE GROWTH OF STATE INVOLVEMENT
IN THE ECONOMY

State intervention in the economy has deep historical
roots in Brazil, as it does in most Latin American societies.

---

* This chapter draws heavily on the following articles:
Werner Baer, Isaac Kerstenetzky, and Annibal V. Villela, "The
Changing Role of the State in the Brazilian Economy," *World
Development*, November 1973; and Werner Baer, Richard Newfarmer
and Thomas Trebat, "On State Capitalism in Brazil: Some New
Issues and Questions," *Inter-American Economic Affairs*,
Vol. 30, No. 3, Winter 1976.

THE PRE-1930 ERA

From colonial times to the present, the government was never removed from the economic sphere to the extent it was in post-mercantilist Europe (especially England) and the United States. In colonial times the crown was the supreme economic patron, and all commercial and productive activities depended on special licenses, grants of monopoly, and trade privileges.[1] During the first century after independence this patrimonial tradition persisted. Describing the activities of the state in the nineteenth century, Faoro has shown how "...the intervention of the state was not restricted to finance and credit. On the contrary, it extended to all commercial, industrial, and public service activities. The state authorized the functioning of limited liability companies, made contracts with banks, granted privileges, made special concessions for the running of railroads and ports, assured supplies of materials and guaranteed interest payments. The sum of these favors and privileges involved the major proportion of economic activities... (which)...could only exist through the life transmitted by the state's umbilical cord..."[2]

The state in nineteenth century Brazil (both under the empire and in the early republican period) was relatively non-interventionist. The government's concern was with tariffs for revenue and, on rare occasions, for protectionist purposes. In the area of incipient industries and infrastructure investments the government acted mainly as the grantor of favors - i.e., special loans for some industrial enterprises[3] and guaranteed rates of return for foreign companies making infrastructure investments.[4] The only other direct participation of the Brazilian government in economic activity was in the financial sector. The Banco do Brasil went through various phases in the nineteenth century, being at times both a commercial bank and a bank of issue, with varying degrees of government participation. In the twentieth century it continued as a commercial bank whose major owner was the Brazilian state. It also exercised many functions of a central bank until the creation of the Banco Central do Brasil in late 1964. Finally, government involvement with savings banks (Caixas Econômicas) dates back to 1861.[5]

Towards the beginning of the 20th century the burden of guaranteeing a minimum rate of return to foreign-owned railroads had become increasingly onerous to the government.[6] It was felt that borrowing money abroad in order to buy a number of railroads would ultimately be less burdensome on the economy. Thus, in 1901 the Brazilian government con-

tracted a large loan in order to nationalize some of the
railroads. This process continued over the years. Already
in 1929 close to half of the railroad network was in government hands, and by the fifties this had grown to 94 percent.[7]

Thus the growth of government ownership in this sector
was not the result of the arbitrary confiscation of private
property, but was the consequence of the lack of profitability and of the government's unwillingness to continue to
guarantee a rate of return. An additional factor leading to
the increasing state control of the railroads and, as will
be seen below, of other public utilities, was the government
control of rates. In setting the latter for public utilities
the government had to balance consideration of returns which
would be adequate for the private investor with concern
about rates which would be considered socially fair to users.
Over the years the second consideration took on increasing
importance. Thus, with controlled prices providing rates of
return which were too low for private companies to warrant
expansion and adequately to maintain the railroad network,
and with the government's unwillingness to guarantee a rate
of return, gradual nationalization became inevitable.

We have already seen in chapter 2 how in the first
decade of the twentieth century state government (mainly
that of São Paulo) became actively engaged in the support
of coffee prices and coffee production.

The 1920s witnessed the growth of state government banks.
Before that time only two state government banks had been
active: the Banco de Crédito Real de Minas Gerais (founded
in 1889) and the Banco da Paraíba (founded in 1912). The
Banco do Estado de Piauí (1926), the Banco do Estado de São
Paulo (1927), the Banco do Estado de Paraná (1928), and the
Banco do Estado de Rio Grande do Sul (1928) were established
with the initial objective of aiding the agricultural sector
of their states. Other state government banks were founded
in the thirties for similar purposes. Many of these became
important commercial banks with branches throughout the
country.

THE THIRTIES

The world depression not only set Brazil on the road
towards import-substitution industrialization, but resulted
also in an increase and change of role of the state in the
country's economy. The institutional changes which led to
a greater role of the state in the economy stemmed from the

Brazilian government's desire to protect the economy from the full impact of the world depression and to support and speed up the process of industrialization.

In order to deal with the immediate impact of the world depression, the federal government took over the coffee support program from the states. This, in effect, meant that for the first time the federal government directly engaged in the pricing and output control of a productive sector.[8] Further direct intervention in the economy occurred through exchange controls, introduced in September 1931 in order to ration scarce foreign exchange.

As the decade wore on, the Vargas regime expanded state intervention to protect and encourage the growth of different sectors through creation of "autarquias."[9] These institutes were created to deal with such sectors as sugar, mate, salt, pinewood, fishing, the merchant marine, etc. In collaboration with producers they regulated production, prices, financed the building of warehouses, etc. Over the years they often expanded from being instruments of government control to being also instruments of pressure for government favors for the specific sector.

One of the first instances of price control (as opposed to price support) in Brazil began in 1934 with the creation of the Código de Aguas, which empowered the government to set electricity rates. These were set in such a way as to permit a maximum return of 10 percent on invested capital. The fact that capital was valued at historical cost for such purpose, as will be seen below, was to lead to the gradual extension of state ownership in this and other public utility sectors. The immediate motive for this control was the fact that rates had been partly based on gold values and partly on domestic paper money in order that foreign companies might protect themselves against exchange rate devaluation. This meant, however, that electricity rates would often rise every month, and when there was a strong devaluation, rates would rise to such an extent as to lower electricity consumption, which, in turn, would adversely affect production. Thus controls were instituted in order to protect industry and consumers. During the following years the welfare aspect in rate setting would become increasingly important.[10]

The initial actions of the government in the thirties to industrialize the country would lead one to believe that it had envisioned the growth of industry as taking place in the private sector, with government providing the necessary protection and finance. The use of exchange controls, of "autarquias," and the creation in 1937 of the Carteira de Crédito Agrícola e Industrial of the Banco do Brasil to provide long term credits to industrial establishments point in this direction. One should also consider the various vain attempts of the Brazilian government to have private domestic and foreign capital establish a large integrated steel mill. The creation of the Companhia Siderúrgica Nacional at Volta Redonda by the state was only a matter of last resort.[11]

A significant indication of the change of government philosophy with respect to state influence over the economy was the creation of the Conselho Federal de Comércio Exterior in 1934. This organ, which consisted of representatives of the foreign and of all the economic ministries, the president's office, the Banco do Brasil, and various specialists, attempted not only to stimulate the country's foreign trade, but also to provide incentives for the development of certain industries (especially cellulose in the thirties). Some have considered this to have been the first attempt at economic planning in Brazil.[12]

The thirties also witnessed the final state take-over of Lloyd Brasileiro, the principal Brazilian shipping firm. The enterprise was founded in 1890 when the government ordered the amalgamation of four shipping lines which were receiving subsidies. Since then the firm was at times in and out of the hands of the government until 1937, when it became a federal "autarquia."[13] The government extended its control over shipping in 1940 by nationalizing and merging two private companies serving the Amazon region (the Company Port of Para and the Amazon River Steam Navigation Company Lts.) into the Serviço de Navegaçao da Amazonia e Administraçao do Porto do Para - SNAAPP). The Companhia Nacional de Navegaçao Costeira was the result of the government take-over of the properties of the Cia. Large e Irmaos, the private shipping firm, in 1942.[14] Finally, the creation of the government firm Serviço de Navegaçao da Bacia do Prata, whose aim it was to promote shipping on the rivers Paraguay and Parana was also the result of the nationalization of a number of private firms serving the region.[15] The motivation for these government actions was twofold: considerations of security during wartime conditions and the promotion of shipping, which had not fared well in private hands.

THE FORTIES: WORLD WAR II AND THE EARLY POST-WAR PERIOD

The years of World War II saw the creation of a number of new government enterprises. Most were founded for national security considerations and some developed into powerful companies in the fifties and sixties.

Besides state expansion into shipping, wartime conditions also led the government to create the Fábrica Nacional de Motores (FNM) in 1943. Its initial purpose was to provide maintenance services for motors and also their production, due to wartime-induced shortages. The firm eventually produced a great variety of products - tractors, trucks, cars, refrigerators. It was always a deficitary enterprise, with many administrative problems, and in 1968 the government sold it to a private foreign firm.

The Companhia Nacional de Álcalis was created by the government in 1943 because of the fear that shortages of soda ash would paralyze industries dependent on this input. Since no foreign or domestic private enterprise was in a position to establish such an undertaking, a government firm was found to be the only solution.

The founding of the Companhia Vale do Rio Doce in 1942 was attributable in large part to nationalistic considerations. For many years foreign interests, often in combination with some local enterpreneurs, were anxious to develop the rich iron ore deposits of Minas Gerais for export. Concessions for mining and export were given and withdrawn a number of times as nationalistic opposition to foreign companies' involvement rose and fell. The forces of nationalism finally won an important victory with the cancellation of mining concessions to a foreign group of the rich Itabira deposits in 1942. This was followed by the creation of the Companhia Vale do Rio Doce, a state-owned enterprise, which was to become Brazil's largest mineral exporting firm.[16]

The immediate postwar period was practically devoid of new experimentations with state involvement in economic activities. The government ownership of the railroad network expanded with the buying out of a number of British railroad companies. Also, as foreign exchange crises brought on renewed exchange controls and as an increasing amount of infrastructure bottlenecks made themselves felt, the government engaged increasingly in planning activites designed to provide for a more balanced growth and to obtain foreign assistance. During the forties a number of plans were drawn up, which would ultimately lead to a further expansion of state economic activities in the fifties.[17]

THE FIFTIES

During the industrialization spurt of the fifties the role of the state in the economy continued to expand. General planning and the occasional appearance of special action groups to spur on the development of specific sectors (the well-known Grupos Executivos) became accepted as a way of government behavior. In fact, with the ambitions of the governments of the fifties to industrialize rapidly, it became clear to the policy-makers that the success of their policies depended on government initiatives in various fields. The protection mechanisms to attract foreign capital and to stimulate private domestic investments have already been described in chapter 4. In order to achieve the industrialization goals, however, state action had to go beyond these measures.

An outstanding event in the early fifties was the establishment of the Banco Nacional de Desenvolvimento Economico (BNDE) in 1952. It has long been recognized that the existence of financial institutions capable of furnishing long-term credits is almost a "sine qua non" in the successful industrialization of a backward economy. Private firms are not sufficiently large and strong to generate internally the funds necessary for the size of investments needed and the financial markets are not sufficiently developed to provide the finance. This has usually necessitated the emergency of investment banks in order to finance and, at times, partake in new and/or expanding industrial enterprises. The well-known generalization about the necessity for investment banks, based on the experience of European countries in the nineteenth century which were latecomers to the industrialization process, is quite applicable to the Brazil of the 1950s and 1960s:

...the more gradual character of the industrialization process (in England) and the more considerable accumulation of capital, first from the earnings in trade and modernized agriculture and later from industry itself, obviated the pressure for developing any special institutional devices for provision of long-term capital to industry. By contrast, in a relatively backward country capital is scarce and diffused. The distrust of industrial activities is considerable, and, finally, there is greater pressure for bigness because of the scope of the industrialization movement, the large average size of plant, and the concentration of industrial output. To these should be added the scarcity of entrepreneurial talent in the backward country.

It is the pressure of these circumstances which essentially gave rise to the divergent development in banking over large portions of the Continent as against England. The continental practices in the field of industrial investment banking must be conceived as specific instruments of industrialization in a backward economy...[18]

The necessity for a government development bank became clear as the Comissão Mista Brasil-Estados Unidos (Brazilian-U.S. Joint Mission) recommended a fairly elaborate plan for the modernization of the country's infrastructure (Programa de Reaparelhamento Econômico) for which no individual enterprise had resources. The BNDE was thus established to provide the finance for the recommended growth and modernization program of the country's infrastructure. Its tasks, however, were also set to include the promotion and finance of heavy industries and certain sectors within agriculture.[19]

Over the fifties and sixties the BNDE fulfilled its tasks in a flexible manner. In its first decade the larger part of its resources (70 percent) went to finance the growth of Brazil's infrastructure, while at a later stage greater emphasis was placed on heavy industry, especially steel. By the late sixties and early seventies the bank also engaged in the administration of special funds to finance the sale of capital goods, the expansion of small and medium-sized firms, etc.[20]

The role of the BNDE in augmenting government participation in the steel industry is especially instructive. The expansion of the productive capacity of that industry was considered an integral part of the industrialization program of the fifties. Except for the enlargement of Volta Redonda, it was expected that a large portion of the increased productive capacity would be built by the private sector and by local (state) governments. This was the case of USIMINAS and COSIPA, two firms created in the early fifties in order to build large integrated steel mills. As it became obvious in each case that local private and government resources were too limited to finance these projects, the federal government committed itself to co-sponsor them through the BNDE. In exchange for the injection of financial resources, the bank received equity participation in each firm. Over the years the BNDE became the dominant shareholder. Thus the government became a reluctant owner of enterprises: i.e., due to the private and local government's inability to come through with projects considered

as keystones in Brazil's industrialization program, its
direct participation became inevitable.[21]

Government takeover through the BNDE was gradual. The
Development Bank seemed to represent a very flexible policy
instrument. It always leaves the door open for gradual
reduction of government participation by the sale of BNDE
shares in enterprises. This, of course, is true of all
government enterprises which operate as "mixed companies"
like the Banco Do Brasil, the Cia. Vale do Rio Doce, etc.
The difference, however, lies in the possibility of a development bank helping in the growth of certain sectors by
direct participation and then selling its equity once the
sectors are functioning smoothly, and then entering other
fields whose development needs strong doses of government
support. Such a "withdrawal," however, might not be very
easy, if at all possible, in an industry like steel which
might be too large to be absorbed entirely by the private
sector.

Another landmark of Brazilian government participation
in economic activities was the creation of Petrobras in
1953. All petroleum exploration and the largest part of
refining activities were declared a monopoly of that state
company. The principal motivation behind this event was a
concern by the government in assuring a domestic source of
supply for emergency situations. As pressure for the
passage of the law creating Petrobras mounted, more nationalistic motivations were gradually introduced - especially
the issue of not handing to foreign companies the exploitation of non-replaceable subsoil wealth.[22]

Besides the creation of the BNDE, government involvement in banking continued to grow. In 1954 the Banco do
Nordeste do Brasil was created to provide both commercial
and development credit facilities. In the sixties it received all deposits of funds from the tax exemption moneys
destined for Northeast Brazil (Law 34/18) and it became the
principal financial agent of SUDENE. Also, a number of
state government development banks made their appearance in
the fifties, while the expansion of the Banco do Brasil,
the Banco do Estado de São Paulo, and other state commercial
banks continued.[23]

The fifties also witnessed the spread of price controls.
Control of public utility rates was extended and soon covered not only electric power, but also telephones, all public
transportation, etc. They were also spread to rents, gasoline, food prices, etc. In the fifties the latter were

controlled by COFAP (Comissão Federal de Abastecimento e Preços), which was supposed to influence the supply and price of food products. This was later turned into the agency called SUNAB (Superintendência Nacional de Abastecimento).

The control of prices was supposed, in part, to dampen the inflationary forces which were rampant in the fifties. In fact, they only succeeded in distorting prices, creating shortages of supplies in many sectors of the economy.

The rapid growth of state enterprises in the public utility sector was due to price controls. The setting of rates for public utilities did not provide a rate of return on investment considered to be adequate by private (mainly foreign) enterprises to warrant the expansion and modernization of their plants. Since controlled rates were considered to be in the national interest, i.e. relatively low rates were thought desirable to encourage industrial growth and to subsidize consumers, the only alternative left was for the state to gradually enter into the field of power generation and distribution, public transportation, telecommunications, etc. This, in part, explains the creation in the fifties of such state enterprises as CHESF (Cia. Hidroelétrica do São Francisco), FURNAS, CEMIG (of the state of Minas Gerais) and in the sixties of CESP (São Paulo) and others, to provide the additional power needed for the expanding economy. Controls also resulted in the decline in quality and rate of growth of the country's telephone system and by the sixties state takeover had also become inevitable.

THE SIXTIES

During the sixties and seventies the expansion of the state in Brazil's economy occurred both through the consolidation and growth of its various activities and through the creation of some new areas of government action. For example, in 1965 the National Housing Bank (BNH) was created. It rapidly became a powerful financial force because of its receipt of part of the workers' retirement funds and its ability to deal with price-indexed financial instruments. The Programa de Integração Social (PIS) created in 1971 strengthened the Caixas Economicas (which had been unified into one organization in the sixties) by obtaining special workers' funds derived from a deduction of 5 percent of taxes owed by the firm and from a contribution of the firm based on 0.5 percent of sales receipts.

During the sixties various state enterprises in the field of power generation were united under the holding company Eletrobras. Also, the state of São Paulo created CESP in order to undertake vast new investments in that sector. Through these massive investments in power the state (both federal and state governments) came to dominate the sector. The newly nationalized telecommunications network was placed in the hands of a state company--Embratel-- which embarked on a huge expansion and modernization program. The government-owned steel mills also began to plan for expansion and in the seventies to execute large investment programs--including the building of new state companies-- e.g. Açominas in Minas Gerais and Tubarão in Vitória.

A remarkable phenomenon in the sixties was the revitalization and rapid expansion of such government firms as the Cia. Vale do Rio Doce and Petrobras. The former's program of modernization and expansion resulted in a remarkable growth of iron ore exports from 5.2 million tons in 1960 to 73 million tons in 1975. Petrobras not only increased substantially the extent of its traditional activities, especially refining and retailing, but it also began to expand into related new fields. Its subsidiary Petroquisa, which was founded in 1968, has been venturing into a number of different enterprises in the petrochemicals sector. Some of these are joining ventures with private domestic and foreign firms. Its subsidiary Braspetro was founded in 1972 in.order to engage in joint ventures abroad in the field of petroleum prospecting and general technical assistance. By the mid-seventies it already had contracts in Ecuador, Iraq, Madagascar, Egypt, and a few other countries.

The sixties also brought drastic changes in the manner of price controls. Attempts at controls in the fifties and early sixties were ineffective in stemming inflation and had the negative effect of distorting relative prices. The founding of CIP (Conselho Interministerial de Preços) in 1968 marked a new chapter in state control over prices. Previous control mechanisms had concentrated exclusively on retail prices, while CIP developed a thoroughgoing mechanism of controls over costs and prices in some of the key productive sectors of the economy.

DEGREE OF STATE CONTROL OVER THE ECONOMY

From the above narrative on the growth of government involvement in the Brazilian economy, it should be obvious

that there is no simple quantitative way to measure the
total control of the state over the country's economic
activities. We shall therefore attempt to verify the degree
of state control in various different quantitative and
qualitative ways.

Government economic controls make themselves felt
through different, but interrelated, institutional channels.
These include: the fiscal system, the central bank, the
government (federal and state) commercial and development
banks, the "autarquias," government (federal and state)
productive enterprises and the price control system. This
multifaceted intervention of the "state" in the economy
is not monolithic. It has often been characterized, in
fact, by a lack of coordination and communication among
the various entities involved.

THE GOVERNMENT AS A REGULATOR

The use of taxation and expenditure powers are the
classic ways through which government tries to attain its
allocative, stabilizing and distributive goals.

FISCAL FUNCTION

As can be seen in Table 34, government expenditures
as a proportion of GDP have risen steadily in the post-
World War II period; they stood at 19.1 percent in 1949
and reached 22.5 percent in 1973 (this refers to all levels
of government, but does not include government enterprises).
It will be noted that most of the gain was due to the almost threefold increase in transfers.

The tax burden has increased sharply in the post-
World War II period. In 1949 total taxes amounted to 14.9
percent of GDP. This proportion rose steadily in the next
decades and by 1973 reached 27 percent. The difference
between the expenditure/GDP and tax/GDP ratios is mainly
due to tax contributions to various types of social security
funds.[24] Although Brazil's tax burden increased rapidly,
it was still substantially below that of a number of industrial countries whose tax burden averaged about 34 percent.
It was high, however, in relation to the average tax burdens
of less developed countries.[25]

Indirect taxes as a percent of GDP have risen from 9.8
percent in 1949 to 15.3 percent in 1973, while direct taxes

TABLE 34

General Government Expenditures (Excl. Public Enterprises)
by Principal Categories as a Percentage of GDP

Category	1949	1959	1970	1973
Current goods and services	5.4	5.4	3.6	2.6
Government workers	6.3	6.5	7.3	7.1
Gross fixed capital formation	4.3	4.1	4.0	3.9
Transfers and subsidies	3.1	5.1	8.5	8.9
Total public sector	19.1	21.1	22.4	22.5

Source: Conjuntura Economica, Junho de 1975.

grew from 5.1 to 11.7 percent in the same period. Thus,
direct taxes which constituted only 34 percent of total
taxes in 1949, climbed to 43 percent in 1973.[26] Another
notable trend in the 1949-73 period has been the growth of
the federal government as the major tax collecting agent.
By 1973 it collected 54.4 percent of all indirect taxes and
94.7 percent of all direct taxes. Through a process of
revenue sharing, state and local governments played a relatively larger role in the distribution of expenditures among
various levels of government; this procedure increased the
power of the federal government, however, in determining
the use of funds transferred to local authorities.

The Brazilian government thus has a pronounced influence
over the distribution of income and resource allocation
through the fiscal system. For example, in 1969 over 36
percent of public expenditures went to social security
programs and education, while almost 17 percent went for
direct infrastructure expenditures (more than half of this
amount going to road construction).

DIRECT REGULATION

We have seen that regulation of prices, production and
foreign trade in one form or another has pervaded the Brazilian economy since the early part of the century.

CIP, created in August 1968, presently controls prices.
Its directors are the ministers of Finance, Planning,
Commerce and Agriculture. It cannot set prices legally,
but acts as a general watchdog commission over prices. Its
indirect powers are substantial. For example, if a firm
raises prices without submitting a justification to CIP,

and/or if the justification is submitted but not accepted
by CIP and if prices are raised anyway, the firm risks
having its credit line eliminated with the Banco do Brasil
and all other government banks, and much of its general
credit-worthiness with the private banking sector will have
been diminished since the Central can refuse to rediscount
the firm's credit instruments. Thus almost all firms of
sectors in which CIP has an interest must obtain permission
for price increases and must justify their request by providing cost information. It seems that until the mid-
seventies CIP avoided creating drastic price distortions in
industry (with the exception of steel prices in the early
seventies) by taking into account cost information and
setting prices with regard to reasonable rates of profit.
In the process the government, through CIP, has gained an
unusual amount of information on the activities of the private sector and thus increased its control thereof.[27]

THE GOVERNMENT AS AN ECONOMIC AGENT

The potential of the government to mobilize public
and private savings and to channel them into desired direc-
tions is an important measure of its overall control of the
economy.

THE STATE AS A BANKER AND FINANCIER

In 1974 the Banco do Brasil, over 60 percent of whose
shares are owned by the government, held 37.1 percent of
all funds on deposit in Brazil's 50 largest commercial
banks. Including commercial banks owned by state governments, the share of total deposits stood at 55.5 percent.

Since it is through their lending that banks directly
influence resource allocation, a brief examination of loan
shares reveals an even greater power of government commercial banks. In 1974 the Banco do Brasil accounted for almost 43 percent of the loans held by the 50 largest banks,
with all government banks accounting for almost 65 percent.[28]

The Banco do Brasil has a unique role. It assumes the
risky burden of providing working capital loans to agriculture. In 1974 almost 44 percent of its loans went to agriculture, while private banks rarely devoted more than 15
percent of their resources to that sector. The Banco do
Brasil has used some of its power over agricultural credit
in an attempt to diversify its loans by agricultural activ-

ities and regions. Although it is also a vehicle to implement monetary policy, it often cushions agriculture in
periods of tight credit. It has been forced by the government, the majority shareholder, to exempt certain types of
agricultural loans from the indexing system which has prevailed in Brazil since the mid-sixties. The interest on
some loans was so low that it was negative in real terms
and thus represented a subsidy program administered through
the Banco do Brasil.

The federal and state governments together constitute
the most powerful investment banker in the Brazilian economy.
Through the National Development Bank (BNDE), the National
Housing Bank (BNH), the Bank of the Northeast, and various
banks of individual states, it provides more

THE STATE AS A PRODUCER

A survey of the 5,113 largest incorporated firms
("sociedades anônimas") in 1974 has shown that over 39 percent of their net assets belonged to public enterprises,
18 percent to multinational corporations and 43 percent to
private Brazilian firms (see Table 35). Using sales as a
measure, state firms controlled 16 percent, multinationals
28 percent and domestic private firms accounted for 56 percent.[29] State investments are highly concentrated in certain basic industries.

In mining, state firms are dominant, controlling about
62 percent of net assets. In the early seventies the state
enterprise Companhia Vale do Rio Doce accounted for the
largest proportion of the value of assets in that sector
and for 80 percent of Brazil's iron ore exports. The government has encouraged the establishment of joint ventures
among state, multinational and private domestic firms in
the seventies, and the Companhia Vale do Rio Doce has, in
effect, formed a number of joint ventures with multinational
enterprises to exploit new iron ore and other mineral deposits and to create new steel, aluminum and other productive concerns.

The sectoral distribution of assets in Table 36 shows
that multinationals and domestic private firms outweigh

TABLE 35

Sectoral Distribution of Net Assets of 5,113 Largest Firms
(percentage distribution)
(1974)

	Total	State enterprise	Multi-national	Private domestic
Mining	100	62	12	26
Manufacturing	100	20	29	51
Non-met. minerals	100	2	35	63
Metal products	100	34	12	54
Machinery	100	1	46	53
Electrical Mach.	100	-	61	39
Transport materials	100	4	63	33
Wood and products	100	-	9	91
Furniture	100	-	-	100
Rubber	100	6	61	33
Leather and goods	100	-	11	89
Chemicals & petroleum	100	55	23	22
Textiles	100	-	13	87
Food products	100	1	31	68
Beverages	100	-	14	86
Tobacco	100	-	99	1
Printing & publishing	100	-	2	98
Miscellaneous	100	-	47	53
Agriculture	100	1	3	96
Construction & engineer.	100	15	3	82
Public utilities	100	88	7	6
Commerce	100	-	5	95
Services	100	27	4	69
Total	100	37	15	48

Source: "Quem é Quem na Economia Brasileira," *Visão*, 31 de agosto de 1975, pp. 28-9.

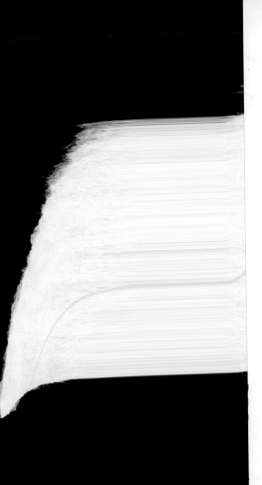

state enterprises in most manufacturing sectors and in agriculture. The state, however, is strongly represented in the metal products sector and in chemicals. In the steel industry, state firms like Companhia Siderúrgica Nacional, Usiminas, Cosipa and a few others are responsible for about two-thirds of sales. Within the chemical sector, Petrobras has dominated petroleum explorations, refining and has steadily increased its share of gasoline distribution. Through subsidiaries, like Petroquisa, it has steadily increased its share in petrochemicals, in part forming joint ~~~~ ~~~~ ~~~~ Over the last decade the ~~~~ ~~~~ an aviation

ization. Both firms have expanded their activities into the production of fertilizer and into shipping; Petrobras into various fields of petrochemicals; and Vale do Rio Doce has gone into pelletizing plants, bauxite mining and aluminum production, pulp manufacture and steel plants. Both firms and some government steel firms have also set up engineering consulting enterprises.

State firms are dominant in the utilities sector. Within a decade power generation changed from a private to a government dominated sector. This reflects the huge amount of investment made by old and new government firms in the sixties. In 1962 the private sector accounted for 64 percent of the country's electric power generating capacity, while by 1977 this proportion had been reduced to less than 20 percent. It can be seen in Table 36 that state firms controlled almost 88 percent of the liquid assets of public utility firms.

At present the state has a quasi-monopoly in railroad transportation, telecommunications, controls almost 70 percent of Brazilian shipping, a large proportion of storage firms and various state governments own companies providing public services.

One characteristic of state enterprises is their much greater size in comparison with domestic private firms and even with multinationals, as is evident from the data in Table 36. Public enterprises in manufacturing are on the average 10 times larger than private firms. Petrobras, Cia.

Vale do Rio Doce and the state steel companies are immense economic units, dwarfing their private counterparts. This is explained in part by the type of technology which was needed in sectors where government firms were established.

TABLE 36
Comparative Measures of Largest* Private Brazilian, Multinational and State Firms, 1972

	Private Brazilian	Multi-nationals	State firms
Fixed assets (1972 Cruzeiros)/Employment	34,978	38,851	150,919
Average size (net assets in billions of 1972 Cruzeiros)	99	217	2,529
Produce per worker (wages, salaries & profits divided by employees - 1972 Cruzeiros)	35	53	99
Exports/total sales	4.8	7.9	11.5
Before tax profitability (before tax profits divided by equity: unweighted average)	16.4	15.8	17.6

*This is based on a sample of 318 of the largest non-financial firms.

Source: Carlos Von Doellinger and Leonardo C. Cavalcanti, *Empresas Multinacionais na Indústria Brasileira* (Rio de Janeiro: IPEA, Coleção Relatórios de Pesquisa, No. 29, 1975).

Table 36 also shows that the performance of state firms in comparison to private Brazilian and multinational firms was quite favorable. In 1972 their product per worker was higher than those of firms in other sectors, they exported relatively more (this is obviously accounted for to a large extent by the specialization of the Cia. Vale do Rio Doce as an iron ore exporter), and their profitability was relatively high.

GOVERNMENT CONTROL O'
AND THEIR DISTRIBU\

We have shown in chapter 5 that n\   ~ble
growth of savings in the sixties and se\   ~
the government sector, i.e., the governm\
and that of government-administered force\
various types of social security funds. T\
percent of savings were due to public firms,
ment and workers' social security funds.

Since government and public enterprise gr\
ment was estimated at about 50 percent of total\
vestment in the years 1970-73, it becomes clear t\
significant amount of private investment was finan\
public resources. That is, private firms received \
tial investment funds from entities like the BNDE, w\
acted as an intermediary in relending funds accumulat\
through workers' social security funds.

In spite of efforts by monetary authorities to develop
a capital market, success has been limited.[31] Little private
capital is raised through the issue of new shares and the
most actively traded stocks are those of government firms.[32]
Most long-term bond issues (with monetary correction) are
those of the government and public authorities. Long-term
outside financing for private firms comes either from abroad,
mostly from parents to subsidiaries of MNC's, or from loans
of government agencies, especially the BNDE and the National
Housing Bank (BNH).

Thus the Brazilian state possesses additional economic
potential by virtue of its position as the most powerful
financial intermediary for long-term financing. In 1973
the loans of the BNH, BNDE, state development banks, and
official savings banks amounted to 41 percent of gross capital formation of enterprises (i.e., capital formation of
private firms and state enterprises). Although no full
national accounts are available for 1974 and 1975, the huge
increase in the resources of the BNDE and other official
financial entities, as a result of the rapid growth of the
various social security funds, would probably show a considerable increase of state financial intermediation.
Whether this intermediation is used to allocate funds on the
basis of government-defined development objectives or in
response to market demands for funds requires further study.

Although the BNDE was the financier of large government
infrastructure and basic industry projects--and in the
process became the owner of some of the country's major

steel mills in the 1950s and early 1960s--its activities
became increasingly directed towards the Brazilian private
sector in the late sixties and seventies. By the mid-
seventies about 80 percent of its loans were directed to
the private sector. Since 1975, however, the bank has
adopted the practice of financing private Brazilian firms
through minority stock purchases. Although the intention
is strictly to strengthen the private sector, the potential
for greater state participation in the future exists,
especially in financially troubled firms where the BNDE is
a minority partner, and where salvation lies in greater
BNDE participation.

TOWARDS AN ANALYSIS OF STATE CAPITALISM

The *ad hoc* nature of the growth of state involvement
in Brazil's economy since the beginning of the century
accounts, in part, for the lack of an analytical framework
which explains the nature and functioning of Brazil's state
capitalist economy. What sort of resource allocation paradigm would be adequate for a society in which private property is prevalent, in which multinationals are an important
part of the economy, but in which the state is both an important regulator and direct agent? An answer to these
questions can emerge only gradually, as economists turn
their efforts toward studying how the system actually functions rather than towards models which say how it ought to
operate, and as they become more receptive to multidisciplin-
ary studies.

ALTERNATIVE PERSPECTIVE ON THE STATE

Although there exist little theory to guide the construction of a new paradigm, a consideration of alternative
"polar" hypotheses about the control of the resource allocation process may provide a starting point.

First, it could be claimed that despite the increasingly large role of the state, market forces in the broadest
sense determine allocation and the direction of development.
State enterprises simply respond to market signals much as
do private enterprises. State planning primarily serves
the purpose of mobilizing and channelling savings to potential bottleneck industries while performing the orchestra-
ting role of macroeconomic policy. In this view the state
is no more than an adjunct to market forces despite its
preponderance, and it makes little difference who controls
the levers of policy.

The weakness of the market allocation theory is that it ignores the many politically set prices throughout the economy, the effects of planning and the role of political factors generally. The above portrait of the state reveals its direct intervention in many markets. The minimum wage, for example, is a political price and has important income distribution ramifications. The government intervenes in many other markets--imports, finance, technology, and final products--through incentives, restrictions and price controls. Moreover, state firms are primarily concerned with growth objectives rather than with financial performance. In sum, public policy and its underlying politics need to be more adequately incorporated into this analysis.

A second perspective is that state policy serves the interests of the foreign and national industrialists and is largely controlled by them. These groups, it is argued, need public planning to ensure the vitality of the private sector. With the government providing needed infrastructure, private firms in industry are free to produce, shape consumption patterns and make a profit. Multinational corporations, in particular, are able to use their considerable market power to capture even greater shares of the national market and orient development in ways that suit their product lines. Government-set prices guarantee market functioning to the ultimate benefit of the private producers. Acting at the behest of private interest groups, the state guarantees the maintenance of social order and political stability.

Although this approach links political to economic theory, it does not account for the aggressive state expansion at the expense of the private sector. In industry and petroleum, private participation among the largest firms declined substantially since 1966. In the regulatory area, the power of public bureaucracies over the private sector has increased substantially. The *estatização* debate in 1975-76 is evidence of the tension between the public and private sectors.[33]

A third hypothesis is that technocrats and military entrepreneurs have assumed the upper hand in the allocation process. The very system of free enterprise which the military and technocrats sought to save with government intervention has now bred new sources of independent economic power: public enterprise and its bureaucracy. State bureaucrats as a group have gained control of both overall allocation and individual markets through direct production. The tail now wags the dog. In this view, the technocrats and public managers form an "independent state" relatively free from the influence of private sector interests, and allocate resources in a way that expands their own power and wealth.

This view may be generalizing from a trend that has not yet matured. It posits the formation of a new "class" and may ignore the degree of decentralization in the federal enterprises and bureaucracies, so that in reality the technocrats hardly work consciously as a group. More importantly, even if state entrepreneurs and bureaucrats occupy positions of widespread power, it is not clear that their interests as a group are fundamentally different from those of the private producers.

These "polar" interpretations all point to areas where future empirical research is warranted. Of necessity, such research must be interdisciplinary. It must consider microeconomic arrangements and the structure of markets, evaluate policy formation and impacts, understand interest groups and their inter-relations, and ultimately come to grips with how the system solves or creates the larger problems of development.

We shall outline how some future research might shed more light on these questions.

AN EXPANDED POLICY APPARATUS

To what extent could and does the state view its directly productive firms, its commercial banks and its public utility enterprises as part of its overall policy apparatus? The more consciously it does, the more difficult it becomes to judge the performance of government enterprises and banks. For example, if the state orders its firms to refrain from price increases in order to support a stabilization program or to provide subsidized inputs to favored sectors or income groups, the traditional criteria of efficiency in terms of profit maximization become irrelevant and some broader social measure of success will have to be found.

Like its growth, the use of the expanded state sector to attain broader policy goals has been on an *ad hoc* basis. In order to attain its stabilization goals in the second half of the sixties, for example, the government ordered its steel firms to raise prices at a rate which was lower than the prevailing inflation. The lag in public utility rates behind price increases prior to 1964 was an implicit redistributive policy favoring both lower income groups and industries. The granting of subsidized loans by state banks to favored sectors reflect government allocational policies. In all these examples there is a subordination of the efficient and/or profitable functioning of government-owned enterprises and banks to broader policy objectives.

Favorable financial performance of the larger public firms, however, suggests that they perceive allocative efficiency as crucial in achieving their specific objectives as firms. Petrobras, the companies composing Eletrobras and Telebras, Vale do Rio Doce and other firms meet operating expenses and generate investment resources independent of budget allocations or other government subsidies. Enterprise managers, anxious to fulfill firm objectives, may be expected to react to this "market discipline" by emphasizing the needs for adequate prices, cost controls, and aggressiveness in markets for loan capital.

DISTRIBUTION OF POWER

When the allocation of resources in a society is influenced to a large extent by non-market forces, the economist, along with other social scientists, needs to search for power groups whose interaction will give an explanation of the actual process of resource allocation. This search is only beginning in state capitalist economies like that of Brazil.

The most vocal critics of the large state role in the economy, mainly representatives of domestic private industry, argue that the state has expanded into areas well served by the private sector. It is claimed that state firms, unchecked by competitive or legislative restraints, use privileged access to capital markets in order to expand into areas which they believe ought to be the preserve of the private sector.

Prime targets of such criticism are some of the giant state conglomerates, especially Petrobras and Vale do Rio Doce. The latter have preferred to form their own transport and construction subsidiaries rather than contract such services from the private sector. State steel companies have organized engineering consulting firms which compete directly with private firms. State commercial banks have aggressively competed with private banks.

THE NEW CLASS OF ENTERPRISE MANAGERS

The recent attention paid to the transformation of government firms into conglomerates has placed in bold relief the dearth of information about the functioning and new interests of such firms. Who are the decision-making groups within government enterprises? What are the ways of attracting and maintaining first-rate technicians and administrators?

It is possible that only a dynamic firm can hope to maintain a first-rate staff. The activities of an enterprise which sticks to the narrow limits of its initial endeavors becomes routinized and thus unattractive to the best talent. Only firms which allow innovations and thus expansion can hope to maintain the best technicians and administrators. Should empirical research confirm this hypothesis, one would be tempted to develop a model which holds that good performance by state enterprises will arise in those which offer challenges to its staff and which are thus expansionary in their activities. In other words, state capitalism must grow in order to stay efficient.

Existing evidence suggests that public firms, in attempting to assemble a well-paid and therefore motivated staff, have brought to their ranks a cadre of well-trained, business-oriented technocrats. Do these constitute a new class? A substantial amount of socioeconomic research is needed in this area. This might establish that much of the recent expansion of state firms may be due to the power-maximizing behavior of these technocrats. In a sense, by deriving satisfaction from the achievement of "their" enterprises, the members of this new class may have contributed toward making the state capitalist sector an independent force. It is also possible that, given their great power in state enterprise hierarchies, these technocrats might be reluctant to move into the administration of the subsidiaries of multinationals, where their decision-making power is restricted, or to tightly-held domestic private firms, whose economic power is small and where the owners are reluctant to delegate decision-making.

THE MILITARY AND THE STATE SECTOR

A discussion of the expanded state sector in Brazil should not overlook the role of the military establishment in the industrialization of the country. The armed forces have had an active interest in the country's industrialization dating back to the nineteenth century, especially in such defense industries as steel and capital goods. The military were in the forefront in training engineers, especially metallurgical and civil engineers.[34]

The large-scale state enterprises in steel-making, petroleum, petrochemicals, mining and public utilities, have in large measure been dominated by military or ex-military technicians and administrators. This is explained by both the policy interests of the military in industry growth and their constituting an important supply of specialized manpower.

CENTRALIZATION VS DECENTRALIZATION

Power struggles are certain to exist within the government sector, especially between central planners and the executives of government enterprises. That the latter are not willing subordinates of the former was well illustrated recently when a presidential decree was necessary to force state enterprises to surrender basic company information to the Ministry of Planning. A number of firms have in the past refused to provide financial data to the government despite statutory legislation. Central government regulatory agencies have in the past been unable to probe into the operations of public firms.

These issues of control suggest that central government use of state firms for macroeconomic purposes, even if such uses are well conceived, is likely to be foredoomed. Government controls over, for example, the volume of imports, the amount of price increases, the feasibility of investment projects, etc., are quite likely to conflict with the microeconomic objectives of the state firm itself. Public enterprise autonomy from central government control will probably increase with the greater size and power of the state firm.

JOINT VENTURES WITH MULTINATIONAL CORPORATIONS

The institutional framework becomes even more complex with the growth of joint ventures, i.e., new companies owned jointly by state enterprises and multinationals. The willingness in the seventies of foreign firms to associate themselves with Petrobras' and the Vale do Rio Doce's subsidiaries in joint ventures opens up newer vistas. It is entirely possible for private foreign capital to prefer

doing business as a partner with a powerful state firm.
This might be considered a profitable and, in the long-run,
a safer investment. It is no simple accident that Fiat's
decision in the mid-seventies to come to Brazil is based
on a joint venture with the government of the state of
Minas Gerais.

The model of state involvement in the Brazilian economy which will emerge in the coming decades may be greatly
different from those models known at present. It may require economists to develop different ways of understanding
such a new system and to develop tools for the policy-maker
to deal with the new reality.

1. Raymundo Faoro, *Os Donos do Poder* (São Paulo: Editora Globo, 1975, 2a, edição) pp. 206-9, 222, 230.
2. Ibid., p. 434.
3. *Mauá, Autobiografia* (Rio de Janeiro: Edições de Oura, Technoprint Gráfica, 1972) p. 107; Nícia Vilela Luz, *A Luta Pela Industrialização no Brasil* (São Paulo, 1960) pp. 170.1 and 190.
4. This was especially the case with railroad construction. Only with government-guaranteed rates of return did foreign companies begin their investment activities. See Annibal V. Villela and Wilson Suzigan, *Política do Governo e Crescimento da Economia Brasileira*, Rio de Janeiro: IPEA/INPES: Série Monográfica, 1973) pp. 392-5.
5. Benedito Ribeiro and Mario Maazei Guimarães, *História dos Bancos e do Desenvolvimento Financeiro do Brasil* (Rio de Janeiro and São Paulo: Pro-Service Ltda. Editôra, 1967) pp. 41-127, 314-5.
6. An estimate for 1887 shows that of ₤ 18 million capital invested in railroads, a guaranteed rate of return of 7 percent per annum amounted to ₤ 1.3 million, which represented 6 percent of total export earnings. See Villela and Suzigan, op. cit., p. 396.
7.

Administration of Railroads (%)		
	Public	Private
1929	49	51
1932	68	32
1945	72	28
1953	94	6

Source: Villela and Suzigan, op. cit., p. 398.
8. Villega and Suzigan, op. cit., pp. 191-200.
9. For a thorough discussion of these entities, especially from a legal and administrative point of view, see: Alberto Venâncio Filho, *A Intervenção do Estado No Domínio Econômico* (Rio de Janeiro: Fundação Getúlio Vargas, 1968) pp. 358-66. Another valuable source on the functioning of "Autarquías" is: Centro de Estudos Fiscais, *O Setor Público Federal Descentralizado* (Fundação Getúlio Vargas, IBRE, 1967).
10. Villela and Suzigan, op. cit., p. 381.
11. Werner Baer, *The Development of the Brazilian Steel Industry* (Nashville, Tennessee: Vanderbilt University Press, 1969) pp. 68-76; John D. Wirth, *The Politics of Brazilian Development, 1930-1954* (Stanford, California: Stanford University Press, 1970) pp. 71-129.

12. Conselho Federal de Comércio Exterior, *Dez Anos de Atividades*, (Rio de Janeiro, Imprensa Nacional, 1944).
13. Annibal V. Villela, Sergio Ramos da Silva, Wilson Suzigan and Maria José Santos, *Aspectos do Crescimento da Economia Brasileira, 1889-1969* (Rio de Janeiro: Fundação Getúlio Vargas, 1971) mineographed, Vol. 1, pp. 382-3.
14. Some of these properties were returned to their former owners after World War II.
15. Villeal et al, op. cit., p. 585.
16. Baer, *The Development of the Brazilian Steel Industry*, pp. 67-8; Wirth, op. cit., chapters 4 and 5.
17. For a review of the different phases of planning in Brazil, see: Jorge Gustavo da Costa, *Planejamento Governamental: A Experiência Brasileira* (Rio de Janeiro: Fundação Getúlio Vargas, 1971); Betty Mindlin Lafer (ed.), *Planejamento no Brasil* (São Paulo: Editora Perspectiva*, Coleção Debates, 1970); Octávio Ianni, *Estado e Planejamento Econômico no Brasil, 1930-70* (Rio de Janeiro: Civilização Brasileira, 1971); Nelson Mello e Souza, "O Planejamento Econômico no Brasil: Consideração Crítica," *Revista de Administração Pública*, 2. semestre 1968, pp. 59-112.
18. Alexander Gerschenkron, *Economic Backwardness in Historical Perspective* (Cambridge, Mass.: Harvard University Press, 1962) p. 14.
19. Wilson Suzigan, José Eduardo de Carvalho Pereira and Ruy Affonso Guimarães de Almeida, *Financiamento de Projetos Industriais no Brasil* (Rio de Janeiro: IPEA, Coleçao Relatórios de Pesquisa, No. 9, 1972) p. 106.
20. Ibid., pp. 106-8.
21. Baer, *The Development of the Brazilian Steel Industry*, pp. 80-3. In similar fashion BNDE acquired the Cia Ferro e Aço de Vitória in the fifties, while the Banco do Brasil became the owner of ACESITA, a special steels firm.
22. For details see Wirth, op. cit., pp. 133-216; Getúlio Carvalho, *Petrobras: do Monopolio aos Contratos de Risco (Rio de Janeiro: Forense-Universitaria, 1976)*.
23. Suzigan et al, op. cit., pp. 166-80.
24. *Conjuntura Econômica*, Junho de 1975, pp. 88-9.
25. John F. Due and Ann F. Friedlaender, *Government Finance: Economics of the Public Sector* (Homewood, Illinois: Richard D. Irwin, Inc., 1973) p. 672.
26. *Conjuntura Econômica*, Junho de 1975, p. 88.
27. The best analysis of price controls in Brazil can be found in: Dionísio Dias Carneiro Netto, "Política de Controle de Preços Industriais," in *Aspectos da Participacão do Governo na Economia*, (Rio de Janeiro: IPEA/ INPES, Série Monográfica No. 26, 1976) pp. 135-69.

28. "Quem é Quem na Economia Brasileria," *Visão*, 31 de agosto de 1975, pp. 573-6.

29. These data, compiled by *Visão* (see footnote 28), should be interpreted with caution. The 5,113 firms include only incorporated firms. Since the unincorporated sector is fairly large in Brazil, the shares of the three sectors (state firms, multinationals and private firms) in the 5,113 firms examined understate the private sector. In the compilation, joint ventures have been treated as a residual category to be located in the private sector, regardless of where control lies. In this case state firms and multinationals are under-represented. Brazil does not require the publication of consolidated balance and income statements. Thus a large firm which owns many subsidiaries has its equity counted twice, once in the parent company, and once in the subsidiary. To the extent that this occurs, it is the state and private Brazilian firms which are over-represented. Additional information on state enterprises can also be obtained from the following sources: Wilson Suzigan, "As Empresas Do Governo e o Papel do Estado Na Economia Brasileira," in *Aspectos da Participação do Governo na Economia* (Rio de Janeiro: IPEA, Série Econogodfica, No. 26, 1976) pp. 77-134; Enrique Saravia, "Aspectos Gerais do Comportamento das Empresas Publicas Brasileiras e sua Ação International," *Revista de Administração Publica*, Vol. 11, Jan./Nov. 1977, pp. 65-142.

30. In 1976 EMBRAER produced 514 planes. See: "A Embraer Em 1975," *Conjuntura Econômica*, Março de 1976, pp. 138-9; "A Indústria Aeronáutica A Um Passo da Maturidade," *EXAME*, 25 de Mavo de 1977, pp. 22-7.

31. Walter L. Ness, Jr., "Financial Markets Innovation as a Development Strategy: Initial Results from the Brazilian Experience," *Economic Development and Cultural Change*, April 1974, pp. 453-72.

32. According to Ness three out of the four most traded shares on the Rio de Janeiro stock exchange were those of government enterprises (Banco do Brasil, Petrobras, Vale do Rio Doce). These accounted for 38 percent of the trading volume in 1972. Ness, op. cit., p. 470.

33. For a summary of the debate, see: *Visão*, April 19, 1976; "O Documento das Industrias Paulistas," *Jornal do Brasil*, 21 de maio de 1976; "Estatização: O Perigo da Desnacionalização," *Opinião*, 4 de Junho de 1976.

34. Werner Baer, *The Development of the Brazilian Steel Industry* (Nashville, Tennessee: Vanderbilt University Press, 1969) pp. 55-76.

8

INFLATION AND
INDEXING

Brazil has been plagued by inflation throughout its history, and during the 1940s and 1950s, under the pressures of rapid industrialization and the policies of populist governments, the rate of inflation accelerated considerably. Although there is some evidence that inflation might have had some positive effects on the economic growth of Brazil in the 1950s, acting as an inflationary tax to redistribute resources from the consumption to the investment (especially government) sector, it nearly went out of control under Goulart's troubled populist regime in the early 1960s. The military government which took power in April 1964 immediately adopted stabilization measures and set about reforming the structure of the economy, giving high priority to eliminating the distortions caused by inflation.[1]

By 1964 inflation had become much more than the treadmill race of income-earners with the price level. Years of inflation had built severe distortions into the Brazilian economy. For example, prices in the controlled sector, particularly public utilities, lagged behind general price increases, resulting in under-investment in a number of critical infrastructure sectors. This underinvestment was partially counterbalanced by large government subsidies which, in turn, led to further inflationary pressures. To the extent that it was not made up for it led to the deterioration of the services in question.[2]

---

* This chapter is based on the article: Werner Baer and Paul Beckerman "Indexing in Brazil," *World Development*, December 1974.

The government deficit, which itself contributed to the inflation, could not be reduced because of the inflation. Besides the growing deficits, the government had to pay higher prices for what it purchased and higher wages to its employees. It could not issue bonds because it was not allowed to pay a high enough interest rate to cover price increases. Taxpayers held off paying as long as they could because inflation ate away the real value of what they owed. The government was forced to divert commercial bank credit to cover some of its deficit. Hence, the deficit persisted and was one of the causes of further inflation.

Demand for credit increasingly exceeded supply, for it bore negative real rates of interest, and it was rationed in ways that had little to do with relative efficiency. Savings were attracted to such areas as real estate and foreign currency to prevent a decline in their real value.[3] Brazil's currency was chronically overvalued, since the frequent devaluations were insufficient and in any case running a treadmill race too.

Brazil's credit markets were on the verge of breaking down altogether in 1964. Two laws dating from 1933 handicapped the capital markets in their ability to deal with inflation: a usury law that prohibited interest charges above 12 percent per year, and a legal tender law that prohibited cortractual payment in anything but domestic currency at its legal value.[4] The usury law was interpreted to refer to nominal interest rates, while the legal tender law prohibited any readjustment of principals for inflation. Hence, whenever the rate of inflation rose above 12 percent per year, as it did in every year after 1951, the effect of the two laws was to turn real interest rates negative. Under these circumstances it was impossible for a long-term credit market to develop. The only sources of long-term credit in 1964 were international agencies such as the U. S. Agency for International Development, the National Development Bank (BNDE) and a number of other government institutions. Their credit was artificially low in cost, but it was heavily rationed by non-market means.[5]

The short- and medium-term credit markets resisted these pressures better by incorporating a number of devices into their operations. Banks were permitted to pay a maximum of 6 percent on time deposits, and these inevitably declined in real terms, but demand deposits remained strong because transactions balances had to be maintained and banks were still the best places to keep them. Hence, banks had a supply of short-term funds. This supply was available to

them for a negative real rate of interest, so that as they
were lending at a higher rate, even a negative one, they
could be making a profit. For their lending operations
they were able to get around the 1933 laws by various devices, including illegal side-payments of extra interest,
collection of high "banking commissions," and the use of
tied accounts.[6] Only through such means could the short-
term credit market be cleared. Banks could make a lot of
money on the difference between negative real rates of interest and so many new banks were established that competition for deposits became intense.[7]

A market for medium-term credit developed through
"credit-and-finance" companies during the 1950s. To get
around the legal restrictions on interest to depositors,
these companies sold shares of their net worth to suppliers
of capital; these shares then earned dividends which were
not affected by the usury laws. The funds obtained were
then loaned out through companies typically owned by the
depositors' companies. The depositors' dividends were
heavily taxed, however, and there were adverse rulings
against this method of operation. Hence, a new instrument
of short- and medium-term credit was adopted by the credit-
and-finance companies - "exchange notes" (Letras de Cambio).
These notes are obtained by the borrower from the finance
company in exchange for his promissory notes, and then sold
by him at a discount on the stock exchange. For the buyer
of the note, the discount, which is not subject to the
usury law, takes the place of interest. Exchange notes remain the principal short- and medium-term credit to this
day, particularly since the 1933 laws are still in effect--
and frequently applies--although since 1964 they have been
interpreted differently. The exchange-note market was badly
squeezed during the high level of inflation in 1964, but the
system remained popular.

The housing market was doubly victimized by inflation.
Like all of Brazil's long-term credit markets, the 1933 laws
made long-term credit for construction and mortgages extremely scarce - the only sources were public institutions
and their credit was severely rationed. Furthermore, between 1950 and 1964 a series of rent-control laws were
passed which had the inevitable effect of discouraging
badly-needed new construction (especially for lower-income
groups) and of permitting the deterioration of existing
properties. The very weakness of the housing market, however, prevented a mass of demand for loans to build inflation-
proof luxury housing.

A more subtle distortion caused by inflation was what has been called "profit illusion."[8] Illusory profits are that part of a firm's profits that represent the amount needed to maintain the real value of a firm's capital. They will arise in an inflationary context if firms depreciate their fixed assets on the basis of historical rather than replacement cost, or if firms provide for the replacement of their working capital (in particular, inventories) at their previous price rather than at their current price. One estimate was made of profits of Brazilian firms that were probably illusory for the period 1958–62: for a small sample of 20 Rio de Janeiro firms, it was found that "...the portion of the balance-sheet profits corresponding to non-accounted depreciation...rose from 19.9 percent to 43.6 percent between 1958 and 1962."[9] For a larger sample of some 7,000 firms, it was calculated that for the same period "more than half of the balance-sheet profits...were absorbed by the replacement of working capital (inventories plus net cash). Inventory replacement was responsible for almost all this illusory profit."[10]

Illusory profits undoubtedly led to various distortions, including irrational pricing and dividend policies, an increased tax obligation due to the excessive profits tax (much of which was in fact evaded), and ironically, an increased demand for credit to replace capital in spite of the "high profits." When inflation was high, a considerable degree of allocative distortion must have resulted from illusory profits. To some extent this was mitigated by the fact that given the difficulty of obtaining outside credit and the traditional preference of Brazilian firms for internal financing, profits were used for new investments in preference to other sources. It is possible that from 1958 to 1960, because of the presence of illusory profits in the retained earnings applied to investment, less than 25 percent of this investment was really new - the rest just restored capital that illusory profits had come from.[11]

The valuation of assets at historical cost was also part of the problem in the pricing of the public service sector. Since firms in the latter were regarded as "natural monopolies," the law set their prices to place a ceiling on their rate of return on capital. Since the capital was valued at historical cost, the rate of return permitted was too low to maintain capital - hence the chronic operating losses and deterioration of services.[12]

THE IMPLEMENTATION OF INDEXING IN BRAZIL

The regime which took power in April 1964 was determined to slow down inflation; hoping, however, to do so without causing a severe depression, it decided on a "gradualist," as opposed to "shock-treatment" approach in its stabilization program. Moreover, the regime was also determined to restore the market as a guide for the allocation of resources, and so the prices which had been artificially held down by previous governments, such as public utility rates, were raised. This had an initial inflationary effect, which was called "corrective inflation."[13] It was thus clear to policy-makers that they would have to put up with high levels of inflation for some time to come. Indexing was therefore seen as a means of eliminating some of the distortions caused by inflation. In other words, the Brazilian authorities decided to "live with inflation," although indexing was apparently conceived of as a temporary measure and not, as is often assumed, as a permanent way of life.[14]

A concept of indexing was first introduced in Brazil in 1951 in a limited and somewhat improvised way. At that time there existed an excess-profits tax on corporate returns to capital. Since inflation was accelerating, and assets were valued at historical cost, the excess-profits tax was clearly unfair. Hence, for calculating taxable profits a special law permitted firms to revalue their fixed assets and their subscribed capital according to rates of inflation. The revaluation was subject to a 10 percent tax; furthermore, depreciation was still permitted only on the basis of historical cost. Later laws, in 1956, 1958, and 1963 made revaluation of assets compulsory in firms subject to the excess profits tax. But until 1964 the revaluation system provided no tax deduction to permit restoration of working capital to its current value; the 10 percent tax remained in force; revaluation was not permitted frequently enough to keep up with the rate of inflation; and depreciation was still calculated on the basis of historical cost.

Indexing was not applied to other economic variables, particularly credit instruments and wages, although some courts began to provide for monetary settlements in current terms. In fact, before 1964 most firms did not revalue their assets, for the sole purpose of the revaluation was to make the incidence of the excess-profits tax more equitable. There was no point for a firm to pay the 10 percent tax on revaluation of its assets if it was not subject to the excess-profits tax or if it could evade it.[15]

After 1964 a series of laws instituted indexing in a large part of the economy. The first law, in July 1964, established indexing as obligatory for all fixed assets, permitting depreciation on the revalued base (this was, in fact, applied gradually to avoid a sudden drop in corporate tax revenue), and gradually eliminated the 10 percent tax on revaluation. The amount of profit that was needed to restore working capital to its previous level was exempted from the excess-profits tax, although this tax itself was abolished in 1966. Indexing was applied to back taxes owed to the federal government to encourage their speedy payment. The same law also authorized the issue of a new series of federal government bonds, "Readjustable National Treasury Obligations," Brazil's first indexed credit instrument. These were bonds of one or two years' maturity whose principals were adjusted monthly according to the three-month moving average of the wholesale price index, lagged three months. (There was also a series of five-year bonds whose principals were readjusted every three months.) The coefficients for adjustment of the principals were set at first by the National Economic Council but, when this institution was dissolved in 1967, the responsibility was transferred to the Planning Ministry. The coefficients were calculated on the basis of the wholesale price index, compiled by the Fundação Getúlio Vargas, a semi-autonomous institute for economic studies.[16]

A law passed in August 1964 created the National Housing Bank to provide mortgage loans. Both the bonds issued by the bank and the loans granted by it were indexed, though much of the financing for the bank was drawn from social security funds. A law passed in November regulated housing rents through a different type of index: rents were adjusted according to the minimum wage, which was itself set by the government. Rents which had been frozen were first allowed to rise, according to the government's corrective-inflation policy. In following years additional laws were added to cover construction loans, non-residential rents, insurance, and back pay owed to employees. The courts continued the application of indexing in adjudicating cases. The principle of indexing was extended to a new series of forced savings.[17]

A "capital markets law" was passed in July 1965. It contained wide-ranging provisions for the reform of Brazil's capital market institutions, including various stimuli for the stock market, the long-term debt market, and investment banks; the law also included some provisions to bring the short-term rate of interest down. The indexing provisions included in the law applied to long-term corporate debt, a large range of time deposits, and the interest rates of medium-term instruments.[18] The hope was that this would lengthen the average term of debt instruments and bring down their real interest rates by removing the uncertainty in the inflation component of the rate. The rate of indexing to be applied would be the same as that applied to the government's readjustable bonds.

The indexing used was "post fixed," that is, credit instruments were adjusted for inflation that had already occurred. It was difficult, however, to use this in the short-term credit market. A series of regulations from 1965 to 1967 created a new concept to be applied to the short-term market: "pre-fixed indexing." A component to account for anticipated inflation was added into the interest rates carried by short-term instruments, including exchange notes and certificates of deposit. The profits on these instruments were calculated ex-post, however, for tax purposes; that is, the taxable interest received on these instruments was the real interest rate plus the pre-fixed index *minus* the rate of inflation which actually occurred during the term of the instrument. In 1970 the government pre-indexed short-term credit notes of its own in addition to its long-term bonds.

The distinction between post-indexed and pre-indexed debt instruments is of some significance. Brazilian law continues to tax them on different bases: post-indexing is treated as capital gains, while pre-indexing is treated as interest income, which in practice means that pre-indexing is taxed and post-indexing is not. A more important point is that post-indexing with a lag may have the effect of impeding the deceleration of inflation (assuming that the rate of inflation is being reduced), since it brings an earlier rate of inflation forward in time to revalue credit instruments. The Brazilian authorities have been preoccupied by this effect and since 1973 a new indexing scheme half-way between post- and pre-indexing has been adopted for all credit instruments. The indexing coefficients are now calculated on a five-month basis, the moving average of inflation for the previous three months plus an official estimate for the next two months.[19] In July 1974 this form of indexing was extended to the short-term credit sector, so that it covered all Brazilian credit instruments.[20]

The adoption in 1968 of a system of minidevaluations, mentioned in previous chapters, must be considered part of the overall indexing policy. Strictly speaking these minidevaluations are only an approximation to an indexing policy, since there is nothing automatic about them. It is a discretionary policy that can be based on factors other than Brazil's inflation relative to that of other countries. But the relative rate of inflation has been the principal determinant; hence it seems fair to regard minidevaluations as part of indexing policy.

Unlike many other countries, Brazil did not index wages, although many wages are directly or indirectly established through guidelines set down by the government. In 1965 it adopted a wage policy which exerted an influence mainly through its coverage of government workers and the minimum wage. In setting wages, a formula was used which based the increase in the nominal wage for the coming year on the anticipated rate of inflation.[21] A 1966 law extended the use of the formula to wage disputes (i.e. where labor and management cannot reach agreement by themselves) and added anticipated productivity increase as a factor in the formula. A further change in 1968 based the new nominal wage not on what it had been previously, but on what it would have been had the inflation and productivity increases that occurred been used to set it in the previous year. Since the principal factors in the formulas have always been *anticipated* rates of increase, and the government did the anticipating, wage increases in Brazil have largely been a matter of discretionary government policy and cannot really be said to have been indexed.

ACCOMPLISHMENTS OF INDEXING IN BRAZIL

Indexing seems to have solved the profit illusion problem. Most inducements to Brazilian firms to consume their own capital on account of profit illusion have apparently disappeared. Prior to the indexing reforms of the sixties there were some factors present which offset the inducements to eat into capital, e.g., the access to long-term credits from the Development Bank at negative rates of interest and low tax liability in real terms due to delays in their payments. Furthermore, the revaluation of the assets of public-service enterprises, in view of the laws basing the prices of their services on the value of their real assets, undoubtedly contributed to the rationalization of their operations.

Table 37 presents various measures of Brazil's inflation since 1951, changes in the exchange rate and the real GDP growth rate. Column 7 gives the percentage by which

TABLE 37

Measures of Inflation, Exchange Rate Changes and Real GDP Growth
(Percentage change over previous year)

Year	Internal price	Wholesale prices	Agricultural prices	Industrial prices	Cost of living, Rio de Janeiro	Implicit GDP deflator	Public Services	Price of US$	Real GDP growth
1951	11.9	17.4	12.8	11.7	10.8	12.0		0.0	6.0
1952	12.9	9.4	15.1	4.8	20.4	13.2		0.0	8.7
1953	20.8	25.0	17.5	32.3	17.6	15.3		136.8	2.5
1954	25.6	22.3	26.5	21.5	25.6	21.4		37.8	10.1
1955	12.4	15.9	7.4	12.9	18.9	16.8		21.0	6.9
1956	24.4	26.2	22.6	29.7	21.8	23.2		-1.4	3.2
1957	7.0	3.8	0.8	6.5	13.4	13.2		2.7	8.1
1958	24.3	35.1	20.5	37.1	17.3	11.1		69.7	7.7
1959	39.5	36.0	42.1	29.8	51.9	29.2		21.7	5.6
1960	30.5	34.5	32.2	33.4	23.8	26.3		21.0	9.7
1961	47.7	53.2	53.0	46.0	42.9	33.3		43.2	10.3
1962	51.3	45.5	44.0	46.9	55.8	54.8	40.9	42.6	5.3
1963	81.3	83.2	90.0	86.1	80.2	78.0	91.2	48.7	1.5
1964	91.9	84.5	86.5	101.3	86.6	87.8	112.4	120.3	2.9
1965	34.5	31.4	25.2	31.5	45.5	55.4	103.4	48.8	2.7
1966	38.2	41.5	42.7	32.0	41.2	38.6	52.8	17.2	3.8
1967	25.0	22.0	21.1	23.1	24.1	28.8	31.7	20.1	4.8
1968	25.5	24.2	16.7	34.6	24.5	27.8	19.5	27.6	11.2
1969	20.1	19.2	31.7	15.1	24.3	20.3	23.9	20.0	10.0
1970	19.3	18.5	20.3	18.9	20.9	18.2	28.9	12.7	8.8
1971	19.5	21.4	24.7	16.7	20.2	17.3	24.0	15.1	13.3
1972	15.7	15.9	22.3	15.4	16.4	17.4	24.4	12.2	11.7
1973	15.5	15.5	19.0	14.7	13.7	20.5	13.0	3.2	14.0
1974	34.5	35.4	29.4	29.3	27.7	31.5	18.7	19.7	9.8
1975	29.4	29.3	24.0	29.4	29.0	32.7	36.5	19.8	5.6
1976	46.3	44.9	59.0	36.6	41.9	41.3	34.5	31.3	9.2

Source: Conjuntura Econômica and Boletim do Banco Central do Brasil.

publicly-controlled prices have been adjusted. The policy of "corrective inflation" from 1964 to 1967 can be observed, i.e., the adjustments of public utility prices which had lagged behind general price increases allowed to rise faster than other prices in order to eliminate distortions.

The indexing of back taxes and of government bonds undoubtedly contributed to the success of the government in closing its deficit. This is shown in Table 38. The federal deficit as a proportion of GDP declined from over 4 percent in the early sixties to 0.17 percent in 1972.

TABLE 38
Federal Government Deficit, Various Measures
(millions of cruzeiros)

Year	Deficit or surplus	Government debt outstanding	Deficit/GDP
1951	+2.4		
1952	+2.5		
1953	-10.7		2.28
1954	-4.0		0.63
1955	-5.7		0.73
1956	-23.9		2.40
1957	-41.2		3.38
1958	-30.7		2.11
1959	-40.5		2.04
1960	-76.6		2.78
1961	-137.5		3.39
1962	-280.9		4.26
1963	-504.7		4.23
1964	-728.2	41	3.16
1965	-592.9	430	1.61
1966	-586.6	1,401	1.09
1967	-1,224.7	2,482	1.71
1968	-1,226.7	3,491	1.23
1969	-755.8	5,881	0.57
1970	-738.3	10,112	0.42
1971	-672.3	15,445	0.29
1972	-516.1	26,179	0.14
1973	+295.1	38,344	
1974	+388.2	47,801	
1975	+73.0	97,548	
1976	+423.0	153,889	

Source: *Boletim,* Banco Central do Brasil.

The notable increase in Brazil's savings and the improvement of their quality can be attributed in large measure to the indexing of savings instruments. Table 39 presents the growth of some of Brazil's principal savings instruments, particularly those that have been indexed. Without indexing the growth of such assets as time deposits, government bonds, housing bonds, etc., would have been unlikely. As Fishlow points out, however, the true magnitude of this growth should not be exaggerated. Some of the savings growth represents substitution among different assets, i.e., channeling of savings through intermediaries, and possibly some double-counting in the composition of the statistics.[22] But there can be little doubt that these savings are more efficiently allocated than they would have been in the absence of indexing. Brazilian savings and investments as a proportion of GDP have grown substantially since the early post-World War II period; they stood at 13.0 and 12.9 percent respectively in 1949, 19.3 and 18.5 percent in 1959, and about 25 and 24 percent in the mid-seventies. Much of the savings increase since the mid-sixties was due to government savings and the social security funds; the latter amounted to almost 40 percent of total savings in 1975.[23]

The elimination of illusory profits has obviated much of the need for bank credit to maintain real capital. Indexed capital instruments have helped form much of the capital base of the National Housing Bank and other savings institutions which have alleviated the housing shortage. Increased workers' savings through the new social security programs were possible because indexing preserves their real value. The one application of savings resources that may be questionable is the considerable growth of consumer credit. Consumer durables, from automobiles to clothing to pocket radios, are now typically purchased by Brazilians in installments at high finance charges. The proportion of total loans of commercial banks going to private individuals grew from 5.6 percent in 1963 to over 16 percent in the mid-seventies; loans of finance companies grew from 7 to 52 billion cruzeiros in São Paulo in the period 1971 to 1976, and from 3 to 13 billion in Rio de Janeiro in the same period; the cost of a 360 day loan in São Paulo in 1976 was 3.56 percent a month and in Rio de Janeiro 3.96 percent.[24]

Government financial market policy has not been successful in the creation of a true long-term debt market. The investment banks created by the 1965 capital-markets law have been reluctant to terminate exchange-notes operations. The 1965 capital-markets law authorized the credit-and-

TABLE 39
Growth of Various Savings Instruments and Money Supply
(in millions of cruzeiros)

Year	Post-indexed treasury bonds outstanding	Post-indexed Nat'l housing Bds outst.	Pre-indexed treasury bills outst.	Pre-indexed exchange notes
1964	41			245
1965	430			695
1966	1,401	7		906
1967	2,482	140		2,105
1968	3,491	461		4,558
1969	5,881	922		6,172
1970	9,412	1,724	700	9,756
1971	11,565	2,762	3,880	14,390
1972	15,975	5,015	10,204	20,973
1973	20,944	6,517	17,400	34,820
1974	32,969	8,287	24,801	42,608
1975	60,112	8,937	37,400	55,809
1976	84,397	9,779	69,404	68,392

	Pre-indexed time deposits	Post-indexed time deposits	Non-indexed time deposits
1966	141	18	127
1967	469	86	138
1968	1,055	330	312
1969	1,938	893	74
1970	4,283	2,081	75
1971	9,319	3,761	88
1972	16,803	7,713	214
1973	25,568	14,122	243
1974	33,341	32,107	130
1975	54,466	55,234	102
1976	72,654	107,539	170

	FGTS	PIS	PASEP	Money supply
1964				4,875
1965				8,750
1966				9,959
1967	597			14,513
1968	1,604			20,174
1969	2,832			26,735
1970	4,345			33,638
1971	6,332	296	729	44,514
1972	9,038	1,628	1,354	61,550
1973	12,907	4,154	4,100	90,490
1974	18,502	10,192	6,748	120,788
1975	26,465	20,594	12,144	172,433
1976	37,479	38,886	20,502	236,506

Source: *Boletim,* Banco Central do Brasil.

finance companies to become investment banks if they phased out their use of exchange notes (which the government hoped to reserve for "finance companies"); the investment banks, however, were reluctant to give up the exchange notes, and the government postponed the date by which they must give them up until 1975.

In addition to the indexing of long-term debt instruments, the capital-markets law provided fiscal incentives for long-term debt, and corporations were authorized to issue indexed *convertible* debentures. These measures, however, have not led to the widespread use of long-term corporate debt. In a recent study of industrial financing it was found that heavy reliance of firms on internal funds for investment purposes did not change in spite of the many financial reforms introduced since 1964. The only changes which occurred were in the sources of external financing, though even these were concentrated in the financing of current production and consumption.[25]

According to Ness, "Businessmen appear to have feared manipulation of the monetary correction index by the government or departure of their industry's prices and costs from national patterns."[26] Brazilians, it seems, are still not prepared to entrust their funds to the uncertainties of the long-run, and indexing alone does not seem to inspire the confidence of people who have seen the economic dislocation of earlier years; furthermore, businessmen prefer not to surrender any control of their enterprises to outside suppliers of capital. Provision of long-term finance remains by default the province of government agencies, such as the BNDE, the Federal Savings Banks in each state, and international agencies. Ness found that "Registered debenture issues have never exceeded 3 percent of the total security issues of non-financial corporations."[27] As Table 39 shows, the growth of the exchange-note market continues to be impressive, the exchange notes will likely remain the principal Brazilian private financial instrument for some time to come.

The long-term debt granted by official agencies has been used mostly as an instrument of development policy. Since it was the government's policy to stimulate industrial growth, these long-term credit instruments were one of the means to provide subsidies to favored sectors. The low and uncorrected rates of interest resulted in negative real rates of interest. In the agricultural sector, even medium-term credit was made available on a subsidized basis, i.e., loans to agriculture fell outside the indexing mechanism.

For example, from 1970 until 1977 the maximum interest charged by commercial banks for "modern inputs" loans to agriculture was held at 7 percent; it was raised to 14 percent in 1977. In 1976, in order to stimulate private investment, the BNDE loans to many sectors were held to a maximum monetary correction of 20 percent; that year the prices index increased by 46 percent.

Indexing has also been instrumental in attracting foreign capital. One of the principal attractions for foreign funds was the relatively high real interest rates which came to prevail under the indexing system. Brazilians were anxious to obtain cheaper Euro-collar funds, while foreigners were attracted by higher earning opportunities in Brazil. For a while an additional attraction was the difference which existed between the indexing rate and the rate at which the cruzeiro was devalued. Since the latter was usually smaller than the former (i.e., the inflation rate being larger than the devaluation rate), foreign lenders gained an additional advantage.

As already noted, Brazil's wage policy is an indexing policy in name only. It is generally agreed that Brazil's income distribution has worsened since 1964, and this may be attributed in part to the government's wage policy, which was intended to check inflation. In the mid-sixties real wages were allowed to decline sharply and their recovery since has been slow. In the seventies real wages rose, but at a rate substantially lower than productivity increases.

EVALUATION

The argument most frequently advanced against indexing is that it is itself a contributor to inflation. Indexing contributes to inflation by institutionalizing price increases. By maintaining real income it keeps demand at inflationary levels.

INDEXING AND INFLATION

The argument that indexing feeds inflation, however, needs to be examined closely. There are circumstances where indexing might actually serve to reduce inflation, and it may be that the net effect of indexing has not been significantly inflationary in Brazil. In general, the net effect depends on the nature of the economy and the system of indexing in use.

When nominal final-goods prices are indexed, inflation is defined into the economy; when factor prices are indexed, inflation is forced into the economy. But, as was observed, relatively few nominal prices of either sort are indexed in Brazil. The indexing of credit instruments also has an inflationary effect in that the price of capital is a cost for firms. Brazilian authorities have felt that indexing might operate against a slowdown of inflation by bringing an earlier rate of inflation forward to make the current adjustment. To diminish this influence post-indexing was changed to a mix of post- and pre-indexing. Indexed credit instruments also contribute to inflation by attracting foreign capital and by increased use of consumer credit.

There are several ways, however, in which indexing may have served to alleviate inflation. The government deficit was one of the principal causes of inflation and its reduction served to reduce demand-pull pressures. The reduction of the deficit was in great measure attributable to the application of indexing to tax debts, which stimulated tax payments on time. To the extent that the deficit was covered by the sale of indexed government bonds to the public, its inflationary force was diminished. The argument that indexing of credit instruments is inflationary must be qualified by the point that if credit instruments were not indexed their real interest rates might be even higher because of the risk component. In the case where credit instruments are not indexed, the interest rate may be described as having three components: a real interest rate, a component reflecting the generally expected rate of inflation, and a component covering risk to the creditor that inflation might be even higher. Indexing eliminates the need for such a risk component. Even if indexing of capital instruments does make the real cost of capital higher, this would serve to hold down new investment demand. Indexing might even tend to reduce demand pressure: in an inflationary context, a person who feels that the purchasing power of his income is eroding will tend to move his current stock of assets out of money and into goods as fast as he can, contributing in the process to demand pressures; indexing his income over the year would relieve the erosion of his purchasing power, and in the aggregate this should reduce inflationary demand pressures.

Asset indexing has probably little inflationary effect since it only serves to make the information that firms use more accurate. The decrease in self-deception of firms as to the true levels of their profits undoubtedly serves to reduce inflationary demand for investment. Partially offsetting this there may be some inflationary effect from the consequent reduction of government revenues from corporate taxes; also, the public service prices that are set on the basis of the value of the firms' capital value are driven up. On the whole, however, indexing of assets has probably reduced inflationary pressures.

INDEXING AND DISTRIBUTION

Indexing in Brazil has been applied to real assets, credit instruments, public service prices, rentals and the price of foreign exchange, but not to wages. It would thus be erroneous to argue that indexing had a definite redistributive effect between labor and capital. The distributional effect which indexing has had in Brazil is essentially between creditors and debtors, not between labor and capital. Classically, creditors lose and debtors gain from unanticipated inflation, but with indexing, to the extent that the price index reflects real purchasing power, creditors are protected from inflation and debtors pay the price of capital that they contracted. This is a more complex distributional effect than that of wage controls; its magnitude and character are quite subtle and a more detailed analysis is necessary.

When we speak of distributional effects, however, more than income is involved. Particularly in a developing country, one must speak of the distribution of savings and of opportunities to obtain credit. In Brazil indexing has opened the possibility for saving to classes of people that never had it before. In an inflationary context it becomes almost pointless for a person of modest means to try to accumulate a stock of savings from his income, particularly if most investment opportunities are for large and lumpy projects. Only if his savings are indexed will their real value be preserved.

Indexing has also made credit available to people to whom it was never available before. This may be a mixed blessing. On the one hand, the expansion of credit has served to make housing and consumer durables available for many who previously had no access to them. On the other hand, it could be claimed that this credit is expensive and has been expanding too rapidly. If a large sector of the economy were unable to meet the obligations imposed by indexing, a large number of partial or total defaults on payments of principal and interest could induce a chain reaction of crises in credit institutions. The government would then face some difficult policy decisions concerning the distribution of income between the creditor and debtor sectors of the economy.

INDEXING AND ALLOCATIONAL EFFICIENCY

It has been observed that indexing can have negative effects on allocational efficiency. If prices are adjusted strictly according to a price index they cannot simultaneously reflect changes in the supply-demand conditions in the markets they clear. Indexing real assets and credit instruments cannot fail to improve allocational efficiency. Indexing of real assets serves to provide firms with more accurate information; indexing of credit instruments establishes the true cost capital. The indexing of nominal prices, however, means that these will be set differently than if the market were allowed to function freely. But this is an argument which applies even more to the entire system of controlling prices in Brazil; any regulation of prices may have distorting effects. In Brazil, indexing the price of foreign exchange was a vast improvement over the previous fixed-rate system, from the point of view of efficiency. In general, choosing the method for setting a particular price frequently entails a controversy between those who want to use the price to allocate efficiently and those who want to assure fixed shares of the national product on the basis of the price. Indexing the price may be, in many cases, the viable compromise between the two.

ENDNOTES

1. For an analysis of the pre-1964 inflation, see: Werner Baer, *Industrialization and Economic Development in Brazil* (Homewood, Illinois: Richard D. Irwin, Inc., 1965) chapter 5; Raouf Kahil, *Inflation and Economic Development in Brazil: 1946-1963* (Oxford University Press, 1973); Samuel Morley, "Inflation and Stagnation in Brazil," *Economic Development and Cultural Change*, January 1971; Syvrud, *Foundations of Brazilian Economic Growth*, chapters 4-6; Werner Baer, "The Inflation Controversy in Latin America: A Survey," *Latin American Research Review*, Winter 1967.

2. See, for instance, the case of transportation: Werner Baer, Isaac Kerstenetzky and Mario H. Simonsen, "Transportation and Inflation: A Study of Irrational Policy-Making in Brazil," *Economic Development and Cultural Change*, January 1965.

3. Walter L. Ness Jr., "Financial Markets Innovation as a Development Strategy: Initial Results from the Brazilian Experience," *Economic Development and Cultural Change*, April 1974, p. 463.

4. These are described in: Julian Chacel, Mario H. Simonsen, and Arnoldo Wald, *A Correção Monetária* (Rio de Janeiro: APEC Editôra S.A. 1970) pp. 19-26.

5. *Ibid.*, pp. 64-5.

6. Tied accounts meant that the borrower would take out a loan larger than he needed, leave the part that he did not need in a demand deposit account with the bank that he agreed not to touch, and pay interest on the whole.

7. Chacel, Simonsen and Wald, op. cit., pp. 61-3.

8. This problem is discussed at length in: Werner Baer and Mario H. Simonsen, "Profit Illusion and Policy-Making in an Inflationary Economy," *Oxford Economic Papers*, July 1965.

9. *Ibid.*, p. 280.

10. *Ibid.*, p. 281.

11. *Ibid.*, p. 287.

12. Chacel, Simonsen and Wald, op. cit., pp. 42-5; also Baer, Kerstenetzky and Simonsen, op. cit.

13. See Baer, Kerstenetzky and Simonsen, op. cit.; Mario H. Simonsen, "Brazilian Inflation: Postwar Experience and Outcome of the 1964 Reforms," *Economic Development Issues, Latin America*, Committee for Economic Development, Supplementary Paper No. 21, August 1967; Howard Ellis, "Corrective Inflation in Brazil," in H. S. Ellis (ed.), *The Economy of Brazil* (Berkeley and Los Angeles: The University of California Press, 1969).

14. In the Chacel, Simonsen and Wald volume on page 301 one reads that "It is evident that indexing was conceived as an artifice of temporary character. This measure forms part of a group of measures that constitute a policy of gradual attack on inflation... when the inflationary tendency falls to a certain critical level (perhaps 10 and 15 percent per year) the correction of past distortions will no longer have great relevance and the real loss can perfectly well be supported by economic agents."

15. Albert Fishlow notes that "Even during the raging inflation of some 80 percent in 1963, only 27 percent of the total corporate capital was revalued." Albert Fishlow, "Indexing Brazilian Style: Inflation Without Tears?", *Brookings Papers on Economic Activity*, No. 1, 1974, p. 265.

16. For more details, see: "Correção Monetária: Tema de Interesse Internacional," *Conjuntura Econômica*, May 1974, p. 111; also Chacel, Simonsen and Wald, op. cit., pp. 101-17.

17. Chacel, Simonsen and Wald describe these laws and their accompanying enabling legislation in detail. The forced savings include: the "Fundo de Garantia de Tempo de Seviço" ("Job Tenure Guarantee Fund"), created in 1965 and financed by an 8 percent payroll tax, administered by the National Housing Bank, and used for workers' indemnization and purchases of housing for workers; the "Programa de Integração Social" ("Social Integration Program"), created in 1971, financed by contributions from firms according to sales and earnings, paying 3 percent plus indexing accruing to workers; and the "Programa de Formação do Patrimônio do Servidor Público," a parallel program also created in 1971 for public servants.

18. Walter Ness, op. cit., p. 458.

19. *Conjuntura Econômica*, May 1974, pp. 111-2.

20. *Jornal do Brasil*, July 23, 1974, p. 23.

21. See also Albert Fishlow, "Some Reflections on Post-1964 Brazilian Economic Policy," in A. Stepan (ed.), *Authoritarian Brazil* (New Haven, Conn: Yale University Press, 1973) pp. 84-97.

22. Fishlow, "Indexing Brazilian Style..." p. 274; see also: Kenneth King, "Recent Brazilian Monetary Policy," Belo Horizonte: CEDEPLAR, October 1972, mimeo.

23. Data taken from national accounts published in the July 1977 issue of *Conjuntura Economica*.

24. More data can be found in the original article by Werner Baer and Paul Beckerman, "Indexing in Brazil,"

World Development, December 1974, pp. 42-3; also in the monthly *Boletim*, of the Banco Central do Brasil.

25. For instance, it was found that the sources of industry's investment funds were divided in the following manner (in percentages):

	1967	1968	1969	1970
Self-financing	47.3	52.9	51.4	45.9
Domestic loans	38.2	24.6	28.6	25.1
Foreign loans	14.5	22.5	20.0	29.0

See: Wilson Suzigan, José Eduardo de C. Pereira and Ruy Afonso Guimarães de Almeida, *Financiamento de Projetos Industriais no Brasil* (Rio de Janeiro: IPEA, Coleção Relatórios de Pesquisa, No. 9, Segunda Edição) pp. 227 and 277.

26. Ness, op. cit., p. 458.
27. Ibid.

9

REGIONAL
IMBALANCES

Inequality in the spatial distribution of income and growth has been a characteristic of the Brazilian economy from colonial times to the present. Each of the past primary product export cycles benefited one specific region or another. The sugar cycle of the sixteenth and seventeenth centuries favored the northeast; the gold export cycle of the seventeenth and eighteenth centuries shifted the economy's dynamism to the area of the present state of Minas Gerais and the regions supplying it, in southeast Brazil; the coffee export boom of the nineteenth century favored at first the backlands of Rio de Janeiro and later the state of São Paulo. By the twentieth century, however, the historic shifting of favored economic regions came to an end. The southeast of the country, which was the dynamic export region when the industrialization process began, also became the center of industrial production. Since the 1930s, when industry became the leading sector of Brazil's economy, the southeast of the country has been the principal beneficiary of economic growth and has substantially increased its share of the GDP.

DEGREE OF REGIONAL INEQUALITY IN BRAZIL

The extent of regional inequality in Brazil can be gauged from Tables 40 and 41. From colonial times until the present Brazil's northeast and southeast have accounted for the bulk of the country's population. It will be noted from the data in Table 40 that until 1872 the largest proportion of the population resided in the northeast. By the turn of the century, however, the southeastern area was the leading population center and remained so until the present. The northeast's share of the country's population declined

TABLE 40
Regional Distribution of Population
1872-1970 (percentages)

	1772-82	1872	1900	1940	1970
North	4.1	3.4	4.0	3.6	3.9
Northeast	47.4	46.7	38.7	35.0	30.3
Southeast	41.8	40.5	44.9	44.5	42.7
South	1.9	7.3	10.3	13.9	17.7
Central-West	4.8	2.2	2.1	3.1	5.5
Total	100.0	100.0	100.0	100.0	100.0
		(993)*	(17,434)*	(41,236)*	(93,135)*

* Numbers in parenthesis represent absolute figures for population in thousands.

Sources: Douglas H. Graham and Thomas W. Merrick, "Population and Economic Growth in Brazil: An Interpretation of the Long-Term Trend (1800-2000)", mimeographed, March 1975, p. 43; besides using the Brazilian census materials, they also used the following sources for the pre-census historical information: Dauriel Alden, "The Population of Brazil in the Late Eighteenth Century: A Preliminary Study," *The Hispanic American Historical Review,* 43, May 1963, pp. 173-205.

continuously after 1872, from 47.4 percent to 30.3 percent in 1970. The redistribution of the population occurred both through internal migration and through the influx of immigrants.

Comparing the regional distribution of the population with the regional distribution of the national income (Table 41) one notes both the high degree of inequality between regions and its persistence over time. Whereas by 1970 the northeast still accounted for over 30 percent of the population, its share of the national income declined from 14.1 percent in 1959 to 12.2 percent in 1970, while the southeast, with 42.7 percent of the population in 1970, accounted for 64.5 of the income. It will also be noted that by 1970 only the south had a share of the national income which was equivalent to its population share. The differences between the major regions are impressive even if the qualification is added that the northeast is more rural, that it therefore has a larger noncommercial sector and thus has an actual real income (including goods which do not enter the market economy) that is somewhat higher than indicated here.

TABLE 41
Regional Distribution of National Income (Renda Interna)
(percentage distribution)

	1949	1959	1970
North	1.7	2.0	2.0
Northeast	14.1	14.1	12.2
Southeast	66.5	64.1	64.5
South	15.9	17.4	17.5
Center-West	1.8	2.4	3.8
Total	100.0	100.0	100.0

Source: Calculated from Fundação Getúlio Vargas, IBRE, Centro de Contas Nacionais, *Sistema de Contas Nacionais, Novas Estimativas,* Setembro de 1974.

Over the period 1960 to 1975 the northeast's per capita income has fluctuated between 40.3 and 48.8 percent of the national per capita income average; it stood at 43.7 percent in 1975. For some individual states the per capita income might be as low as 20 percent of the national average, while for others in the more advanced region this proportion reached over 135 percent. As a rough indication of the actual magnitudes involved, it has been estimated that the per capita GDP of Brazil in 1960 was about US$420 and in 1976 about US$1,190 (in current US$).

An indication of a strong association between the industrialization process and increased regional disparities can be obtained from an examination of changes in the regional distribution of the agricultural, industrial and service sectors in Table 42. It will be noted that the degree of regional concentration is much less pronounced in agriculture than in the other sectors. Since the latter (especially industry), however, have been growing more rapidly than agriculture, and since they are basically urban sectors, it would seem that the increased regional concentration of economic activity is due in great part to the nature of the industrialization process. It should also be noted, however, that it is in the agricultural sector where one finds the greatest regional disparities in income and economically active population. In other words, a region like the northeast not only has a much smaller share of industry in relation to its population share, but it also has a per capita income in agriculture which is much smaller than that of the southeast.

TABLE 42
Regional Distribution of Income by Sectors
(percentage distribution)

	Agriculture			Industry			Services		
	1949	1959	1970	1949	1959	1970	1949	1959	197
North	1.6	1.7	2.3	1.0	1.7	1.3	2.0	2.2	2.
Northeast	18.7	21.0	20.9	9.4	8.3	5.6	13.1	13.0	12.
Southeast	54.2	43.7	40.0	75.4	76.9	80.6	70.7	69.1	65.
South	22.2	28.8	29.6	13.5	12.3	11.7	12.9	13.8	16.
Center-West	3.3	4.8	7.2	0.7	0.8	0.8	1.3	1.9	3.
Total	100.0	100.0	100.0	100.0	100.0	100.0	100.0	100.0	100.

Source: Same as Table 41.

Tables 43 and 44 reveal substantial differences in the sectoral distribution of income and labor force in the different geographical areas. Whereas in 1970 the national average for the proportion of the national income generated by agriculture was 19.5 percent, this proportion varied between 12.1 in the southeast, 37.4 in the center-west, and it amounted to 33.4 in the northeast. The national average for the industrial sector was 25.3 percent, varying considerably among regions - 31 percent in the southeast, 11.6 in the northeast and 5.5 in the center-west. The regional variation for services was much smaller.

In 1970 the economically active population as a proportion of total population of ten years and over was highest in the southeast (32.4 percent) and stood at only 29.1 percent in the northeast. The sectoral distribution of the labor force presented in Table 44 also indicates substantial regional variations. In 1970 the national average for the share of the labor force in agriculture was 44.3 percent, while it stood at 61.1 percent in the northeast and 26.9 in the southeast. For industrial employment the national average was 17.9 percent, with variations from 25 percent in the southeast (31.4 and 47.3 percent in the states of São Paulo and Guanabara respectively) to 10.7 percent in the northeast. The proportion of the working population employed in the service sector was much above the national average in the southeast (48.1 percent) and was lowest in the poorest regions (28.2 percent in the northeast).

TABLE 43
Sectoral Distribution of Income of Principal Macro Regions
(percentage distribution)

	1949				1959			
	A	I	S	T	A	I	S	T
North	30.0	12.3	57.7	100.0	22.8	19.6	57.6	100.0
Northeast	41.0	13.8	45.2	100.0	39.5	13.4	47.1	100.0
Southeast	25.2	23.3	51.5	100.0	18.0	27.2	54.8	100.0
South	43.0	17.5	39.5	100.0	43.7	16.1	40.2	100.0
Center-West	46.8	7.0	36.2	100.0	53.0	7.3	39.7	100.0
Brazil	30.9	20.6	48.2	100.0	26.4	22.7	50.9	100.0

	1970			
North	22.4	15.8	61.8	100.0
Northeast	33.4	11.6	55.0	100.0
Southeast	12.1	31.7	56.2	100.0
South	32.9	16.9	50.2	100.0
Center-West	37.4	5.5	57.1	100.0
Brazil	19.5	25.3	55.2	100.0

Source: Calculated from Censuses of 1950, 1960, and 1970.

Table 44 also shows that, over the years, labor was transferred from agriculture to the other two sectors in all regions. However, whereas in the southeast the share of industrial employment almost doubled, the service sector grew more slowly. In the northeast the service sector grew slightly more in relative terms – industry from 7.3 to 10.7 percent and services from 18.4 to 28.2 percent.

A comparison of the share of the three main sectors in the major regions of Brazil in the national income and economically active population (EAP) reveal some striking features (Table 45). While 24 percent of the EAP of Brazil was engaged in northeastern agriculture in 1950, it contributed only 5.7 percent to the national income; by 1970, 17.6 percent of the EAP was working in northeastern agriculture, contributing 3.9 percent to the national income. This means that northeastern agricultural productivity worsened, since the ratio of the EAP share to the income share of agriculture in the northeast rose from 4.2 to 4.5 in the period examined. It will be noted that although in the southeast and south the share of the EAP occupied in agriculture was also higher than the share of these sectors in the national income, the discrepancy was much smaller than that of the northeast.[1]

TABLE 44

Sectoral Distribution of Labor Force by Regions

	Agriculture	Industry	Services	Total
Brazil - 1970	44.3	17.9	37.8	100.0
North & Center-West				
1940	70.4	8.2	21.4	100.0
1950	72.8	7.5	19.7	100.0
1960	62.8	9.1	28.1	100.0
1970	55.2	11.3	33.5	100.0
Northeast				
1940	74.3	7.3	18.4	100.0
1950	73.8	8.0	18.2	100.0
1960	69.6	8.0	22.4	100.0
1970	61.1	10.7	28.2	100.0
Southeast				
1940	55.4	12.7	31.9	100.0
1950	47.1	19.0	33.9	100.0
1960	38.8	18.4	42.8	100.0
1970	26.9	25.0	48.1	100.0
South				
1940	63.9	9.4	26.7	100.0
1950	63.3	12.6	24.1	100.0
1960	59.4	10.2	30.4	100.0
1970	54.0	14.3	31.7	100.0

Source: IBGE, various Demographic Censuses.

Turning to the urban sectors, one is struck by the contrasts of productivities in the industrial sectors of the northeast and the southeast. In the former the share of the national EAP was larger than the share of national income in 1950 and this gap widened even more by 1970. In the southeast the share of industrial labor force in the national EAP was much smaller than the share in national income in 1950 and this gap widened by 1970.

TABLE 45
Shares in National Income and
Economically Active Population(EAP)

	Agriculture	Industry	Services
Northeast			
Income			
1950	5.7	1.9	6.2
1970	3.9	1.3	6.4
EAP			
1950	24.0	2.7	6.1
1970	17.6	3.0	7.6
Southeast			
Income			
1950	16.5	15.2	33.6
1970	7.4	19.5	34.6
EAP			
1950	21.4	8.7	15.6
1970	11.9	11.3	21.5
South			
Income			
1950	6.7	2.7	6.2
1970	5.5	2.8	8.4
EAP			
1950	9.5	1.9	3.6
1970	9.9	3.0	7.6

Source: Calculated from Fundação Getúlio Vargas, Centro de Contas Nacionais, *Sistema de Contas Nacionais*, Setembro de 1974; and IBGE, various censuses.

Examining the service sector, one notes that within the northeast the share gap (EAP versus National Income) was smaller than in other sectors, though the EAP share in 1970 was larger than that of income. In the southeast service productivity was substantially higher than in the northeast, the EAP share being much smaller than that of income. In the south the gap was quite large in 1950 (EAP being much smaller than income), but narrowed by 1970.

THE DYNAMICS OF REGIONAL INEQUALITIES

As long as Brazil's economy was primarily export-oriented, the regional distribution of income was determined by the type of primary exports which were dominant. When the principal source of growth became internalized, however, unequal regional growth and development rates tended to perpetuate themselves or even increase at times.

GENERAL CONSIDERATIONS

Hicks, among others, has observed that once unequal rates of growth develop they tend to perpetuate themselves, or the disparity in growth rates might even increase because "...as industry and trade become concentrated in a particular center, they themselves give to that center an advantage for further development."[2] New firms will tend to settle in the already growing regions, unless there are some special reasons to go to another region, since external economies will make investment in those areas more remunerative. Such external economies consist of more readily available skilled labor, a wide variety of auxiliary goods and services which do not have to be imported from elsewhere, etc. Although the initial reason for the faster growth of such a region might have been some geographic advantage "...it is perfectly possible that they may lose their geographical advantage, and yet they continue to grow, through this advantage of concentration. They grow, that is, by an internal economic momentum."[3]

Although the growth momentum is usually cumulative in the dynamic area, it could under certain conditions spread some of its dynamism to other areas. In other words, the growth of the dynamic area can act as a centrifugal force in certain cicumstances, but it could also act as a centripetal force and drain the marginal areas of any growth potential they might have had.

Growth can be transmitted from the dynamic to the static region through three basic channels: the movement of goods, of capital and of labor. Growth transmissions through trade take place when the dynamic region is not self-sufficient, leading to part of the incremental wealth being spent in another complementary region. Capital will have an incentive to move from the dynamic to the stagnant area only in case a vital source of supply to the former needs development. Such movement might create new centers of self-sustaining growth; though it might also simply

create an enclave economy in a distant region with little
local linkages. With the exception of such an incentive,
it is probable that the dynamic center will act centri-
petally as far as capital is concerned, for with all the
available externalities, rates of return on investment will
probably be much higher in the growing than in the stagnant
region.

One would also expect labor mobility to be in the
direction of the growing region. It is most likely that
productivity and earnings of labor are higher in the latter
than in the stagnant area and that labor will therefore
move from the stagnant to the growing area. The margin of
difference in labor remuneration, or the expectation thereof, will have to be enough to overcome the inertia due to
change of patterns of living involved in the movement. On
the positive side, labor movement might ease the pressure
in the stagnant area and even raise per capita income,
especially if there existed a considerable amount of dis-
guised unemployment in the area. Such a movement might also
benefit the dynamic center by keeping a steady labor supply
on hand, thus preventing labor costs from rising too fast.
Labor movement can also be a considerable drain on the stagnant region since there is usually a greater tendency for
younger, more vigorous, and better trained or trainable individuals to move.

It can also be argued that if the growing area does
not attract labor fast enough from other regions, this might
ultimately make the latter seem more attractive to capital
than previously. It is more likely, however, that relatively lower wages in the stagnant regions will be offset by
lower labor productivity and higher costs in other fields,
such as transportation, power, etc.

If the dynamics of the situation are such as to result
in centripetal forces being dominant, equity considerations
might force the government to undertake actions to redress
regional inequalities. To what extent can this be done
without impairing the growth of the dynamic region? Public
policy measures of geographical redistribution can be
achieved through fiscal policy and/or direct official
measures to encourage firms to settle in the more backward
regions.

One obvious redistributive measure is for the government to expand its building of social and economic infrastructure in the stagnant region, financed either by a curtailment of its activities in the dynamic area or by in-

creasing the tax burden of the latter. The first method might be harmful to the continued growth of the dynamic region because of the bottlenecks in infrastructure that might appear. If the expansion of government investment in the stagnant region should be financed by additional expenditures based on increased taxation in the dynamic area, the harm to the latter will depend on the tax structure. If it is progressive in nature, the source of capital and the incentive to invest might be substantially reduced, leading to a diminishing rate of growth in that region. But if the tax structure is regressive, which is the case in many developing countries, the effect might be less harmful or even neutral. In this case, the finance of development in the stagnant region would come from a curtailment of consumption in the dynamic region. Under certain circumstances this would be a healthy phenomenon, though growth in the latter region could be curtailed if decreased consumption would be of such a magnitude as to affect the investment incentive.

INTERNAL POPULATION MIGRATION

It will be noted from Table 46 that some adjustments in the regional imbalances took place through migration.

Foreign immigrants had an important impact on the state of São Paulo and the·southern states in the second half of the nineteenth century and first two decades of the twentieth century. In the case of São Paulo, immigration was linked to the expansion of the coffee sector. In the south it was related to the opening of new lands where, after the exploitation of forest products, there developed commercial agriculture which served the growing urban markets.

Thereafter internal migration took on increasing importance. This was especially the case when import substitutive industrialization became the principal dynamic force and, located in the southeast, attracted large numbers of·migrants. Improvements in the communications between various parts of the country, which occurred as a byproduct of the industrialization process and the opening of new frontier areas for increased agricultural production, made internal migration easier. As with the foreign immigration, the internal migration benefitted mainly São Paulo and the frontier states of Parana, Mato Grosso and Goias (see Table 46).

TABLE 46
National and Regional Rates of Net Internal Migration Expressed as a % of Population in Initial Census Years, 1890-1970

A. National Rates

Ten-year intercensal years	Rate	Twenty-year	Rate
1890-1900	2.97	1900-1920	3.79
1940-1950	2.94	1920-1940	4.99
1950-1960	5.51		
1960-1970	4.49		

B. Regional Rates*

	1890-00	1900-20	1920-40	1940-50	1950-60	1960-70
North	27.38	16.66	-13.72	-3.38	0.39	2.78
Northeast	-1.42	-1.68	-0.84	-2.67	-9.78	-5.08
East	-0.64	-4.81	-5.37	-3.26	-3.10	-5.57
South	-0.97	5.24	11.73	6.07	8.25	5.61
São Paulo	5.43	1.13	11.54	5.70	7.80	7.66
Parana	-7.47	13.43	19.58	29.28	43.58	18.39
Central-west	2.64	11.88	13.37	7.27	22.52	23.22
Goias	2.17	10.33	9.92	11.15	21.34	21.42
Matos Grosso	3.81	15.60	21.30	-0.55	23.59	27.38

* It should be noted that this table uses old Macro-Regional divisions.

Source: Graham and Merrick, op. cit., p. 49.

INTERACTION BETWEEN THE NORTHEAST AND THE CENTER-SOUTH

It has been argued that the ISI process worsened Brazil's regional imbalances, especially between the northeast and the center-south.[4] Prior to ISI the northeast of Brazil was an exporter of primary products (sugar, cotton, cocoa, etc.) and an importer of manufactured products from abroad. The policies which led to the intensification of ISI not only resulted in the establishment of most of the country's industrial capacity in the center-south of the country, but it also led to the worsening of the northeast's absolute position. While that region continued to export its traditional primary products, it was forced through the country's protective policies to import its manufactured products from the center-south instead of abroad. And since the relative prices of products of newly-established firms was higher than those formerly imported, the northeast suffered a decline in its terms of trade. In effect, the northeast was helping to subsidize the industrialization of the center-south of the country.

The available evidence suggests these trends existed in the 1950s. Table 47 contains the foreign trade position of the northeast and the regional distribution of exports and imports. The average value of exports from the northeast rose from US$165 million in 1948-49 to US$232 million in 1959-60, while during that time the average value of

TABLE 47
(a) Foreign Trade of Northeast
(in millions of US$)

	Exports	Imports	Balance
1948	197.6	93.2	104.4
1949	133.0	100.3	32.7
1950	174.1	86.9	87.2
1951	197.6	166.4	31.2
1952	114.5	173.3	-58.8
1953	169.6	95.3	74.3
1954	235.4	86.9	148.5
1955	238.5	86.2	152.3
1956	163.9	97.7	66.2
1957	212.1	131.9	80.2
1958	246.1	94.4	151.7
1959	216.1	79.3	136.8
1960	247.7	85.3	162.4

Source: Conselho de Desenvolvimento do Nordeste, op. cit., p. 20; Banco do Brasil, *Relatorio*, 1960.

(b) Regional Percentage Distribution of Exports and Imports

	Exports 1947	Exports 1960	Imports 1947	Imports 1960
North	2.4	1.7	1.3	1.2
Northeast	9.8	7.7	6.4	4.5
East	22.2	39.2	42.6	33.9
South	65.6	48.3	49.6	60.3
Center-west	-	3.1	0.1	0.1
	100.0	100.0	100.0	100.0

Source: Calculated from various issues of Banco do Brasil, *Relatorio*.

imports of the northeast fell from US$97 million to US$82 million. During many of the post-World War II years the northeastern foreign trade surplus was enough to cover the deficits incurred by the rest of the country in its trade balance; at times it was even large enough to cover other deficits in the balance of payments.

The increased foreign trade surplus of the northeast was due primarily to the general industrialization policies pursued by the federal government. Since the northeast was not industrializing at as fast a rate as the southeast, the structure of its import demand was oriented toward goods against which restrictions were heavy. Thus "...the northeast did not use the total of foreign exchange earnings generated by its exports. About 40 percent of such foreign earnings were transferred to other regions of the country."[5]

Table 48 contains interregional trade figures for the 1948-59 period. It will be noted that the northeast has had perennial deficits with the rest of the country, mainly the center-south, and that these deficits were growing during the latter part of the fifties.

TABLE 48

Value of the Northeast's Trade with the Center-South
(in millions of Cruzeiros)

	Exports	Imports	Balance
1948	4,069	5,541	-1,472
1949	4,579	6,630	-2,051
1950	5,349	7,141	-1,792
1951	6,843	8,298	-1,455
1952	6,687	8,159	-1,472
1953	7,975	10,792	-2,817
1954	10,804	12,871	-2,067
1955	13,495	16,477	-2,982
1956	19,845	19,692	153
1957	17,892	21,078	-3,186
1958	16,878	22,732	-5,854
1959	21,857	26,699	-4,842

Source: Conselho de Desenvolvimento do Nordeste, op. cit., p. 121; Banco do Brasil, *Relatorio*. These data refer to coastal shipping between states.

These data have led the northeastern development authorities to conclude that "...by supplying foreign credits to the center-south, the northeast has been contributing towards the development of the former, with a factor which is scarce for southerners, capacity for importing." Also, with a growing deficit of the northeast vis-a-vis the center-south in trade and "...as the center-south exports to the northeast are made up chiefly of manufactured merchandise, whereas raw materials have much more weight in northeastern exports, it is proper to surmise that the discrepancy favoring the center-south is still greater, if the barter is measured in terms of the volume of employment created for both regions."[6]

The foreign export surplus of the northeast resulting from the industrialization centered in the southeast--the former being forced to buy from the latter at less favorable terms of trade--implies a transfer of income from the poorer to the richer region of the country. Attempts have been made to measure the magnitude of this income transfer. Table 49 contains the index of Brazilian export and wholesale prices, excluding coffee. The ratio of the first to the second indicates the terms of trade for the region on the assumption that only domestic goods can be purchased with export earnings.[7] Since the period until 1953 was one of stable exchange rates, column C reflects quite adequately the loss of purchasing power of the northeast. After that date, however, the ratios had to be corrected for changes in the exchange rate. This was done in the last column. Thus, in the period 1948-60, the price ratio declined from 100 to only 48 instead of 10. This means that "...foreign exchange proceeds which the northeast did not spend for imports, but used for buying in the center-south, suffered a drop in purchasing power of the magnitude indicated."[8]

In Table 49 we also present a measure of the actual transfer of assets. Column F contains the net earnings of foreign exchange by the northeast. This is multiplied by the index of buying power of foreign earnings in the center-south region. We thus obtain an approximation of the actual buying power of net foreign exchange earnings, and the difference between this and the initial foreign exchange earnings (the last column) reveals the amount of assets transferred to the southeast.

In the period 1948-60 over US$413 million of capital assets were transferred, or an average of 32 million a year. Thus, the transfer of assets occurred because the price at

TABLE 49

Estimated Transfer of Resources from Northeast to Center-South
Through Trade: 1948-60 and 1960-68

	Price index of Brazilian exports A	Wholesale prices B	Ratio of A/B C	Index of exchange rate D	Corrected by C × D / 100 E	Net NE foreign trade income F	Index of buying power from foreign income in C-S G	F × G / 100 H	Transfer of assets F-H I
1948	100	100	100	100	100	104.4	100	104.4	-
1949	86	105	82	100	82	32.7	82	26.8	5.9
1950	78	105	72	100	72	87.2	72	62.8	24.4
1951	96	130	74	100	74	31.2	74	23.1	8.1
1952	106	147	72	100	72	-	-	-	-
1953	98	169	58	112	65	74.3	65	48.3	26.0
1954	84	213	39	169	66	148.4	66	97.9	50.5
1955	85	252	34	225	77	152.3	77	117.3	35.0
1956	88	307	29	255	74	66.3	74	49.1	17.2
1957	89	352	25	255	64	80.2	64	51.3	28.9
1958	83	403	20	255	51	151.7	51	77.4	74.3
1959	79	573	14	406	57	136.8	57	78.0	58.8
1960	73	756	10	481	48	162.4	48	78.0	84.4
1960	100(73)*	100(756)*	100	100(481)*	100(48)*	161.0	100(48)*	161(78)*	-44.0(77)*
1961	110(80)	140(1,058)	78	158(760)	124(61)	181.0	124(61)	225(110)	-33.0(49)
1962	106(77)	210(1,588)	51	252(1,212)	127(61)	121.0	127(61)	154(74)	-23.0(76)
1963	109(80)	371(2,805)	29	390(1,876)	114(56)	163.0	114(56)	186(91)	-30.0(53)
1964	112(82)	673(5,088)	17	745(3,583)	124(72)	126.0	124(72)	156(91)	-50.0(59)
1965	107(78)	1,030(7,787)	10	1,270(6,109)	132(61)	153.0	133(61)	203(93)	-21.0(78)
1966	105(77)	1,460(11,038)	7	1,560(7,504)	112(52)	164.0	113(52)	185(85)	-47.0(64)
1967	128(93)	1,840(13,910)	7	1,850(8,899)	129(62)	158.0	130(62)	205(98)	-41.0(53)
1968	123(90)	2,190(16,556)	6	2,330(11,207)	131(56)	134.0	134(56)	175(75)	

* Numbers in parentheses in the lower half of table are calculated on 1948 base.

Note: Columns F and H and I in millions of US$; column A index based on prices on US$.

Sources: First part of table, 1948-60, from Conselho de Desenvolvimento do Nordeste, op. cit., p. 23; also calculated from data in *Conjuntura Economica* and IMF's *International Financial Statistics*. The calculations for the second period, 1960-68, are taken from: Roberto Cavalcanti de Albuquerque and Clovis de Vasconcelos Cavalcanti, *Desenvolvimento Regional no Brasil* (Brasília: IPEA, Serie Estudos Para o Planejamento, 16, 1976), p. 50.

which the northeast sold its foreign assets rose less than
the price of the merchandise it bought in the center-south.

There was no obvious flow of capital between the northeast and the center-south in the 1950s, when one discounts
the capital transfer implied in the analysis of the price
deterioration. The large internal trade deficits of the
northeast, especially the ones in 1953 and the second half
of the 1950s, reflect federal aid to relieve the effects
of drought conditions and the attempts by SUDENE, the development agency for the northeast, to carry out special
investment plans. In times of drought, however, there
occurs a considerable amount of private capital flows to
the richer area. For example, in 1953 the federal government spent 1.6 billion cruzeiros more than it collected
from the northeast; but in that year net inflow of capital
amounted to only a little more than one billion. It can
thus be surmised that substantial private capital outflows
must have taken place.[9]

A further burden on the northeastern economy during
the industrialization process of the fifties was the effect
of the exchange system. Northeastern importers had to pay
high rates relative to rates for "subsidized" imports like
capital goods. Proceeds from these rates were used by exchange authorities to prop up the coffee economy, which is
centered in the southeast. Excess balances from the exchange rate system also increased the capacity of the Banco
do Brasil to make loans, a high proportion of which were
made in the south. The degree of "taxation" of the northeast implied in this operation can be estimated in the
following way. In Column A of Table 50 are listed the value
of imports of the northeast in cruzeiros and in the next
column are listed the dollar value of these imports. Dividing column A by column B, one obtains the actual exchange
rate paid by importers. In column D are listed the exchange rate of exports for the type of goods exported from
the northeast. Multiplying the dollar value of imports by
column D, one obtains (column E) the cruzeiro value of imports if the exchange rate for imports had been the same
as for exports. Subtracting this value of actual cruzeiros
spent, we obtain an estimate of the loss of purchasing
power which goes to support other sections of the country.

The resource transfer through trade relationships was
reversed in the sixties (see the lower half of Table 49),
approximately 36 million dollars a year entering the northeast. This was due to a more favorable evolution of the
exchange rate for the type of products exported by the

TABLE 50
Losses of the Northeast
Incurred through the Exchange Rate System

Year	A Value of imports (millions of Cr$)	B Value of imports (thousands US$)	C A/B	D Exchange rate for NE-types exports	E B x D	A - E Losses due to exchange rate system
1955	3,830	87,292	43.87	37.06	3,235	595
1956	4,933	98,933	49.86	43.06	4,260	673
1957	6,782	131,928	51.41	43.06	5,681	1,101
1958	6,340	94,357	67.19	43.06	4,063	2,277
1959	8,537	79,292	107.66	76.00	6,026	2,511
1960	10,147	85,308	118.94	90.00	7,678	2,469

Source: Calculated from data in Banco do Brasil, *Relatorio,*
1960 and 1957; IMF, *International Financial
Statistics.*

by the northeast and for their prices in relation to the
rise of the country's general price level.[10] It should be
noted, however, that if 1948 had been used as the base year
for the 1960–68 calculations (see numbers in parentheses in
Table 48), there would have been a continued asset transfer
from the northeast to the south; the relative purchasing
power would have been based on 1948 rather than 1960 relative
prices.

RESOURCE TRANSFERS THROUGH THE FISCAL MECHANISM

Brazil's federal fiscal mechanism has acted as a means
of resource transfer to the less favored regions of Brazil
for many decades. It has never been fully established,
however, to what extent this mechanism was large enough to
counter other resource flows to the wealthier regions.[11]

The federal tax burden of the northeast has traditionally
been much lighter than that of the country as a whole (see
Table 51), though the increase of that burden since the mid-
1960s has been faster for the northeast than for the rest of
the country. The total tax burden (i.e., including state
and municipal taxes) amounted to 11.3% for the northeast in
1974 (taxes as a % of regional GDP) and 20.7% for the country
(taxes as a % of national GDP). Estimates for federal government expenditures in the northeast have shown these to
have been larger as a proportion of the GDP of the northeast
than taxes, which means that the federal fiscal mechanism
resulted in a net transfer of resources to the northeast.
It will be noted, however, that in 1974 the tax burden was
greater than expenditures.

TABLE 51

Tax Burden and Various Transfers to Northeast Brazil

	Northeast Fed. Tax/ GDP_{NE}	Brazil Fed. Tax/ GDP_{BR}	Fed. Exp. in Northeast/ GDP_{NE}	Inter-Govt Transfers to NE/GDP_{NE}	Tax Incentive granted/GDP_{NE}
1947	5.0	9.6			
1950	4.0	8.1			
1955	4.0	8.0			
1960	3.4	7.8	7.4	0.46	0.01
1965	3.1	8.5	5.0	0.88	0.15
1970	6.0	10.5	9.6	4.07	3.11
1974	5.9	12.2	5.8	4.21	1.81

Source: Roberto Cavalcanti de Albuquerque and Clovis de Vasconcelos Cavalcanti, op. cit., pp. 123-5.

Another net resource inflow occurred through the transfer of federal taxes to state and municipal governments. In the period 1964 to 1974 such transfers to the northeast rose from 13 percent of federal tax receipts in the northeast to almost 68 percent (in 1970 this proportion was as high as 98 percent), or from 0.5 percent of the northeastern GDP to 4.2 percent.

The use of tax incentives to attract private investment funds to the northeast was a major policy instrument of regional redistribution of income in the second half of the sixties and early seventies. As can be seen in Table 51, funds released under this program rose to 68 percent of federal tax revenue in the northeast in 1970 and 3.1 percent of northeastern GDP. By the mid-seventies, however, funds declined again as tax incentives for other regions and sectors diluted the availability of funds for the northeast.[12]

Summing federal expenditures in the northeast, transfer of taxes to state and local governments, and tax incentives, and subtracting the tax burden, one finds that the net transfer through the fiscal mechanism increased from a yearly average of 4.4 percent of northeastern GDP in the early sixties to over 6 percent in the first half of the seventies.[13]

REGIONAL POLICIES

Regional equity in the economic development process has

not always been a major concern of Brazil's policy-makers. It has usually been an explicit objective of the government in times of regional calamities (like the periodic droughts in the northeast) or when it has been politically useful as a counter balancing measure to develop programs which have blatantly favored the more advanced regions of the country. In times of major national economic crises—often linked to the balance of payments—the programs formulated to deal with them have usually been devoid of concern with regional equity. The most notable cases are the import substitution industrialization programs since the 1930s, which were adopted as a result of balance of payments crises.

Prior to World War II Brazilian governments had no regional economic policies. Specific regional programs surfaced only in times of natural disasters, usually in connection with the recurrent droughts of the northeast.[14] To the extent that there existed some national economic programs, these were directed towards the protection and development of specific sectors—e.g., the coffee support programs, which date to the early part of the century and which were taken over by the federal government in the thirties, or the measures taken to develop the steel industry in the thirties—and their regional effect was usually to concentrate economic growth in the more advanced areas of the country, mainly the center-south.

Since World War II the formulation of "explicit" regional policies has become more frequent, especially from the late fifties on. These policies were aimed at the redistribution of income and investment resources from the richer to the poorer regions. Regional equity as a policy goal, however, has usually been viewed as just one of a series of objectives which the government has striven for. In other words, the attainment of other objectives—such as rapid growth of certain industrial sectors, the control of inflation etc.—were not conditioned by a desire for regional equity. Programs for the attainment of each goal have usually been formulated with little attention paid to their effects on other goals. This has led to contradictory policies, especially with regard to regional equity goals.

Brazil's national development plans in the late 1940s and 1950s do not contain explicit regional programs. The regional impact of the sectoral investment programs contained in them (e.g. transportation, health, basic industries, energy) was greatest on the more developed southeast.[15] The obvious bias of the Programa de Metas in the second half of the 1950s in favor of the southeast region, combined

with a severe drought in the northeast in 1958, forced the
government to formulate an explicit policy in relation to
the northeast. In 1959 a study group was thus created,
under the leadership of Celso Furtado, to formulate a development program for the northeast. The analysis of the resulting document on the nature of the region's backwardness
(some of the above analysis was based on this document), led
the government to create the Superintendency for the Development of the Northeast (SUDENE) in 1959.

SUDENE was supposed to direct and coordinate all activities of the federal government in the region. The basic
aims of the new agency in its first plan (which were always
repeated in all subsequent plans) were: 1) Intensification
of industrial investments with a view to creating sources of
employment in urban areas. This was to be achieved through
a special tax incentive law (known as law 34/18) permitting
firms to use 50 percent of taxes due the federal government
for investment in the region. 2) Changing the agrarian
structure of the humid coastal zone of the northeast, aimed
at a more intensive utilization of the land which would increase productivity of the sugar economy and allow the establishment of family units specialized in staple food
production (and thus diminish the region's dependence on
food imported from the south). 3) Progressive change in the
economy of the semiarid zones, by increasing productivity and
bringing it more into line with ecological conditions. 4)
Shifting the agricultural frontier, so as to integrate the
humid lands of southern Bahia and of Maranhão into the economy of the region and open up the latter through road construction, which would also lead to the possibility of
migrants moving into the Amazon region.

The accomplishments of the four SUDENE development
plans in the sixties and seventies fell substantially below
these original goals. Little was accomplished in changing
the region's agrarian structure. Great reliance was placed
on the tax incentive scheme (articles 34/18 programs) to
increase private investment in the northeast, and much investment in industry took place in the second half of the
sixties and early seventies. However, most of the firms
located in the cities of Salvador and Recife and their
activities generated relatively little employment.[16] Thus
the industrialization process of the northeast did little
to solve the region's endemic underemployment problems.

Some critics have faulted SUDENE's planning with a lack
of precise schemes to deal with the region's problems. For
example, general preoccupation with employment and income

distribution have never been tied to specific programs and policy instruments. The Third Plan of SUDENE specifically admits to a general deficiency in the organization's administrative apparatus.[17]

Returning to the national level, the government's economic plans in the 1960s were still mainly concerned with sectoral programs and general problems of stabilization. They referred to regional problems explicitly as worthy of national concern, but did not develop specific projects. In the late sixties some institutional changes with respect to regional policy-making took place. The creation of the Ministry of the Interior centralized federal decision-making. Such regional agencies as SUDENE, SUDAM (for the Amazon region), the Banco do Nordeste, etc., were made subject to its control. It was hoped that this institutional change would help in the formulation of more coherent regional policies.

The calamitous northeastern drought of 1970 spurred the government into renewed efforts towards a more active explicit regional policy. The importance of SUDENE was downgraded somewhat as a result of that institution's late and inadequate response to the drought emergency, which seemed to dramatize many of its weaknesses as a regional development agency.[18] The direct action of the government in the early seventies consisted of a three-pronged program - the National Integration Program (PIN), the modernization program for agriculture (PROTERRA) and the special development program for the São Francisco River area (PROVALE). PIN sought a solution to the northeastern problem through the development of the Amazon region. It was hoped that the building of the Transamazon road system, the construction of communities along it, the modernizing of the port facilities along the Amazon river, would create conditions to effectively absorb the excess northeastern population. PROTERRA was supposed to inject resources into the rural sector to both redistribute land and increase agricultural productivity in the northeast, while PROVALE was supposed to accelerate the agricultural development of the empty areas around the São Francisco river. Few of these objectives were accomplished by the mid-seventies.

The National Development Plan spanning 1975 to 1979 stated that regional problems, especially of the northeast, would be tackled by a program of federal investments and private investments induced by the fiscal incentive system. Emphasis was also given to the creation of various "development poles" for backward regions - e.g., the petrochemical pole in Bahia, a fertilizer pole, a metal and electrical machinery complex, and the strengthening of the more traditional industries (like textiles, shoes, etc.).

Federal funds were supposed to be allocated for the growth and modernization of the northeast's agricultural sector - the plan specifically mentions the projects to industrialize cotton, manioc, regional fruits, and other goods; to irrigate new areas; to develop the cattle sector, etc. These projects aimed at both modernizing northeastern agriculture and diversifying it.

THE REGIONAL DIMENSION OF SECTORAL PROGRAMS

Explicit regional programs have made up a relatively small proportion of the federal government's investment plans (they were always below 10 percent). A recent study has shown that the combined sectoral and regional expenditure programs of the federal government do not have much of a redistributive impact.[18] The estimates show that the southeast receives more from the government than its population share, yet slightly less than its share in the national income, while the northeast receives substantially less than its population share, yet slightly more than its share of the national income. However, one cannot even say that the total federal government program was even slightly redistributive. The study considered only planned investment programs and it is likely that, given the more developed nature of the southeastern economy, the multiplier repercussions of investment expenditures favor the latter more than the northeast. That is, one can expect substantial leakages from the less developed to the more developed regions as these investment programs make themselves felt. It may thus be likely that if we could measure the total impact of government programs, the secondary repercussions would swamp the initial slight degree of regional redistribution.

ENDNOTES

1. Werner Baer and Pedro Pinchas Geiger, "Industrialização, Urbanização e a Persistência das Desigualdades Regionais do Brasil," *Revista Brasileira de Geografia,* Ano 38, No. 2, Abril/Junho 1976, pp. 3-99.
2. J. R. Hicks, *Essays in World Economics* (Oxford: At the Clarendon Press, 1959) p. 163; other well-known analyses of regional inequalities can be found in: Gunnar Myrdal, *Economic Theory and Under-Developed Regions* (London: Gerald Duckworth Co., Ltd., 1957); A. O. Hirschman, *The Strategy of Economic Development* (New Haven, Conn.: Yale University Press, 1958), p. 183; François Perroux, "Note Sur La Notion de 'Pole de Croissance'," *Économie Appliquée,* Tome VIII, Numeros 1-2 (Janvier-Juin, 1955), pp. 307-20.
3. Hicks, op. cit., p. 163.
4. Conselho de Desenvolvimento do Nordeste, *A Policy for the Economic Development of the Northeast,* 1959. This document was written by Celso Furtado and led to the creation of the Superintendency for the Development of the Northeast (SUDENE). A similar analysis had also been undertaken somewhat earlier by the research section of the Banco do Nordeste. - The analysis in this section also appeared in part in the author's previous book: *Industrialization and Econonomic Development in Brazil,* (Homewood, Illinois: Richard D. Irwin, Inc., 1965), pp. 174-183.
5. Conselho de Desenvolvimento do Nordeste, op. cit., p. 18.
6. Ibid., p. 19.
7. Although prices of exports and imports are measured in dollars and prices of internally traded commodities in cruzeiros, the ratios are significant, since we are interested in relative changes.
8. Conselho de Desenvolvimento do Nordeste, op. cit., p. 24.
9. Ibid., p. 26.
10. Roberto Cavalcanti de Albuquerque and Clovis de Vasconcelos Cavalcanti, *Desenvolvimento Regional no Brasil* (Brasília: IPEA, Série Estudos Para o Planejamento, 16, 1976), p. 49.
11. There exist no data on the geographical distribution of federal government expenditures. Some special estimates were made for the northeast. See: Roberto Cavalcanti de Albuquerque and Clovis de Vaconcelos Cavalcanti, op. cit., p. 122.
12. The best and most thorough analysis of these incentives can be found in: David E. Goodman and Roberto Cavalcanti de Albuquerque, *Incentivos a Industrialização do Nordeste* (Rio de Janeiro: IPEA, Coleção Relatórios de Pesquisas, No. 20, 1974).

13. Roberto Cavalcanti de Albuquerque and Clovis de Vasconcelos Cavalcanti, op. cit., pp. 125-6.

14. For an historical analysis of Brazil's policies with regard to the northeast, see: Roberto Cavalcanti de Albuquerque and Clovis de Vasconcelos Cavalcanti, op. cit., pp. 50-62; Alberto O. Hirschman, *Journeys Toward Progress: Studies of Economic Policy-Making in Latin America* (New York: The Twentieth Century Fund, 1963) chapter 1, "Brazil's Northeast," pp. 11-92.

15. Dalia Maimon, Werner Baer and Pedro P. Geiger, "O Impacto Regional Das Politicas Economicas no Brasil," *Revista Brasileira de Geografia*, Ano 39, #3, Jul./Set. 1977.

16. Roberto Cavalcanti de Albuquerque and Clovis de Vasconcelos Cavalcanti, op. cit., p. 78; David E. Goodman and Roberto Cavalcanti de Albuquerque, op. cit., chapters VIII and IX.

17. Roberto Cavalcanti de Albuquerque and Clovic de Vasconcelos Cavalcanti, op. cit., pp. 74-5.

18. Maimon, Baer and Geiger, op. cit.

10

THE PERFORMANCE OF THE AGRICULTURAL SECTOR

From the early post-World War II years until the 1960s the agricultural sector was neglected by policy-makers and some of the measures to promote industrialization even discriminated against it. Since the mid-sixties, however, agricultural modernization has been one of the major goals of government planners, and considerable efforts were made to transfer resources into that sector and to make some institutional changes designed to increase productivity. In this chapter we shall first examine the performance of the sector since World War II. We shall then briefly review the changes in economic policies vis-a-vis agriculture since the early fifties.[1]

GROWTH OF AGRICULTURAL OUTPUT

Despite the long neglect of the agricultural sector, the growth rate of its output seems to have been adequate throughout most of the post-World War II period (see Table 52(a)), i.e., the average yearly growth rate of agricultural production was mostly ahead of the population growth rate (which stood at 3 and 2.7 percent per year in the fifties and sixties respectively). It is also clear from Table 52(a) that agriculture was never the leading sector since the forties; industrial growth was usually substantially greater (often at double the rate as that of agriculture).

An examination of some individual agricultural products (Table 52(b)) reveals substantial variations of growth rates among products and also for specific products in different periods of time. Some of the major export products (coffee, cocoa) experienced slow rates of growth in the years 1948/52 to 1962/66, and the coffee growth continued to

TABLE 52

Growth of Agricultural Output

(a) Average Yearly Growth Rates of Real Output by Sectors

Period	Agriculture Total	Crops	Livestock	Industry	Real GDP
1947-50	4.3	4.4	6.2	11.0	6.8
1951-54	4.5	3.0	9.4	7.2	6.8
1955-58	4.2	5.6	1.5	9.9	6.5
1959-62	5.8	5.7	4.9	10.0	7.7
1963-66	3.2	3.0	4.7	3.1	3.1
1967-70	4.7	5.1	2.3	10.1	8.2
1970-76	5.9	5.5.	6.3	14.0	12.2

Source: Fundaçao Getulio Vargas, *Conjuntura Economica.*

(b) Yearly Growth Rates of Some Individual Products

	1948-52/1962/66	1962-66/1966-70	1970/1976
Coffee	2.2	7.1	1.4
Cocoa	1.3	1.3	4.3
Sugar	4.6	3.7	3.8
Beans	3.2	4.7	-1.9
Rice	5.2	2.2	7.6
Soybeans	16.5	31.8	41.0
Corn	3.8	6.5	5.2
Milk	6.0	4.6	6.3
Beef	1.3	5.3	7.1
Pork	3.2	5.3	8.9

Source: Ruy Miller Paiva, Salomão Schattan and Claus F. R.
De Freitas, *Setor Agrícola do Brasil,* (São Paulo:
Secretaría de Agricultura, 1973) p. 32; IBGE,
Anuário Estatístico do Brasil, various issues.

(c) Regional Growth Rates of Agricultural Output and
Regional Shares

Regions	Growth rates 1947-65	1965-71	Regional shares 1947-49	1963-65	1970
North	3.8	-	2	2	2.4
Northeast	4.7	3.2	15	16	20.9
Southeast	3.2		31	24	
South	4.8	5.9	48	50	69.6
Center-West	8.4		4	8	7.1
Brazil	4.6	4.5	100	100	100.0

Source: Farm Growth in Brazil, (Columbus, Ohio: The Ohio State
University, June 1975),pp. 3-9; José R. Mendonça de
Barros, Affonso C. Pastore, and Juarez A. B. Rizzieri,
"A Evolução Recente da Agricultural Brasileira," in
Estudos Sobre a Modernização da Agricultura Brasileira,
edited by José R. Mendonça de Barros and Douglas H.
Graham, (Sao Paulo: IPE, 1977) pp. 115-7.

be slow in the seventies. This says little, of course, about the impact of the sectors, since international prices often more than compensate for small production increases. The spectacular growth of soybeans is explained partially by the small base from which the product started, but in the 1970s the output increase was large even in absolute terms (by the mid-1970s Brazil had become the world's third largest soybean producer and second largest exporter). The growth of staple products has been mixed: meat products, milk and corn grew at rates substantially higher than the population in the 1960s and 1970s, while the performance of beans was poor in most years.

It was also noteworthy that there was no accentuated difference in the growth rate of agricultural output between various regions.[2] One observes in Table 52(c) that in the 1947-65 period the yearly growth rate of northeastern agriculture was superior to that of the southeast and about the same as that of the south. The high rates for the center-west reflect the opening of vast new productive regions in the states of Mato Grosso and Goias.

The adequacy of Brazil's agricultural sector in supplying the population can also be gauged from the behavior of food prices relative to changes in the general price level and the prices of non-agricultural products. This can be observed in Table 53. It will be noted that in the cost of living data, food prices were ahead of the general price level only in the 1958-62 period, while throughout most of the 1960s they were actually lagging behind. The wholesale price changes also show no pronounced leading influence in agricultural prices.[3]

SOURCES OF AGRICULTURAL GROWTH

Most of Brazil's agricultural growth occurred on the extensive margin, that is, more land was brought under cultivation. The number of farms increased by over 60 percent in the fifties and by almost 50 percent in the sixties. In 1950 there existed a little over 2 million farms and by 1970 this had grown to almost 5 million.[4] The amount of land under cultivation in the 1950-70 period grew by 124 percent. In 1950, 6.5 percent of the land belonging to agricultural establishments was under cultivation; by 1970 this percentage had grown to 11.6 percent.[5]

Productivity increase contributed relatively little to the growth of Brazilian agriculture. This is clear from the

TABLE 53
Price Changes in Agriculture and Other Sectors
(Average Yearly Percentage Price Increases)

(a) Cost of Living (Rio de Janeiro)

Period	Total	Food	Clothing	Housing	Public Services
1948-50	6.7	6.8	4.3	10.7	10.5
1950-54	16.5	18.1	12.0	19.1	11.3
1954-58	18.3	19.4	15.4	16.8	27.7
1958-62	38.3	43.0	40.7	23.1	35.0
1962-66	67.4	61.9	65.6	69.1	89.8
1966-70	24.4	21.0	22.9	33.6	26.0
1971-76	24.7	26.4	15.2	16.2	25.1

(b) Wholesale Prices

Period	Products for Domestic Use				Aggregate Supply		
	Total	Raw Mats.	Food	Construc-tion Mats.	Total	Agri-culture	Industrial Products
1948-50	3.4	16.9	1.0	12.3	18.1	17.7	4.1
1950-54	18.6	19.1	19.8	18.0	19.0	19.3	18.3
1954-58	17.6	12.1	16.3	20.0	14.2	11.2	18.0
1958-62	41.2	41.0	44.2	33.1	40.0	41.4	38.7
1962-66	63.0	63.1	62.8	66.5	63.5	62.4	65.0
1966-70	21.9	20.5	22.0	26.3	22.7	23.0	23.3
1970-76	25.3	24.4	28.0	25.6	25.9	29.8	23.9

Source: Ruy Miller Paiva et al, op. cit., pp. 37-8; and *Conjuntura Economica.*

data in Table 54. From the forties to the seventies there has been no change (and even some retrogression) in the productivity (as measured by output per hectare) of such staple products as rice, beans and manioc; among export products, cotton was stagnant, cocoa was stagnant until the mid-seventies, while only coffee and sugar showed some notable productivity increases.

A comparison of productivity between Brazil as a whole and the state of São Paulo (Table 54(a) and (b)) is quite instructive. It will be noted that productivity in São Paulo's cotton sector was not only superior to that of the country, but it also increased substantially, while that of the country as a whole stagnated. São Paulo's rice produc-

TABLE 54
Agricultural Productivity
(Kilograms per Hectare)

(a) Brazil	1947-49	1961-63	1964-66	1968-70	1972-74	1974-76
Cotton	442	554	482	490	526	446
Peanuts	1,004	1,347	1,286	1,286	1,196	1,302
Rice	1,552	1,634	1,536	1,464	1,533	1,461
Cocoa	450	312	341	378	436	528
Coffee	411	415	771	811	1,192	1,009
Sugar cane	38,333	42,773	44,841	45,551	43,806	47,785
Beans	685	659	656	634	593	566
Manioc	13,347	13,404	14,120	14,662	13,168	12,278
Corn	1,256	1,311	1,283	1,365	1,462	1,650
Wheat	789	658	833	945	1,110	892

(b) São Paulo State					1970-72
Cotton	576	985	1,147	1,550	1,077
Peanuts	948	1,160	1,257	1,126	1,308
Rice	1,357	1,126	865	874	1,054
Coffee	943	903	1,036	1,118	1,324
Sugar cane	47,117	48,747	52,294	47,597	55,131
Beans	670	377	474	432	505
Manioc	9,481	16,875	17,351	17,533	17,136
Corn	1,262	1,620	1,565	1,602	1,846

Sources: Ruy Miller Paiva, et al, op. cit., pp. 64-5; IBGE, *Anuario Estatistico*.

tivity lagged behind the national average; this crop progressed much more in the state of Rio Grande do Sul. In sugar cane São Paulo's absolute productivity was greater than the national average, but its rate of growth was less than the latter. The state's performance in staples was mixed – beans performing worse than the national average, while manioc and corn progressed more.

The mediocre productivity performance of Brazil's agriculture could be attributed, in part, to the relative slowness in increasing the use of modern inputs. It will be noted in Table 55 that the use of fertilizer per hectare in the mid-sixties was extremely low by international standards. It increased in the following ten years, but even in the mid-1970s it had not yet reached the standards of advanced countries in the 1960s. On a regional level one observes an enormous difference of fertilizer use between the northeast,

TABLE 55
Agriculture Inputs

(a) Use of Fertilizer, (Kg./ha) - Brazil

1960	11.5
1964	8.3
1968	17.9
1970	27.8
1975	44.6

(b) Use of Fertilizer - Regional and International Comparisons (kg./ha)

Brazil (1970)	27.8
Northeast	5.6
Southeast	34.4
South	46.6
São Paulo	72.8
U. S. (1964)	54.6
France (1966)	167.1
Taiwan (1967)	282.7
Italy (1967)	73.8

(c) Hectares of Cultivated Land per Tractor

Brazil 1960	430
1965	344
1970	218
1975	137
São Paulo (1970)	90

Russia (1967)	139
U. S. (1967)	27
France (1966)	19
W. Germany (1967)	36
Italy (1967)	30
Norway (1967)	11

Source: Ruy Miller Paiva, op. cit., p. 77; *Indice do Brasil*, 1977-78, (Rio de Janeiro: Banco Denasa de Investimento S. A., 1977), p. 341.

the southeast, the south and the state of São Paulo. The greater use of modern inputs in a state like São Paulo is related to a longer tradition of the state government in promoting agricultural research and encouraging greater use of fertilizer, chemicals and improved seeds.[6]

Although the mechanization of Brazilian agriculture grew substantially in the 1960s, it was still far behind most advanced countries' standards by the mid-seventies, when measured in terms of hectares of cultivated land per tractor (Table 55(c)). São Paulo had made the greatest advances in agricultural mechanization.

Increased mechanization, however, leads to a diminished capacity of agriculture to absorb labor. This, in turn, leads to a continued or even accelerated rate of rural-urban migration.

DISTRIBUTION OF LAND

As can be observed in Table 56, the concentration of
rural holdings is very large in Brazil and there has been
little change over the period 1950 to 1970. Since the concept for holdings used is not property, but establishment,
the table understates the degree of inequality of land
holdings. In considering the high degree of concentration
of rural holdings one should also take into account that
there is a great amount of variation in the quality of land
in a country as large as Brazil. Thus, many large agricultural establishments often contain a high proportion of poor
land which is used for extensive cattle raising.

TABLE 56
Size Distribution of Rural Properties
by Number of Establishments and Total Area
(percentage distribution)

Size of Properties (hectares	Number of Establishments			Area		
	1950	1960	1970	1950	1960	1970
Less than 10	34.0	44.7	51.2	1.3	2.4	3.1
10 - 100	50.9	44.6	39.3	15.3	19.0	20.4
100 - 1,000	12.9	9.4	8.4	32.5	34.4	37.0
1,000 - 10,000	1.5	0.9	0.7	31.5	28.6	27.2
10,000 - 100,000	0.7	0.4	0.1	19.4	15.6	12.3
No declaration	-	-	0.3	-	-	-
Total	100.0	100.0	100.0	100.0	100.0	100.0

Source: Calculated from IBGE, *Anuário Estatístico,* 1976,
p. 161.

Calculations of Gini coefficients for concentration in
land distribution for the census years 1950, 1960 and 1970
have shown these to have hardly changed – hovering around
0.84. This compares with coefficients of 0.72 in the U. S.
in 1959, 0.57 in Canada in 1961, 0.51 in India in 1960 and
0.71 in the U. K. in 1960.[7] Gini coefficients for different
regions in Brazil show that ownership concentration is larger
in the north, northeast and center-west and smallest in the
south. This reflects both the great variety of socio-
economic conditions and the different types of agricultural
activities found in the different regions of Brazil – ranging
from small family farms of descendents of European immigrants

in southern Brazil, to the cooperatives of Japanese-
Brazilians in Sao Paulo and Parana, to the giant ranches of
Mato Grosso, and to the traditional sugar estates in north-
eastern Brazil.[8]

RURAL POVERTY

One of the leading authorities on Brazilian agriculture
has stated that the increase of the country's agricultural
product at the extensive margin without a drastic increase
of relative food prices has been possible, in part, due to
the adequacy of the rural labor supply at relatively low
wages.[9] This has meant that the traditional conditions of
poverty to be found in rural Brazil did not change over
the years. In 1960 the estimated income per worker in agriculture was Cr$121 (in 1970 Cr$ prices), as compared to
Cr$263 for the urban workers; by 1970 the rural workers' in-
come had grown only by 14.2 percent to Cr$138, while that
of the urban worker had grown by 43.4 percent by Cr$378[10].
A study has shown that, with the exception of São Paulo, in
the early 1970s the average rural worker's salary was below
the legal minimum wage. Ruy Miller Paiva has observed that
these income levels "...do not make it possible to have
satisfactory welfare conditions in agriculture."[11] Some
social surveys have shown that in 1970 only 2.5 percent of
Brazil's rural homes had running water, that only 25 percent
had adequate sanitary installations and that only 5 percent
had access to gas.[12]

Poverty extends beyond rural workers' earnings. We
have seen that a large proportion of rural establishments
are of less than 10 hectares (increasing from 34 percent of
total establishments in 1950 to 51.2 percent in 1970).
Various studies have shown that the income generated by such
properties is extremely small and in many cases the income
produced was calculated as being even negative.[13]

AGRICULTURAL POLICIES

Throughout the 1950s agricultural policies were subordinate to the major goal of industrialization. According
to Nicholls "...the principal objective of public policy
during that decade had been the exploitation of its exportable surplus (coffee, cotton and cocoa) to finance industrial development through an elaborate system of multiple-
exchange rates which discriminated against the traditional
exports while favoring imports of machinery and producer

goods."[14] This was partially offset by occasional favorable exchange rates granted for the importation of some agricultural inputs (like fertilizers) going to the major export crops. Attempts were also made to develop agricultural extension services, but by 1960 only 11.5 percent of the country's municipalities were reached by them (excluding the state of São Paulo).

The extensive growth of Brazil's agricultural output in the 1950s could not have taken place without the government's road construction program. In the period 1952–60 the federal highway system increased from 12.3 to 32.4 thousand kilometers and the state highway system from 51 to 75.9 thousand kilometers. Although this was "...still grossly inadequate for so vast a nation, the expansion in the federal and state highway networks was accompanied during the 1950s by a fourfold increase in the volume of commodities transported by truck..."[15]

A minimum price guaranty program was used in the 1950s, but it was not very effective since "...with prices rising at rates in excess of 25 percent per year, the floor price set for agricultural commodities was unrealistically low by the time the farmer sold his crops. The rural credit program was limited almost entirely to the financing of crop marketing, not for fixed investment or production loans. Much of the credit, it appears, went to middlemen to finance the movement of goods to market, or at times to withhold goods from the market pending further rises in prices."[16]

After 1964 government policies were more supportive of the agricultural sector than previously. Much emphasis was placed on the market mechanism to stimulate production. Price controls on many products were gradually removed (on beans, milk, beef, and other products). For a number of years the government relied on a minimum price program as an incentive to agricultural production. The high cost and inflationary impact of this program, however, led to increased reliance on non-recourse financing as a substitute to the outright purchase of crops. This approach "...left to the farmer to withhold his crops from the market and to arrange for storage and for sales when the market seemed most profitable..."[17]

In the sixties and seventies one of the major policy instruments to stimulate agriculture was the use of credit. From 1960 to the mid-1970s the real value of new agricultural loans increased more than sixfold. The ratio of agricultural credit as a proportion to total credit rose from 11 percent in 1960 to almost 25 percent in the mid-1970s. Most of the credit to agriculture originates with the Banco do Brasil, but various measures have also been taken to induce private banks to increase their loans to that sector. Most agricultural loans have been made on a concessional basis, that is the interest charged has usually been substantially below the rate of inflation. For instance, in the mid-seventies loans for agricultural inputs carried interest rates of 7 percent, while the rate of inflation was higher than 35 percent. This means that a substantial amount of income was transferred to the agricultural sector.[18]

This transfer has been of mixed benefit to the rural sector. While it has helped a substantial increase in mechanization in certain areas and improved farming techniques, the distribution of the subsidy through negative interest credit has been quite lopsided, i.e., the larger farmers have usually been the greatest beneficiaries of this credit. Some studies have also shown that not all rural subsidized credit has been wisely used. It has often been indirectly used to acquire more land or even consumption goods (when rural credit increases the sale of automobiles in the interior usually rises considerably).[19]

It is now generally admitted that various types of rural subsidy programs have had only a limited impact. For instance, in analyzing the fertilizer subsidy program, Syvrud comes to the conclusion that it "...met with a small measure of success as Brazilian farmers responded with increased use of fertilizer. But the methods used to implement the program had serious shortcomings. Since it was not supervised or tied to any meaningful standards which would limit diversion of the funds to other uses, it benefitted only about 5 percent of Brazilian farmers, probably the more technologically advanced producers. The great majority of farmers were not touched by the program. As with the minimum price and rural credit programs, the effectiveness of an input subsidy program as an instrument for improving farm productivity and output was limited to the modern segments of agriculture which respond to market incentives. For the majority of Brazilian farmers market incentives are not sufficient; they must be supplemented with rural extension services, education, research and, in some cases, changes in the land tenure system."[20]

Although the rural credit subsidy system, the extensive road construction program, and some investment in marketing has helped to both increase and diversify Brazil's agricultural production, there seems to be a need for more basic institutional reforms to increase the productivity of the sector and to increase equity in the distribution of the product. Effective land reform in some of the more backward regions has not been instituted[21] and not enough has been done to date to change the quality of the rural credit and extension service system.

In 1973 the government decided that a breakthrough in productivity could be achieved by massive investment in research. To that end the Empresa Brasileira de Pesquisa Agropecuaria (EMBRAPA) was created.[22] It remains to be seen at this writing if the activities of this new institution can effect the type of structural changes which are needed in order to modernize the whole agricultural system.

ENDNOTES

1. For the reader interested in more detailed information on Brazil's agriculture than is provided in this chapter, the following sources are recommended: G. Edward Schuh, *The Agricultural Development of Brazil* (New York: Praeger Publishers, 1970); *Farm Growth in Brazil,* (Columbus, Ohio: The Ohio State University, Department of Agricultural Economics, June 1975); Claudio Roberto Contador (editor), *Tecnologia e Desenvolvimento Agricola* (Rio de Janeiro: IPEA/INPES, Serio Monografica, 1975).

2. José Roberto Mendoca de Barros, Affonso Celso Pastore, and Juarez A. Baldini Rizzieri, "A Evolução Recente da Agricultura Brasileira," in José R. Mendonça de Barros and Douglas H. Graham (editors), *Estudos Sobre a Modernização da Agricultura Brasileira,* (São Paulo: Serie IPE Monografias, 1977) pp. 107–38.

3. Ruy Miller Paiva, Salomão Schattan, and Claus R. T. De Freitas, *Setor Agricola do Brasil: Comportamento Economico, Problemas e Possibilidades* (São Paulo: Secretaria da Agricultura, 1973), pp. 37–43.

4. Richard Meyer, "Agricultural Policies and Growth, 1947–1974," in *Farm Growth in Brazil* (Columbus, Ohio: The Ohio State University, Department of Agricultural Economics, 1975), pp. 3–9.

5. Calculated from data in IBGE, *Anuario Estatistico, 1966.*

6. Richard Meyer, op. cit., pp. 3–14; Schuh, op. cit., chapter 5; Ruy Miller Paiva, et al, op. cit., chapter 4.

7. Rodolfo Hoffmann e José F. Graziano Da Silva, "A Estrutura Agraria Brasileira," in Claudio Contador (editor) op. cit., pp. 248–51. In other Latin American countries the coefficients stood at 0.84 in Colombia in 1960, 0.93 in Venezuela in 1961 and 0.95 in Mexico in 1960.

8. On a macro-regional basis the highest Gini coefficient was found in the northeast in 1970. It stood at 0.87. For the center-west it stood at 0.86 and for the south at 0.75. On a state basis, the highest concentration was in Mato Grosso (0.93) and the lowest in Espirito Santo (0.61). Results for some other states are: Ceara - 0.79; Pernambuco - 0.84; Bahia - 0.80; São Paulo - 0.78; Minas Gerais - 0.75; Parana - 0.71; Rio Grande do Sul - 0.76. Ibid., p. 251.

9. G. Edward Schuh, "A Modernizaçao Da Agricultura Brasileira; Uma Interpretaçao," in Claudio Contador, op. cit., p. 12.

10. Richard Meyer, op. cit., pp. 21–22.

11. Ruy Miller Paiva, "Os Baixos Niveis De Renda e de Salarios Na Agricultura Brasileira," in Claudio Contador, op. cit., pp. 105–9.

12. Ibid.
13. Ibid., pp. 201-2.
14. William H. Nicholls, "The Brazilian Agricultural Economy: Recent Performance and Policy," in Riordan Roett (editor), *Brazil in the Sixties* (Nashville, Tennessee: Vanderbilt University Press, 1972), p. 151.
15. Ibid., p. 156.
16. Donald E. Syvrud, *Foundations of Brazilian Economic Growth* (Stanford, California: Hoover Institution Press, 1974) p. 219.
17. Ibid., p. 231.
18. Ibid., pp. 231-5; Richard Meyer, op. cit., pp. 10/5 - 10/11.
19. Richard Meyer, op. cit., pp. 10/38 - 10/40.
20. Syvrud, op. cit., p. 236.
21. Rodolfo Hoffmann and Jose F. Graziano Da Silva, "A Estrutura Agraria Brasileira," in Claudio R. Contador (editor) op. cit., p. 248.
22. José Pastore e Eliseu R. A. Alves, "A Reforma do Sistema Brasileiro de Pesquisa Agricola," in Claudio R. Contador (editor), op. cit., pp. 111-129.

Bibliography

Alden, Dauriel, "The Population of Brazil in the Late Eighteenth Century: A Preliminary Study," *The Hispanic American Historical Review.* 43, May 1963, pp. 173-205.

Almeida, Jose, *Industrializaçao e Emprego no Brasil.* (Rio de Janeiro; IPEA, Colaçao Relatorio de Pesquisa, No. 24, 1974).

Bacha, Edmar L., *Os Mitos de Uma Decada: Ensaios de Economia Brasileira.* Rio de Janeiro: Ed. Paz e Terra, 1976).

Bacha, Edmar L., "Issues and Evidence on Recent Brazilian Economic Growth," *World Development,* January-February 1977.

Baer, Werner, *Industrialization and Economic Development in Brazil.* (Homewood, Illinois: Richard D. Irwin, Inc., 1965).

Baer, Werner, *The Development of the Brazilian Steel Industry.* (Nashville, Tennessee: Vanderbilt University Press, 1969).

Baer, Werner, "Import Substitution in Latin America," *Latin American Research Review,* Spring 1972.

Baer, Werner, "The Inflation Controversy in Latin America," *Latin American Research Review,* Spring 1967.

Baer, Werner, "Furtado on Development: A Review Essay," *The Journal of Developing Areas,* January 1969.

Baer, Werner, "Furtado Revisited," *Luso-Brazilian Review,* Summer 1974.

Baer, Werner, I. Kerstenetzky and Mario H. Simonsen, "Transportation and Inflation: A Study of Irrational Policy-Making in Brazil," *Economic Development and Cultural Change,* June 1965.

Baer, Werner, and Mario H. Simonsen, "Profit Illusion and Policy-Making in an Inflationary Economy," *Oxford Economic Papers,* July 1965.

Baer, Werner, "The Brazilian Economic Miracle: The Issues and the Literature," *Bulletin of the Society for Latin American Studies,* No. 24, March 1976.

Baer, Werner, and Pedro P. Geiger, "Industrializacao, Urban-icacao e a Persistencia das Desigualdades Regionais do Brasil," *Revista Brasileira de Geografia*, Ano 38, No. 2, 1976.

Baer, Werner, Pedro Geiger and Paulo Haddad (editors), *Dimensões Do Desenbolvimento Brasileiro* (Rio de Janeiro: Editõra Campus, 1978.)

Baklanoff, Eric N., *New Perspectives of Brazil*. (Nashville, Tennessee: Vanderbilt University Press, 1966.)

Baklanoff, Eric. N., *The Shaping of Modern Brazil*. (Baton Rouge: Louisiana State University Press, 1969.)

Bergsman, Joel, *Brazil: Industrialization and Trade Policies*. (London: Oxford University Press, 1970.)

Buescu, Mircea, and Vincente Tapajos, *Historia Do Desenvolvimento Economico do Brasil*. (Rio de Janeiro: A Casa do Livro, Ltda., 1969.)

Carvalho, Getulio, *Petrobras: Do Monopolio aos Contratos de Risco*. (Rio de Janeiro: Forense-Universitaria, 1976.)

Castro, Claudio M., *Investimento em Educação no Brasil: Um Estudo Socio-Economico de Duas Comunidades Industriais*. (Rio de Janeiro: IPEA/INPES, Serie Monografica, No. 12, 1974.)

Castro, Claudio M., and Alberto de Mello e Souza, *Mao-De-Obra Industrial No Brasil: Mobilidade, Treinamento e Produtividade*. (Rio de Janeiro: IPEA/INPES, Relatorio de Pesquisa No. 25, 1974.)

Cavalcanti, Clovis de Vasconcelos, "Uma Avaliação das Estimativas de Renda e Produto do Brasil," *Pesquisa e Planejamento Economico*, Dezembro de 1972.

Cavalcanti, Roberto de Albuquerque and Clovis V. Cavalcanti, *Desenvolvimento Regional no Brasil*. (Brasilia: IPEA, Serie Estudos Para o Planejamento, 16, 1976.)

Chacel, Julian M., Mario H. Simonsen, and Arnoldo Wald, *A Correção Monetaria*. (Rio de Janeiro: APEC Editora S.A., 1970.)

Conceicao Tavares, Maria da, *Da Substituicao de Importaçoes ao Capitalismo Financeiro* (Rio de Janeiro: Zahar Editora, 1972.)

Conselho Federal de Comercio Exterior, *Dez Anos de Atividades.* (Rio de Janeiro: 1944.)

Contador, Claudio Roberto (editor) *Tecnologia e Desenvolvimento Agricola.* (Rio de Janeiro: IPEA/INPES, Serie Monografica No. 17, 1975.)

Contador, Claudio Roberto, *Os Investidores Institucionais no Brasil.* (Rio de Janeiro: IBMEC, 1975.)

Costa, Margaret H., "Atividade Empresarial dos Governos Federal e Estaduais," *Conjuntura Economica,* Junho de 1973.

Da Costa, Jorge Gustavo, *Planejamento Governamental: A Experiencia Brasileira.* (Rio de Janeiro: Fundacao Getulio Vargas, 1971.)

De Oliveira, Francisco, "A Economia Brasileira: Critica a Razao Dualista," *Estudos CEBRAP,* Outubro 1972.

Dean, Warren, *The Industrialization of Sao Paulo, 1880-1945.* (Austin, Texas: University of Texas Press, 1969.)

De Almeida, Wanderly J. M., and Maria da Conceição Silva, *Dinamica do Setor Servicos no Brasil - Emprego e Produto.* (Rio de Janeiro: IPEA/INPES, Coleção Relatorio de Pesquisa No. 18, 1973.)

De Almeida, Wanderly J.M., *Servicos e Desenvolvimento Economico no Brasil: Aspectos Setoriais e Suas Implicacoes.* (Rio de Janeiro: IPEA/INPES, Coleção Relatorio de Pesquisa, No. 23, 1974.)

Delfim Netto, A., *O Problema do Cafe no Brasil.* (São Paulo: Universidade de São Paulo, 1959.)

Dias Carneiro, Dionisio, "Politica de Controle de Precos Industriais," in *Aspectos da Participacao do Governo na Economia,* (Rio de Janeiro: IPEA/INPES, Serie Monografica No. 26, 1976.)

Dias Carneiro, Dionisio (editor), *Brasil: Dilemas Da Politica Econômica.* (Rio de Janeiro: Editora Campus, 1977.)

Ellis, Howard S. (editor), *The Economy of Brazil*. Berkeley and Los Angeles: The University of California Press, 1969.)

Faoro, Raymundo, *Os Donos do Poder: Formação do Patronato Politico Brasileiro*. (São Paulo: Editora Globo/Editora da Universidade de São Paulo, 1975.)

Farm Growth in Brazil. (Columbus, Ohio: The Ohio State University, Department of Agricultural Economics, June 1975.)

Fishlow, Albert, "Brazilian Size Distribution of Income," *American Economic Review*, May 1972.

Fishlow, Albert, "Origins and Consequences of Import Substitution in Brazil," in *International Economics and Development*, edited by Luis Eugenio Di Marco. (New York: Academic Press, 1972.)

Fundação Getulio Vargas, *A Missão Cooke no Brasil*. (Rio de Janeiro, 1949.)

Fundação Getulio Vargas, *O Setor Publico Federal Descentralizado*. (Rio de Janeiro, 1967.)

Fundação IBGE, *Anuário Estatistico* (yearly publication).

Fundação IBGE, *Censuses*.

Fundação IBGE, *Matriz de Relações Interindustriais, Brasil 1970* (Rio de Janeiro, 1976.)

Fundaçao IBGE, *Pesquisa Nacional Por Amostra de Domicilios* (Rio de Janeiro, 1972, 1973.)

Furtado, Celso, *Formação Economica do Brasil*. (São Paulo: Companhia Editora Nacional Décima Primeira Edição, 1972.)

Furtado, Celso, *Analise do Modelo Brasileiro*. (Rio de Janeiro: Editora Civilizacao Brasileira, 1972.)

Furtado, Celso, *Desenvolvimento e Subdesenvolvimento*. (Rio de Janeiro: Editora Fundo de Cultura, 1961.)

Glade, William P., *The Latin American Economies: A Study of Their Institutional Evolution*. (New York: American Book-Van Nostrand, 1969.)

Goodman, David E., and Roberto de Albuquerque Cavalcanti, *Incentivos a Industrialização e Desenvolvimento do Nordeste.* (Rio de Janeiro: IPEA/INPÊS, Coleção Relatorios de Pesquisa, No. 20, 1974.)

Gordon, Lincoln, and Engelbert L. Grommers, *United States Manufacturing Investment in Brazil: The Impact of Brazilian Government Policies, 1946-1960.* (Boston: Division of Research, Graduate School of Business Administration, Harvard University, 1962.)

Graham, Douglas H., and Thomas W. Merrick, *Population and Economic Growth in Brazil: An Interpretation of the Long-Term Trend (1800-2000),* mimeographed, 1975.

Haddad, Paulo Roberto, *Contabilidade Social e Economia Regional.* (Rio de Janeiro: Azhar Editores, 1976.)

Haddad, Paulo Roberto, (editor), *Desquilibrios Regionais e Descentralização Industrial.* (Rio de Janeiro: IPEA/INPES, Serie Monografica, No. 16, 1975.)

Hirschman, Albert O., *The Strategy of Economic Development.* (New Haven, Conn.: Yale University Press, 1958.)

Holloway, Thomas H., *The Brazilian Coffee Valorization of 1906: Regional Politics and Economic Dependence.* (Madison, Wisconsin: The State Historical Society of Wisconsin for the Department of History, University of Wisconsin, 1975.)

Hirschman, Albert O., *Journeys Toward Progress: Studies of Economic Policy-Making in Latin America.* New York: The Twentieth Century Fund, 1963.)

Huddle, Donald, "Balanço de Pagamentos e Controle de Cambio no Brasil," *Revista Brasileira de Economia,* Março de 1964 and Junho de 1964.

Huddle, Donald, "Review Article: Essay on the Economy of Brasil," *Economic Development and Cultural Change,* April 1972.

Ianni, Octavio, *Estado e Planejamento Economico no Brasil, 1930-70.* (Rio de Janeiro: Civilização Brasileira, 1971.)

Kafka, A., "The Brazilian Exchange Auction System," *The Review of Economics and Statistics,* August 1956.

Kafka, A., "The Brazilian Stabilization Program," *The Journal of Political Economy*, August 1967, Supplement.

Kahil, Raouf, *Inflation and Economic Development in Brazil, 1946-1963* (Oxford University Press, 1973.)

Katzman, Martin T., "Urbanicação e Concentração Industrial: 1940/70," *Pesquisa e Planejamento Economico*, Dezembro 1974.

Katzman, Martin T., "Regional Development Policy in Brazil: The Role of Growth Poles and Development of Highways in Goias," *Economic Development and Cultural Change*, October 1975.

Katzman, Martin T., *Cities and Frontiers in Brazil*. (Cambridge, Mass.: Harvard University Press, 1977.)

Kershaw, Joseph, "Postwar Brazilian Economic Problems," *The American Economic Review*, June 1948.

King, Kenneth, "Recent Brazilian Monetary Policy." (Belo Horizonte: DEDEPLAR, September 1972, mimeo.)

Lafer, Betty Mindlin (editor), *Planejamento no Brasil*. São Paulo: Editora Perspectiva, Coleção Debates, 1970.)

Langoni, Carlos G., *Distribuição da Renda e Desenvolvimento Economico do Brasil*. (Rio de Janeiro: Editora Expressão e Cultura, 1973.)

Leff, Nathaniel, *The Capital Goods Sector in Brazilian Economic Growth*. (Cambridge, Mass.: Harvard University Press, 1968.)

Leff, Nathaniel, *Economic Policy-Making and Development in Brazil*. (New York: John Wiley & Sons, 1968.)

Leff, Nathaniel, "Export Stagnation and Autarkic Development, *The Quarterly Journal of Economics*, May 1967.

Leff, Nathaniel, "Import Constraints and Development," *Review of Economics and Statistics*, November 1967.

Leff, Nathaniel, "Long-Term Brazilian Economic Development," *The Journal of Economic History*, September 1969.

Lopes, Francisco L., "Subsidios a Formulação de um Modelo de Desenvolvimento e Estagnação no Brasil," *Revista Brasileira de Economia*, Junhe de 1969.

Lopes, Francisco L., "Desigualdade e Crescimento: Um Modelo de Programacao com Aplicacao ao Brasil," *Pesquisa e Planejamento Economico*, Dezembro 1972.

Loeb, G. F., *Industrialization and Balanced Growth: With Special Reference to Brazil*. (Groningen, Netherlands, 1957.)

Luz, Nicia Vilela, *A Luta Pela Industrialização do Brasil*. (São Paulo: Corpo e Alma do Brasil, Difusão European do Livro, 1961.)

Malan, Pedro S., and Regis Bonelli, "The Brazilian Economy in the Seventies: Old and New Developments," *World Development*, January-February 1977.

Malan, Pedro S., R. Bonelli, M. P. Abreu, and J. E. C. Pereira, *Politica Econômica Externa e Industrialização no Brasil (1939-1952)*. (Rio de Janeiro: IPEA, Coleção Relatorio de Pesquisa, No. 36, 1977.)

Maimon, Dalia, Werner Baer and Pedro P. Geiger, "O Impacto Regional Das Politicas Economicas no Brasil," *Revista Brasileira de Geografia*, 1977.

Mello e Souza, Nelson, "O Planejamento Economico no Brasil: Considerações Criticas," *Revista de Administração Publica*, 2. semestre, 1968.

Merrick, Thomas W., "Population, Development, and Planning in Brazil," *Population and Development Review*, June 1976.

Morley, Samuel, "Inflation and Stagnation in Brazil," *Economic Development and Cultural Change*, January 1971.

Morley, Samuel, and Gordon W. Smith. "On the Measurement of Import Substitution," *American Economic Review*, September 1970.

Morley, Samuel, and Gordon W. Smith, "Import Substitution and Foreign Investment in Brazil," *Oxford Economic Papers*, March 1971.

Morley, Samuel, and Gordon W. Smith, "Limited Search and the Technology Choices of Multinational Firms in Brazil," *The Quarterly Journal of Economics*, May 1977.

Morley, Samuel, and Gordon W. Smith, "The Choice of Technology: Multinational Firms in Brazil," *Economic Development and Cultural Change*, January 1977.

Ness, Walter, "Financial Markets Innovation as a Development Strategy: Initial Results from the Brazilian Experience," *Economic Development and Cultural Change*, April 1974.

Neuhaus, Paulo, *Historia Monetaria do Brasil, 1900-45*. (Rio de Janeiro: IBMEC, 1975.)

Newfarmer, Richard S., and Willard F. Mueller, *Multinational Corporations in Brazil and Mexico*. (Washington D.C.: U.S. Government Printing Office, 1975, Report to the Subcommittee on Multinational Corporations of the Committee on Foreign Relations, United States Senate.)

Normano, J. F. *Brazil, A Study of Economic Types*. (Chapel Hill, N.C.: University of North Carolina Press, 1935.)

Paiva, Ruy Miller, Salomão Schattan and Claus R. T. De Freitas, *Setor Agricola Do Brasil: Comportamento Economico, Problemas e Possibilidades*. (São Paulo: Secretaria do Agricultura, 1973.)

Pastore, Affonso Celso, Jose Roberto M. de Barros and Decio Kadota, "A Teoria da Paridade do Poder de Compra, Minidesvalorizações e o Equilibrio da Balança Comercial Brasileira," *Pesquisa e Planejamento Economico*, Agosto 1976.

Pastore, Affonso Celso, "A Oferta de Moeda no Brasil 1971/2," *Pesquisa e Planejamento Economico*, Dezembro 1973.

Pastore, Affonso Celso, *Observações Sobre a Politica Monetaria no Programa Brasileiro de Estabilização*. (Sao Paulo: Faculdade de Economia e Administraçao, Universidade de São Paulo, Livre Docencia, 1973.)

Pastore, José, "Emprego, Renda e Mobilidade Social no Brasil," *Pesquisa e Planejamento Economico*, Dezembro 1976.

Pelaez, Carlos M., "A Balança Comercial, A Grande Depressao, e a Industrializaçao Brasileira," *Revista Brasileira de Economia*, Março 1968.

Pelaez, Carlos M., *Historia da Industrializacao Brasileira*. (Rio de Janeiro: APEC Editora S.A., 1972.)

Pereira, Jose Eduardo C., *Financiamento Externos e Crescimento do Brasil, 1966/73*. (Rio de Janeiro: IPEA/INPES, Coleção Relatorios de Pesquisa, No. 27, 1974.)

Prado Junior, Caio, *Historia Economica do Brasil* (São Paulo: Editora Brasiliense, 12. edição, 1970.)

Prado, Junior, Caio, *The Colonial Background of Modern Brazil*. (Berkeley and Los Angeles: University of California Press, 1967.)

Reynolds, Clark W., and Robert T. Carpenter, "Housing Finance in Brazil: Toward a New Distribution of Wealth," in Wayne A. Cornelius and Felicity M. Trueblood (editors), *Latin American Urban Research*, Vol. 5 (Beverly Hills: SAGE Publications, 1975.)

Rezende da Silva, Fernando A., and Dennis Mahar, *Saude e Previdencia Social: Uma Analise Economica*. (Rio de Janeiro: IPEA/INPES, Coleçao Relatorios de Pesquisa, No. 21, 1974.)

Rezende da Silva, Fernando A., *Avaliação do Setor Publico na Economia Brasileira-Estrutura Funcional da Despesa*. (Rio de Janeiro: Coleção Relatorios de Pesquisa No. 13, 1972.)

Rezende da Silva, Fernando M., *O Sistema Tributario d As Desigualdades Regionais: Uma Analise da Recente Controversia Sobre o ICM*. (Rio de Janeiro: IPEA/INPES, Serie Monografica, No. 13, 1974.)

Ribeiro, Benedito, and Mario M. Guimarães, *Historia dos Bancos e do Desenvolvimento Financeiro do Brasil* (Rio de Janeiro and São Paulo: Pro-Service Ltda. Editora, 1967.)

Robock, Stefan H., *Brazil's Developing Northeast*. (Washington, D.C.: The Brookings Institution, 1963.)

Robock, Stefan H., *Brazil: A Study in Development Progress*. (Lexington, Mass.: Lexington Books, D.C. Heath and Company, 1975.)

Rocca, Carlos A., "O ICM e O Desenvolvimento Nacional," *Finanças Publicas*, No. 308, Marco/Abril, 1972, Ministerio da Fazenda, Brasil.

Roett, Riordan, *Brazil: Politics in a Patrimonial Society*. (Boston: Allyn and Bacon, 1972.)

Roett, Riordan, *The Politics of Foreign Aid in the Brazilian Northeast*. (Nashville, Tennessee, Vanderbilt University Press, 1972.)

Roett, Riordan, (editor), *Brazil in the Sixties*. (Nashville, Tennessee: Vanderbilt University Press, 1972.)

Roett, Riordan, (editor), *Brazil in the Seventies*. (Washington, D.C.: American Enterprise Institute, December 1976.)

Rosenbaum, H. J. and W. G. Typer, (editors), *Contemporary Brazil: Issues in Economic and Political Development*, (New York: Praeger Publishers, 1972.)

Saraiva, Enrique, "Aspectos Gerais do Comportamento das Empresas Publicas Brasileiras e sua Açao Internacional," *Revista de Administracao Publica*, Jan./Marco 1977.

Sayad, Joao, "Planejamento, Credito e Distribuicao de Renda," *Estudos Economicos*, Vol. 7, No. 1, 1977.

Saunders, John, (editor), *Modern Brazil: New Patters and Development* (Gainesville, Florida: University of Florida Press, 1971.)

Schlittler Silva, Helio, "Comercio Exterior do Brasil e Desenvolvimento Economico," *Revista Brasileira de Ciencias Sociais*, Marco 1962.

Schuh, G. Edward, *The Agricultural Development of Brazil*. (New York: Praeger Press, 1970.)

Silveira, A. N., "Interest Rates and Rapid Inflation: The Evidence from the Brazilian Economy," *Journal of Money, Credit and Banking*, Vol. 5, 1973.

Simonsen, Mario H., *Brasil 2001*. (Rio de Janeiro: APEC Editora S. A., 1972.)

Simonsen, Mario H., "Brazilian Inflation: Postwar Experience and Outcome of the 1964 Reform." *Economic Development Issues: Latin America*. (New York: Committee for Economic Development, Supplementary Paper No. 21, August 1967.)

Simonsen, Mario H., and Roberto de Oliveira Campos, *A Nova Economia Brasileira*. (Rio de Janeiro: Livraria José Olympio Editora, 1974.)

Simonsen, Roberto C., *A Evoluçao Industrial do Brasil*. (São Paulo: Empresa Grafica da Revista dos Tribunais, 1939.)

Singer, Hans W., "The Brazilian SALTE Plan," *Economic Development and Cultural Change*, February 1953.

Skidmore, Thomas E., *Politics in Brazil 1930-1964: An Experiment in Democracy*. (New York: Oxford University Press, 1967.)

Smith, T. Lynn, and Alexander Marchant (editors), *Brazil: Portrait of Half a Continent*. (New York: The Dryden Press, 1951.)

Smith, T. Lynn, *Brazil: People and Institutions*. (Baton Rouge: Louisiana State University Press, 1963.)

Stein, Stanley J., *The Brazilian Cotton: Textile Enterprise in an underdeveloped Area, 1850-1950*. Cambridge, Mass.: Harvard University Press, 1957.)

Stein, Stanley J., *Vassouras: A Brazilian Coffee Country, 1850-1900*. (Cambridge, Mass.: Harvard University Press, 1973.)

Stepan, A. (editor), *Authoritarian Brazil: Origins, Policy and Future*. (New Haven: Yale University Press, 1973.)

Suplicy, Eduardo Matarazzo, *Os Efeitos das Minidesvalorizacoes Na Economia Brasileira*. (Rio de Janeiro: Fundaçao Getulio Vargas, 1976.)

Suzigan, Wilson, et al, *Financiamento de Projetos Industriais no Brasil*. (Rio de Janeiro: IPEA/INPES, Coleção Relatorios de Pesquisa, No. 19, 1972.)

Suzigan, Wilson, "As Empresas do Governo e o Papel do Estado na Economia Brasileira," in *Aspectos da Participacao do Governo na Economia* (Rio de Janeiro: IPEA/INPES, Serie Monografica, No. 26, 1976.)

Syvrud, Donald E., *Foundations of Brazilian Economic Growth*. (Stanford, California: AEI-Hoover Research Publications, Hoover Institution Press, 1974.)

Tendler, Judith, *The Electric Power Industry in Brazil*. (Cambridge, Mass.: Harvard University Press, 1968.)

Tolipan, Ricardo, and Arthur Carlos Tirelly (editors), *A Controversia Sobre Distribuição de Renda e Desenvolvimento*. (Rio de Janeiro: Zahar Editores, 1975.)

Tolosa, Hamilton C., "Politica Urbana e Redistribuição de Renda," *Pesquisa e Planejamento Economico, Abril* 1977.

Tolosa, Hamilton, "Dimensão e Causas da Pobreza Urbana," *Estudos Economicos,* Vol. 7, No. 1, 1977.

Tyler, William G., *Manufactured Export Expansion and Industrialization in Brazil.* (Tubingen: J. C. B. Mohr, Kieler Studien No. 134, 1976.)

Venancio Filho, Alberto, *A Intervencao do Estado no Dominio Publico.* (Rio de Janeiro: Fundacao Getulio Vargas, 1968.)

Versiani, Flavio, "Industrialização e Emprego: O Problema de Reposição de Equipamentos," *Pesquisa e Planejamento Economico,* Junho 1972.

Versiani, Flavio R., and Jose Roberto M. de Barros (editors), *Formação Economica do Brasil: A Experiencia da Industrialização.* (São Paulo: Editora Saraiva, 1977.)

Vieira, Dorival Teixeira, *O Desenvolvimento Economico do Brasil e a Inflacao.* (São Paulo: Faculdade de Ciencias Economicas e Administrativas, Universidade de São Paulo, 1962.)

Villela, Annibal V., and Wilson Suzigan, *Politica do Governo e Crescimento da Economia Brasileira 1889-1945.* (Rio de Janeiro: IPEA/INPES, Serie Monografica, No. 10, 1973.)

Villela, Annibal V., Sergio Ramos da Silva, Wilson Suzigan, and Mario Jose Santos, *Aspectos do Crescimento da Economia Brasileira, 1889-1969.* (Rio de Janeiro: Fundação Getulio Vargas, mimeographed, 1971.)

Villela, Annibal V., "As Empresas do Governo Federal e sua Importancia na Economia Nacional: 1956-1960," *Revista Brasileira de Economia,* Marco 1962.

Von Doellinger, Carlos, et al, *A Politica Brasileira de Comercio Exterior e Seus Efeitos: 1967/73.* (Rio de Janeiro: INPEA/INPES, Coleção Relatorio de Pesquisa, No. 22, 1974.)

Von Doellinger, Carlos, Leonardo C. Cavalcanti, and Flavio Castelo Branco, *Politica e Estrutura Das Importações Brasileiras.* (Rio de Janeiro: IPEA/INPES, 1977).

Von Doellinger, Carlos, et al, *Empresas Multinacionais na Industria Brasileira.* (Rio de Janeiro: IPEA/INPES, Coleção Relatorios de Pesquisa, No. 29, 1975.)

Wagley, Charles, *An Introduction to Brazil*. (New York: Columbia University Press, 1971.)

Wells, John, "Distribution of Earnings, Growth and the Structure of Demand in Brazil During the Sixties," *World Development*, January 1974.

Wells, John, "Under consumption, Market Size and Expenditure Patterns in Brazil," *Bulletin of the Society for Latin American Studies*, No. 24, March 1976.

Wells, John, "Euro-Dollars, Foreign Debt and the Brazilian Boom," Centre of Latin American Studies, University of Cambridge, England, Working Paper, No. 13, 1973.

Wirth, John D., *The Politics of Brazilian Development, 1930-1954*. (Stanford: Stanford University Press, 1970.)

Index